3/00

WITHDRAWN

THE
UFO
ENIGMA

T H E
U F O
ENIGMA

A NEW REVIEW OF THE PHYSICAL EVIDENCE

PETER A. STURROCK

WARNER BOOKS

A Time Warner Company

Warner Books, Inc., 1271 Avenue of the Americas,
New York, NY 10020
Visit our Web site at www.warnerbooks.com

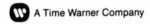 A Time Warner Company

Printed in the United States of America
First Warner Books Printing: November 1999
10 9 8 7 6 5 4 3 2 1

ISBN: 0-446-52565-0
LCCN: 99-066643

Book design and composition by L&G McRee

CONTENTS

FOREWORD

As a lifetime student of philosophy and religion, I have long been interested as to whether we, as conscious beings, have potentials beyond those we now know. Among other questions, I have sought to learn whether we are alone in the universe. In this regard, I became fascinated with the possible relationship between extraterrestrial intelligence and what are known as "Unidentified Flying Objects." Should this connection be established objectively and conclusively, we would know that we are not alone.

In this quest, in view of the extensive anecdotal evidence that exists, I have worked with a number of individuals and organizations, but I was never satisfied that we were able to establish unqualified scientific evidence as to the existence of UFOs.

Thus, I was encouraged when Dr. Peter A. Sturrock, a distinguished astrophysicist at Stanford University, agreed to conduct a study concerning physical evidence related to the UFO phenomenon. Under his leadership, nine impartial scientists were brought together to hear presentations by experienced investigators and render their opinions and advice.

I am most grateful to the scientists and investigators who

took part in this project and produced this report. While their findings were not conclusive, I hope that this study will raise the level of the debate and will be helpful, in particular, to other scientists who might be encouraged to undertake their own research and so further contribute to our knowledge of what is truly an enigma.

Laurance S. Rockefeller

PREFACE

This book has its origins in a study that was carried out at the Pocantico Conference Center in Tarrytown, New York, from September 29 to October 3, 1997. It is a pleasure to acknowledge the initiative, support, and wise counsel of Mr. Laurance S. Rockefeller, the efficient administrative support of Mr. Rockefeller's colleague Mr. Henry Diamond, and the support of the officers of the Society for Scientific Exploration, notably SSE Treasurer Dr. Charles R. Tolbert. For assistance in planning the study, I am indebted to members of the Scientific Steering Committee: Dr. Thomas E. Holzer, Dr. Robert Jahn, Dr. David E. Pritchard, Dr. Harold E. Puthoff, Dr. Yervant Terzian, and Dr. Charles R. Tolbert. Thanks are due to the investigators who tried to present a crash course on the UFO problem in the space of only a few days: Dr. Richard F. Haines, Dr. Illobrand Von Ludwiger, Dr. Mark Rodeghier, Mr. John F. Schuessler, Dr. Erling Strand, Dr. Michael D. Swords, Dr. Jacques F. Vallee and Mr. Jean-Jacques Velasco; and to the scientists who made a brave attempt to assess the subject in that very short time: Dr. Von R. Eshleman, Dr. Thomas E. Holzer, Dr. J. R. (Randy) Jokipii, Dr. François Louange, Dr. H. J. (Jay) Melosh, Dr. James J. Papike, Dr. Guenther Reitz, Dr. Charles R. Tolbert, and Dr. Bernard Veyret.

This book incorporates material, itemized in the Acknowledgments section, that was previously published by the Society for Scientific Exploration in its journal, *Journal of Scientific Exploration*, and by the Center for UFO Studies as a CUFOS Report, and I wish to thank the following authors who have generously allowed me to incorporate their work in this book: Dr. Von R. Eshleman, Dr. Richard F. Haines, Dr. Thomas E. Holzer, Dr. J. R. (Randy) Jokipii, Dr. François Louange, Dr. H. J. (Jay) Melosh, Dr. James J. Papike, Dr. Guenther Reitz, Dr. Charles R. Tolbert, Dr. Jacques F. Vallee, Mr. Jean-Jacques Velasco, Dr. Bernard Veyret, and Ms. Jennie Zeidman.

For support in preparing the original report and the resulting book, I am indebted to my assistant Ms. Diane Kohlman, to my local editor Ms. Kathleen Erickson, and to our editorial assistant Mr. Marcel Kuijsten. This book also owes much to the sound judgment of Warner Books editor Ms. Betsy Mitchell.

In order to be useful, a book should read easily. However, if any book on the UFO topic reads too easily, it does not reflect the difficulty and complexity of the problem it is supposed to address. This book is at best a brief introduction to an extensive and recalcitrant subject. (My dictionary defines "recalcitrant" as "obstinate in defying constituted authority.") For those who wish to go further, I give my own short list of recommended reading at the end of this book.

I hope this book will help encourage more scientists to study this subject, develop their own ideas, and test those ideas by independent research. This is I believe our best hope—and may be our only hope—for finally arriving at a full resolution of the problem posed by UFO reports which have persisted worldwide for over fifty years.

Peter A. Sturrock
Stanford, California
June 1999

PART ONE

——

HISTORY

CHAPTER 1

Introduction

The word "UFO" presents an enigma—a puzzle concerning which everyone has an opinion but no one has an answer. Ordinary citizens are typically curious and open-minded. By contrast, professional people (administrators, policy makers, journalists, scientists, and most other scholars) are typically very guarded in their response.

In 1976, I carried out a survey of the members of the American Astronomical Society to assess their level of interest in the subject, whether they thought it deserves scientific investigation, and whether any members could report observations similar to those of typical UFO reports (Sturrock, 1994 a, b, c). I learned that most of the respondents were as curious as most citizens; most considered that the subject does indeed deserve scientific investigation; and a few percent had witnessed events similar to those described in the UFO literature.

When speaking in public, however, scientists tend to be dismissive of the UFO question. The great physicist Richard P. Feynman, one of the most open-minded and articulate scientists of the twentieth century, made the following remarks in the course of a lecture entitled "This Unscientific Age," presented at the University of Washington in April 1963:

> If we come to the problem of flying saucers, . . .
> we have the difficulty that almost everybody who
> observes flying saucers sees something different . . .
> orange balls of light, blue spheres which bounce on
> the floor, gray fogs which disappear, gossamer-like
> streams which evaporate into the air, tin [*sic*], round
> flat things out of which objects come with funny
> shapes that are something like a human being. . . .
> Just think a few minutes about the variety of life that
> there is. And then you see that the thing that comes
> out of the flying saucer isn't going to be anything like
> what anybody describes. . . . It is very unlikely that
> flying saucers would arrive here, in this particular
> era. . . . Just when we're getting scientific enough to
> appreciate the possibility of traveling from one place
> to another, here come the flying saucers (Feynman,
> 1998).

The problem of trying to understand the cause or causes of UFO reports has become more difficult since Feynman gave his lecture in Seattle. Now a citizen may ask a scientist not only about "flying saucers," and not only about possible extraterrestrial occupants, but also about reports that some objects have crashed and been retrieved, that some human beings are being subjected to examination by extraterrestrial visitors, and that federal agencies are hiding important relevant information from the public. Such prospects are so mind-boggling and so close to science fiction, and the issues so very far removed from conventional scientific research, that nowadays scientists are even less willing to become involved in this subject than they were in 1963. This has resulted in considerable polarization: citizens are keenly interested in the problem and want answers, but scientists who could help provide answers have little interest and no incentive to cooperate in this endeavor.

These were some of the thoughts that came to mind in December 1996, when Mr. Laurance Rockefeller asked about my thoughts on what might be done to learn what lies behind UFO reports. I had come to recognize the complexity of the issue, and I had also learned something about what works and what does not work in scientific research.

For the last thirty years, I have been involved in theoretical research into solar physics, wrestling with a number of puzzles such as why the Sun's outer atmosphere, the corona, has a temperature of a million degrees, and what happens during a solar explosion called a flare. I have learned that it is helpful to break down each of these complex issues into a number of simpler phenomena that raise more specific questions. It is always tempting to develop a theory to answer such a question and then immediately check that theory against the data. Sometimes that procedure works, but more often it does not. If I try four or five ideas and none of them work, I finally realize that I must change my attitude and adopt a different strategy. At that stage, my best option is to recognize that (a) I do not understand the phenomenon; (b) I need to study the data much more carefully; and (c) the best question to ask is, What is the Sun trying to tell me? I believe that the UFO problem needs a similar approach. Scientists need to ask, first, What are the facts? and second, What are those facts trying to tell us?

However, this is not so easy. Concerning the UFO problem, Richard Feynman did not see any solid, clear-cut facts in 1963, and most scientists do not see any such facts today, beyond the obvious one that reports continue. Social scientists and detectives are used to dealing with anecdotal reports; physical scientists are not. If a witness is taken to a scientific research institution and asked to describe his or her observations, it is highly unlikely that this will lead to any significant relevant research. On the other hand, if the witness can produce some physical evidence, such as a photograph, a tape recording, or a piece of metal, there is a great deal that the staff of a well-equipped laboratory could do. If careful field investigation of ten separate UFO events, each with strong witness testimony, were to produce ten items of physical evidence, if each item were analyzed in several different laboratories, and if the resulting reports showed that the items were (a) very similar, and

(b) very unusual, then we would have not only evidence, but a pattern among the evidence. We would have established a fact.

If it does indeed turn out that there is relevant physical evidence, if this evidence is carefully collected and analyzed, and if this analysis leads to the identification of several facts concerning the UFO phenomenon, then will be the time for scientists to step back and ask, What are these facts trying to tell us? If those facts are strong enough to lead to a firm conclusion, then will be the time to confront the more bizarre questions. If, for instance, it turns out that all physical evidence is consistent with a mundane interpretation of the causes of UFO reports, there will be little reason to continue to speculate about the role of extraterrestrial beings. If, on the other hand, the analysis of physical evidence turns up very strong evidence that objects related with UFO reports were manufactured outside the solar system, then one must obviously consider very seriously that the phenomenon involves not only extraterrestrial vehicles but probably also extraterrestrial beings.

For these reasons, it was my opinion that the very first step in the direction of scientific research into the UFO problem would be a determination of whether or not there even exists physical evidence related to UFO reports. This specific question could be addressed by means of a panel review, as we discuss further in Chapter 5, "Introduction to Pocantico." The review and the resulting report are contained in this book, together with some selected case studies.

Experienced UFO investigators find that the majority of reports that come to their attention can be attributed to natural occurrences, familiar objects seen under unusual circumstances, et cetera. A very small percentage of reports will be recognized as due to hoaxes perpetrated on or by the witnesses. Of the remaining reports, many will be uninteresting because they contain little information, or conflicting information, and little or no supporting evidence. A very small fraction of the cases have good documentation (but usually not as good as one might like) and some form of physical evidence (but never as much as one might like). A few of these interesting and challenging cases (drawn from those presented in summary form to the review panel) may be found in Part Five of this book. However, before getting into this review, it may be helpful to go back to the very beginning of the UFO story.

CHAPTER 2

UFO History: 1947 to 1967

The term "UFO" began as an acronym formed from the term "unidentified flying object," which appears to have been introduced into the vocabulary of the United States Air Force some time in 1948. Edward J. Ruppelt, who played an important role in the Air Force investigations, claims to be the originator of this term (Ruppelt, 1956, p. 1). An interim report (Project Sign, 1949) of the progress of "Project Sign" tells us that this project of the Air Material Command (at Wright-Patterson Air Force Base in Dayton, Ohio) came into being on January 22, 1948. The subject of the study was originally referred to as "Flying Disks." However, on February 11, 1948, the project received further instructions referring to their mission as the "Evaluation of Unidentified Flying Objects."

According to a press release issued by the Office of Public Information of the National Military Establishment on April 27, 1949, Project Sign (referred to in the press release as "Project Saucer") came into being in response to a "veritable celestial chain reaction" of "fabulous flying saucers," that followed the publication on Tuesday, June 25, 1947, of a story concerning "a Boise, Idaho, businessman named Kenneth Arnold." Since the Arnold incident is widely regarded as the beginning of the current UFO phenomenon (using that term in its widest possible sense), it is interesting to read the original story (Clark, 1998, pp. 139–43), written by reporters of the *East Oregonian* in Pendleton, Oregon, on June 25, 1947:

> PENDLETON, Ore., June 25 (AP)—Nine bright saucer-like objects flying at "incredible speed" at 10,000 feet altitude were reported here today by Kenneth Arnold, a Boise, Idaho, pilot who said he could not hazard a guess as to what they were.
>
> Arnold, a United States Forest Service employee [an incorrect identification] engaged in searching for a missing plane, said he sighted the mysterious objects yesterday at three p.m. They were flying between Mount Rainier and Mount Adams, in Washington State, he said, and appeared to weave in and out of formation. Arnold said that he clocked and estimated their speed at 1200 miles per hour.
>
> Enquiries at Yakima last night brought only blank stares, he said, but he added he talked today with an unidentified man from Ukiah, south of here, who said he had seen similar objects over the mountains near Ukiah yesterday.
>
> "It seems impossible," Arnold said, "But there it is."

The National Military Establishment (1949) press release gave the following account of the Arnold incident:

> On Tuesday, June 24, 1947, a Boise, Idaho, businessman named Kenneth Arnold looked from his private plane and spotted a chain of nine saucer-like objects playing tag with the jagged peaks of Washington's Mt. Rainier at what he described as a "fantastic speed." . . .
>
> Arnold, representative of a fire control equipment firm in Boise, Idaho, was en route from Chehalis, Washington, to Yakima, Washington, on June 24, in

a privately owned plane when he saw the reflection of a bright flash on his wing. Arnold said he looked around and observed a chain of nine peculiar aircraft approaching Mt. Rainier.

"I could see their outline quite plainly against the snow as they approached the mountain," he reported. "They flew very close to the mountaintops, directly south to southeast down the hog's back of the range, flying like geese in a diagonal chain-like line, as if they were linked together."

Arnold observed that the objects seemed smaller than a DC-4 on his left, but he judged their wing span to be as wide as the furtherest engines on either side of the DC-4's fuselage.

"I never saw anything so fast," he told investigators.

Arnold said he clocked the "Saucers" [sic] speed at about 1,200 miles an hour. Later, however, Aero-Medical Laboratory men stated that an object travelling that fast would not have been visible to the naked eye.

It is noteworthy that, although this press release was prepared almost two years after the Arnold event and presumably was based on an official investigation, it is both inaccurate and misleading. Arnold never said he saw "saucer-like" objects. He described and drew the objects as crescent-shaped. The term "flying saucer" arose not from Arnold's description of their appearance but his description of their motion: he said that they moved with an undulating motion, like a "saucer skipping across the water." Furthermore, the judgment attributed to the "Aero-Medical Laboratory men," that the objects would not have been visible, does not stand up to scrutiny. There are many factors that influence the visibility of an object—angular size, angular speed, brightness, contrast, color—but speed itself is not a determining factor. In a clear atmosphere, it is as easy to see an object of a given size and speed at twenty miles as it is to see an object half its size and half its speed at ten miles.

Arnold's observation (Arnold and Palmer, 1952) has never been satisfactorily explained, although many suggestions have been advanced. The distinguished astrophysicist Donald H. Menzel offered three different interpretations in his three books (Menzel, 1953; Menzel and Boyd, 1963; Menzel and Taves, 1977) on "flying saucers." Developing a list of hypotheses is an important stage in scientific research, but it is only one stage. It is then necessary to draw upon the evidence to reduce the list—hopefully to just one surviving hypothesis. One gets the impression from reading his books that Menzel really regarded unidentified flying objects as a joke unworthy of the impressive caliber of scientific research for which he was renowned.

The authors of the Project Sign report (Project Sign, 1949) made a number of interesting observations. Concerning the shapes of objects, they stated:

> Unidentified aerial objects appear to be grouped as follows:
> (1) Flying disks (saucers)
> (2) Torpedo or Cigar Shaped Bodies (no wings or fins visible in flight)
> (3) Spherical or Balloon-Shaped Objects (capable of hovering, descending, ascending or traveling at high speed
> (4) Balls of light (no apparent physical form attached). Capable of maneuvering, climbing and traveling at high speed.

Concerning the possible origin of the objects, they stated:

> Consideration has been given to the possibility that these unidentified aircraft represent scientific developments beyond the level of knowledge attained in this country. [They argued that such development could come only from the USSR, and they considered that unlikely.] . . . Another possibility is

> that these aerial objects are visitors from another
> planet. . . . The commentary on this possibility by
> Dr. James Lipp of the Rand Project . . . indicates that
> this solution of the mystery connected with the
> sighting of unidentified flying objects is extremely
> improbable. Pending elimination of all other solu-
> tions or definite proof of the nature of these objects,
> this possibility will not be further explored.

The above classification of shapes associated with UFO reports
has stood the test of time. The French scientist Claude Poher
(1973), in a document written when he headed the Sounding
Rockets Division of the French National Center for Space Research (CNES) in Toulouse, analyzed 220 reports from France
and 825 reports from other countries, finding similar patterns
in both groups, including the following prevalent shapes: disk-
like, round like a ball, cigar-shaped, and egg-shaped.

Whether or not UFO reports have anything to do with secret
weapons or extraterrestrial spacecraft is still being vigorously
debated.

From January 1948 to December 1969, there was an almost
continuous UFO research project in the U.S. Air Force, but the
level of support and the name of the project both changed over
the years. David M. Jacobs's *The UFO Controversy in America*
(Jacobs, 1975) provides a thorough account of these and other
developments up to 1974. The level of effort was never very
great: Typically, a project had only a few staff members. The
level of classification, typically 2A, was not very high. There
appears to have been little or no attempt to conceal the fact that
the projects existed. Project Sign was terminated in December
1948 and replaced by Project Grudge, with the goal of a "Detailed Study of Flying Discs." Project Grudge (1949) issued its
final report in August, and the Air Force released a summary to
the news media in December 1949. The project's main conclusion was that "there is no evidence that objects reported upon
are the result of an advanced scientific foreign development;
and therefore, they constitute no direct threat to the national
security. . . . All evidence and analysis indicated that UFOs

were the result of the misinterpretation of various conventional objects [or] a mild form of mass hysteria and war nerves" or hoaxes perpetrated by publicity seekers and "psychopathological persons."

Project Grudge continued as a low-level activity until September 1951. During that month, there was a dramatic sighting of an object described as thirty to fifty feet in diameter by the pilot of a T-33 plane and his passenger, an Air Force major, of Fort Monmouth, New Jersey. This event attracted the attention of Major General C. B. Cabell, director of Air Force intelligence. Lieutenant Jerry Cummings, then head of Project Grudge, was released from active duty, and Captain Edward J. Ruppelt was appointed to head the project. One of his first steps was to appoint the astronomer Professor J. Allen Hynek as his chief scientific consultant. In March 1952, the Air Force changed the code name to Project Blue Book and gave it the formal title Aerial Phenomena Group. The Air Force also instituted a new reporting procedure by which Blue Book received prompt notice of new sightings. According to Jacobs, "By June 1952 Project Blue Book was a dynamic, ongoing organization."

However, June 1952 was also a time of great stress for the new organization since in that one month, the Air Technical Intelligence Center (ATIC) received 149 reports, more than in any previous month of its history. The next month ATIC received 536 reports—nearly 50 in one day (July 28) alone. During that summer, several series of sensational sightings were reported on the East Coast, notably in the vicinity of Washington, D.C. The Pentagon was besieged with inquiries from the press and congressional offices, and its telephone lines were jammed for several days—a valid cause for great concern. In response to this pressure, the Air Force held the largest and longest press conference since World War II, on July 29, 1952. Major General John A. Samford, director of Air Force Intelligence, acknowledged that the Air Force had received a number of reports from "credible observers of relatively incredible things." Some of these reports were accompanied by radar returns that the Air Force attributed to unusual meteorological conditions.

The 1952 wave of sightings attracted the interest of the Central Intelligence Agency, since a deluge of UFO reports could compromise the valid reporting of hostile air activity. This led the CIA to consult a panel of five distinguished scientists: Luis Alvarez, Lloyd Berkner, Samuel A. Goudsmit, Thornton Page, and H. P. Robertson. The panel, headed by Robertson, met in January 1953. After receiving presentations from Blue Book staff and from Hynek for two days, the panel prepared its report, then classified Secret. The Robertson panel (Condon and Gillmor, 1969, pp. 905–19) concluded that:

> The evidence presented on Unidentified Flying Objects shows no indication that these phenomena constitute a threat to national security [and] the continued emphasis on the reporting of these phenomena does, in these parlous times, result in a threat to the orderly functioning of the protective organs of the body politic.

The panel therefore recommended:

> That the national security agencies take immediate steps to strip the Unidentified Flying Objects of the special status they have been given and the aura of mystery they have acquired [and] that the national security agencies institute policies on intelligence, training and public education designed to prepare the material defenses and morale of the country to recognize most promptly and to react most effectively to true indications of hostile intent or action.

Possibly as a result of the Robertson panel report, the Air Force appears to have lost interest in Blue Book from 1953 on. The staff dwindled, and when Ruppelt left Blue Book in August 1953, the management of the project was turned over to Airman First Class Max Futch. Captain Charles Hardin was appointed head of Blue Book in March 1954. Hardin was replaced by Captain George T. Gregory in April 1956, Major Robert J. Friend in October 1958, and Major Hector Quintanilla sometime in 1963.

Project Blue Book issued a number of reports during its lifetime. The most interesting one was Blue Book Special Report Number 14 (originally classified Secret), which was prepared for the Air Force by the Battelle Memorial Institute. It was primarily a statistical analysis of data that had been accumulated in Blue Book files. Unlike the Poher analysis of 1973, the report claims that "the data as a whole failed to reveal any marked patterns or trends" and concluded that "on the basis of this evaluation of the information, it is considered to be highly improbable that any of the reports of unidentified aerial objects examined in this study represent observations of technological developments outside the range of present-day scientific knowledge." This report was released by the Air Force on October 25, 1955 (Project Blue Book, 1955).

Between 1952 and 1956, two civilian UFO groups came into existence: APRO (Aerial Phenomena Research Organization), led by James and Coral Lorenzen, and NICAP (National Investigating Committee for Aerial Phenomena), led during its formative years by Donald E. Keyhoe, a retired Marine Corps major. These organizations, especially NICAP, lobbied Congress to hold hearings on the UFO question.

In 1965, Hynek wrote to Lieutenant Colonel J. F. Spaulding, of the Office of the Secretary of the Air Force, proposing that the Air Force submit the problem to a panel of civilian scientists. On September 28, 1965, Director of Information General E. B. LeBailly wrote to the director of the Air Force scientific advisory board and requested "that a working scientific panel composed of both physical and social scientists be organized to review Project Blue Book . . . and to advise the Air Force of any improvements that should be made." This panel, called the Ad Hoc Committee to Review Project Blue Book, was convened (for one day only) in February 1966. Its members were Dr. Brian O'Brien (chairman), Dr. Launor Carter, Dr. Jesse Orlansky, Dr. Carl Sagan, and Dr. Willis A. Ware. All but Sagan were members of the Air Force scientific advisory board. The report of this committee (Condon and Gillmor, 1969, pp. 811–15) was issued in March 1966. The key recommendations were that the Air Force should negotiate contracts "with a few selected universities to provide selected teams to investigate promptly and in depth certain selected sightings of UFOs" and that a single university should coordinate the teams. The Air Force did not immediately respond to these recommendations.

On March 20, 1966, eighty-seven women students and a civil defense director at Hillsdale College in Hillsdale, Michigan, saw (according to their reports) a glowing football-shaped object hovering over a swampy area a few hundred yards from the women's dormitory. The witnesses watched the object for four hours. The next night, five people, including two police officers, watched (again according to their reports) a large glowing object rise from a swampy area near Dexter, Michigan. Project Blue Book dispatched its scientific consultant, Hynek, to the scene.

After his investigation, Hynek held a press conference and suggested that the lights could have been the result of decaying vegetation that spontaneously ignited, a phenomenon known as "marsh gas." This proposal became the subject of intense ridicule. The uproar led two congressmen from Michigan, Weston E. Vivian and Gerald R. Ford (then House Republican minority leader), to call for congressional hearings.

The House Armed Services Committee held an open hearing on April 5, 1966. The chairman, L. Mendel Rivers, invited testimony from Secretary of the Air Force Harold D. Brown, Project Blue Book Chief Hector Quintanilla, and Hynek. NICAP submitted written testimony. Hynek defended his investigation of the Michigan sightings, but also called for a civilian panel of scientists to examine the UFO problem. Secretary Brown allowed that he was considering this possibility, which had been recommended to the Air Force by the O'Brien committee. The congressmen gave their strong support to this proposal.

Following the Rivers hearings, Secretary Brown instructed the Air Force chief of staff to accept the O'Brien committee recommendations. Responsibility for implementing the recommendations was assigned to General James Ferguson, deputy chief of staff for research and development. Responsibility for university participation was assigned to Lieutenant Colonel Robert Hippler of the Air Force Office of Scientific Research. It was not easy for Hippler to find a taker, but eventually, through the good offices of Dr. Walter Orr Roberts, director of the National Center for Atmospheric Research in Boulder, Colorado, the University of Colorado agreed to undertake the project.

The "Colorado Project" and its resulting report are the subject of the next chapter.

CHAPTER 3

The Colorado Project and the Condon Report

On October 6, 1966, Thurston E. Manning, Vice President at the University of Colorado in Boulder, signed a contract with the Air Force for a "Scientific Study of Unidentified Flying Objects." The final report of that project (the Colorado Project) was transmitted to the Air Force by J. R. Smiley, then president of the university, on October 31, 1968. The project director was Professor Edward U. Condon, a distinguished physicist and a man of strong and independent character. The report, subsequently edited for publication by Daniel S. Gillmor, is known as the Condon Report (Condon and Gillmor, 1969).

The project and the report are often referred to as the work of a "Condon Committee," but this is a serious error that completely misrepresents the nature of both the project and the report. Neither the Air Force nor the University of Colorado put the project or the report in the hands of a committee and, as we shall see, the Condon Report is not a consensus document. It was never debated and ratified by a committee.

Sections I and II, the "Conclusions and Recommendations" and the "Summary of the Study," were written by Condon. Section III, "The Work of the Colorado Project," comprises summaries of different aspects of the research written by staff members and a summary of opinion polls conducted by the American Institute of Public Opinion, more familiarly known as the Gallup Poll. Section IV contains 240 pages of "Case Studies." The entire report, with additional sections and appendices, is almost 1,000 pages in length.

The general impression given by Condon's summary is that there is nothing unusual or significant in the UFO phenomenon. This view gains significant additional weight from the fact that the Condon Report was reviewed by a panel of eminent scientists (led by Professor G. H. Clemence) of the National Academy of Sciences (NAS), who endorsed both the methodology and findings of the report (Clemence, 1969). This chapter presents an overview of the Condon Report, a comparison of Condon's "Summary of the Study" with the six staff summaries, a comparison of each staff summary with the case summaries on which it was based, and a discussion of scientific methodology.

OVERVIEW

The Condon Report, presenting the results of the Colorado Project, does not give the impression of a tightly integrated research program. The total budget over a two-year period was $500,000, but the report lists thirty-seven members of the project staff, and a number of other individuals were consulted. It is clear that the Air Force was receiving a very high return of scientific manpower for its money, even though most of the staff must have been contributing only a small fraction of their time to the project. One would have expected that such a large research effort would have been organized into teams led by the other principal investigators or by members of the full-time staff, but there is no indication that such a structure was set up.

Professor Condon is listed as the Scientific Director of the project. Dr. Stuart W. Cook, Professor of Psychology; Dr. Franklin E. Roach, Professor of Astrogeophysics; and Dr. David R. Saunders, Professor of Psychology, are listed as Principal Investigators, and Dr. William A. Scott, Professor of Psychology, is listed as Co-Principal Investigator. Mr. Robert J. Low, with degrees in electrical engineering and business administration, was the Project Coordinator. In addition, the report lists five Research Associates: Dr. Norman E. Levine (Ph.D., Engineering), Mr. Ronald I. Presnell (M.S., Engineering), Dr. Gerald M. Rothberg (Ph.D., Physics), Mr. Herbert J. Strentz (M.A., Journalism), and Mr. James E. Wadsworth (B.A., Behavioral Science).

The core of the report is Section IV, which presents fifty-nine cases. In this work, the director took no part; one principal investigator worked on two cases, another principal investigator on one case; the co-principal investigator took no part; the project coordinator worked on eight cases; one research associate (Dr. Levine) worked on eight cases; Dr. Rothberg on one case; and Mr. Wadsworth on seventeen cases. Important contributions were made by Dr. Roy Craig (Ph.D., Physical Chemistry) and Dr. William K. Hartmann (Ph.D., Astronomy, who was actually located at the University of Arizona in Tucson), who are listed simply as "staff members." Craig and Hartmann each worked on fourteen cases.

The next most important section is Section III, which represents six summaries of the work of the Colorado Project, together with a review of opinion polls by Dr. Aldora Lee (Ph.D., Social Psychology). None was written by the director, one was written by a principal investigator (Roach), and none by the research associates. Three chapters were written by Craig, one by Hartmann, and one by Gordon Thayer (B.S., Physics), who had also worked on a radar-visual case (Case 2) (CR, pp. 248–56).*

Section V, dealing with historical aspects of UFO phenomena, comprises three chapters, and Section VI, dealing with "The Scientific Context," comprises ten chapters. Of these thirteen chapters, one was written by the director. The remaining twelve chapters were written by staff members not previously listed in this discussion.

It is instructive to see what specific contributions were made

---

*CR refers to the Condon Report (Condon and Gillmor, 1969).

by different staff members of the Colorado Project. These contributions are summarized in the following table:

Table 3-1. Breakdown of Activities among Staff

		Condon Report			
		Sec. IV 59 cases	Sec. III 7 Summaries	Sec. V, VI 13 Chapters	Sec. I, II
Condon	Director	0	0	1	2
Cook	Principal Investigator	1	0	0	0
Roach	Principal Investigator	2	1	0	0
Scott	Co-Principal Investigator	0	0	0	0
Low	Project Coordinator	8	0	0	0
Levine	Research Associate	8	0	0	0
Presnell	Research Associate	0	0	0	0
Rothberg	Research Associate	1	0	0	0
Strentz	Research Associate	0	0	0	0
Wadsworth	Research Associate	17	0	0	0
Craig	"Staff"	13	3	0	0
Hartmann	"Staff"	14	1	0	0
Lee	"Staff"	0	1	0	0
Thayer	"Staff"	0	1	0	0
Others		≥30	0	12	0

The overall impression we get is that one group did the work and a different group did the writing. For instance, Condon prepared Section I, "Conclusions and Recommendations," and Section II, "Summary of the Study," but took no part whatever in the case studies. (The historical account "UFOs, 1947–1968" in Section V is attributed to Condon but, in its style and level of detail with incident numbers, report numbers, and initials of people being cited, much of it reads as if it had been produced in an Air Force office.) Most of the casework was done by Low, the project coordinator, by three of the five research associates, and by staff members Craig and

Hartmann. Of these, only Craig and Hartmann contributed to the summaries in Section III and, as we have noted, no one other than Condon actually contributed to the "Conclusions and Recommendations" or to the "Summary of the Study."

Another important part of any scientific study is the definition of the scope of the study and the definitions of the principal terms involved. Condon states that "the emphasis of the study has been on attempting to learn from UFO reports anything that could be considered as adding to scientific knowledge." His conclusion (CR, p. 1) was that "nothing has come from the study of UFOs in the last twenty years that has added to scientific knowledge. . . . Further extensive study of UFOs probably cannot be justified in the expectation that science will be advanced thereby." The key definition is given by Condon:

> An unidentified flying object (UFO, pronounced OO-FO*) is here defined as the stimulus for a report made by one or more individuals of something seen in the sky (or an object thought to be capable of flight but seen when landed on the earth) which the observer could not identify as having an ordinary natural origin, which seemed to him sufficiently puzzling that he undertook to make a report of it to the police, to government officials, to the press, or perhaps to a representative of a private organization devoted to the study of such objects. Defined in this way, there is no question as to the existence of UFOs because UFO reports exist in very large numbers, and the stimulus for each report is, by this definition, an UFO. The problem then becomes that of learning to recognize the various kinds of stimuli that give rise to UFO reports.

---

*The pronunciation originated with Condon and appears to have been used only by him.

Most scientists who study UFOs adopt a more restricted definition that rules out reports that are readily explainable (Hynek, 1972, pp. 3–4). Furthermore, some members of the project staff must have adopted a different definition of the term "UFO" since one finds elsewhere in the report the statement "The preponderance of evidence indicates the possibility of a genuine UFO in this case" (CR, p. 248) and the statement "The probability that at least one UFO was involved appears to be fairly high" (CR, p. 256).

In most scientific research, investigators have in mind one or more considered hypotheses. Condon writes:

> The idea that some UFOs *may* be spacecraft sent to Earth from another civilization, residing on another planet of the solar system, or on a planet associated with a more distant star than the Sun, is called the Extra-terrestrial Hypothesis (ETH).

It is somewhat confusing that Condon also introduces the term "extraterrestrial actuality" (ETA), which apparently represents the belief that ETH is true. Condon's finding is that "no direct evidence whatever of a convincing nature now exists for the claim that any UFOs represent spacecraft visiting Earth from another civilization" (CR, p. 25). In reaching this conclusion, Condon takes the position that "if an [*sic*] UFO report can be plausibly explained in ordinary terms, then we accept that explanation, even though not enough evidence may be available to prove it beyond all doubt" (CR, p. 19).

In assessing the basis for Condon's conclusion, we may refer to the staff summaries that comprise Section III; the staff summaries are based, in turn, on the case studies. In the next section, we shall consider the evidence as categorized in the staff summaries, referring to specific cases as seems appropriate. In the remainder of this section, we shall categorize cases according to the conclusions drawn by the project staff.

Some fifty-nine cases are listed in Section IV, entitled "Case Studies." (There are in addition three observations by astronauts that will be discussed separately.) One of these fifty-nine cases (Case 14) actually involves six separate events. Another "case" (Case 38) is in fact a discussion of "over 800 sightings of UFOs." The analysts made the following assessments of these cases:

1. No event: one case—Case No. 19.
2. Inconsistent data, possible hoaxes, or otherwise of no probative value: 17 cases—Case Nos. 4, 7, 14.4, 22, 23, 24, 26, 32, 33, 39, 42, 44, 48, 52, 53, 56, and 58.
3. Identified (anything from "conclusively" to "inconclusively"): 25 cases—Case Nos. 3, 9, 11, 14.3, 14.5, 14.6, 15, 18, 20, 25, 27, 28, 29, 35, 36, 37, 40, 41, 43, 45, 49, 50, 51, 54, and 55.
4. Not identified: 14 cases—Case Nos. 1, 5, 6, 8, 10, 12, 13, 14.2, 17, 21, 31, 34, 47, and 59.
5. Delusions: 2 cases—Case Nos. 16 and 38.
6. Not appraised due to evasion by Air Force: 1 case—Case No. 30.
7. Possible UFOs: 2 cases—Case Nos. 14.1 and 57.
8. Probable UFOs: 2 cases—Case Nos. 2 and 46.

A reference guide to cases listed in the Condon Report has been provided by Dr. Willy Smith (Smith, 1996).

EVALUATION OF EVIDENCE BY CATEGORY

We now consider evidence by category, drawing from both Section III (staff summaries) and Section IV (case studies) of the report.

NARRATIVE EVIDENCE

The staff gave special weight to cases that involved some form of physical evidence such as photographs or radar returns.

However, there was one case that involved only witness testimony, but nevertheless seemed impressive. Staff member Craig writes (CR, pp. 72–73):

> While the current cases investigated did not yield impressive residual evidence, even in the narrative content, to support an [*sic*] hypothesis that an alien vehicle was physically present, narratives of past events, such as the 1966 incident at Beverly, Mass. (Case 6), would fit no other explanation if the testimony of witnesses is taken at face value.

The abstract of Case 6 (CR, pp. 266–70) is as follows:

> Three adult women went onto the high school athletic field to check the identity of a bright light which had frightened an 11-year-old girl in her home nearby, and reported that one of three lights they saw maneuvering in the sky above the school flew noiselessly toward them, coming directly overhead, 20–30 ft. above one of them. It was described as a flowing [*sic*], solid disc-like, automobile-sized object. Two policemen who responded to a telephone message that a UFO was under observation verified that an extraordinary object was flying over the high school. The object has not been identified. Most of the extended observation, however, apparently was an observation of the planet Jupiter.

PHOTOGRAPHIC EVIDENCE

In his summary of this category, Hartmann describes a "residual group of unidentifieds" that "is not inconsistent with the hypothesis that unknown and extraordinary aircraft have penetrated the airspace of the United States," although "none yields sufficient evidence to establish this hypothesis" (CR, p. 86). A little later, Hartmann remarks:

> After investigation, there remains a small residual of the order of 2% of all cases, that appears to represent well recorded but unidentified or unidentifiable objects that are airborne—i.e., UFOs. . . . The present data are compatible with, but do not establish either the hypothesis that (1) the entire UFO phenomenon is a product of misidentification, poor reporting, and fabrication, or that (2) a very small part of the UFO phenomenon involves extraordinary events.

As examples of the "small residual" cases, we may refer to Cases 46 and 47. Concerning Case 46 (McMinnville, Oregon, May 11, 1950), Hartmann reaches these conclusions (CR, p. 407):

> This is one of the few UFO reports in which all factors investigated, geometric, psychological, and physical appear to be consistent with the assertion that an extraordinary flying object, silvery, metallic, disc-shaped, tens of meters in diameter, and evidently artificial, flew within the sight of two witnesses. It cannot be said that the evidence positively rules out fabrication, although there are some factors such as the accuracy of certain photometric measures of the original negatives which argue against a fabrication.

Hartmann gives the following summary of Case 47 (Great Falls, Montana, August 15, 1950):

> Witness I, General Manager of a Great Falls baseball team, and Witness II, Secretary, observed two white lights moving slowly across the sky. Witness I made 16 mm motion pictures of the lights. Both in-

dividuals have recently reaffirmed the observation, and there is little reason to question its validity. The case remains unexplained. Analysis indicates that the images on the film are difficult to reconcile with aircraft or other known phenomena, although aircraft cannot be entirely ruled out.

It is interesting to compare Hartmann's report and case studies with Condon's two-page summary of "Study of UFO Photographs" (CR, pp. 35–37). Only one paragraph is clearly based on Hartmann's work. This reads:

> Hartmann made a detailed study of 35 photographic cases (Section IV, Chapter 3) referring to the period 1966–1968, and a selection of eighteen older cases, some of which have been widely acclaimed in the UFO literature. This photographic study led to the identification of a number of widely publicized photographs as being ordinary objects, others as fabrications, and others as innocent misidentifications of things photographed under unusual conditions.

In fact, Hartmann discusses fourteen cases, of which six are from the period 1966–1968. Concerning the McMinnville, Oregon, case (Case 46), it is puzzling that Condon refers not to the analysis made by Hartmann, but to an analysis made by Everitt Merritt, who was not a member of the project staff, but a photogrammatrist on the staff of the Autometrics Division of the Raytheon Company of Alexandria, Virginia. Merritt found that "the UFO images turned out to be too fuzzy to allow worthwhile further parametric analysis." Condon reports at length Merritt's analysis of another case (Zanesville, Ohio; not discussed anywhere else in the report) that was considered to be a hoax, and also discusses two photographs published in *Look* magazine, quoting the analysis of Staff Sergeant Earl Schroeder of the Wright-Patterson Air Force Base. Schroeder is not listed as being affiliated with the Colorado UFO project, and the case he analyzed was not considered by the project staff.

Apart from generalizations, Condon devotes only one and a half pages to discussion of photographic evidence. Of this total, 60 percent is devoted to the work of Merritt, 30 percent to the work of Schroeder, and only 10 percent to the work of Hartmann. Further, as we have seen, Condon's summary of the work of his own staff member (Hartmann) was quite inadequate and—for whatever reasons—misleading.

RADAR-VISUAL CASES

Special importance may be attached to cases in which both visual and radar observations were made, and in which these observations were consistent. Such cases will typically involve several witnesses: They involve observations made at two or more "channels" of the electromagnetic spectrum; and the radar observations provide distance measurements and possibly height measurements also. Such cases are discussed in two staff summaries: Section III, Chapter 2, "Field Studies" by Craig (CR, pp. 51–75), and Section III, Chapter 5, "Optical and Radar Analysis of Field Cases" by Thayer (CR, pp. 115–76).

Thayer, in his summary of radar-visual cases, states: "There is a small, but significant, residue of cases from the radar-visual files (i.e., 1482N, Case 2) that have no plausible explanation such as propagation phenomena and/or misinterpreted man-made objects" (CR, p. 175). Earlier in his summary (CR, pp. 163–64), Thayer offers this comment on the case (referred to as "Lakenheath, England, August 13–14, 1956, 2230-0330 LST"): "The probability that anomalous propagation of radar signals may have been involved in this case seems to be small." Later, he adds: "The apparently rational, intelligent behavior of the UFO suggests a mechanical device of unknown origin as the most probable explanation of this sighting."

Case 2 (listed, rather cryptically, as "Greenwich, summer

1956") is presented in the Condon Report (CR, pp. 248–56). The abstract reads:

At least one UFO was tracked by air traffic control radar (GCA) at two USAF-RAF stations, with apparently corresponding visual sightings of round, white rapidly moving objects which changed directions abruptly. Interception by RAF fighter aircraft was attempted; one aircraft was vectored to the UFO by GCA radar and the pilot reported airborne radar contact and radar "gunlock." The UFO appeared to circle around behind the aircraft and followed it in spite of the pilot's evasive maneuvers. Contact was broken when the aircraft returned to base, low on fuel. The preponderance of evidence indicates the possibility of a genuine UFO in this case. The weather was generally clear with good visibility.

This case was later discussed in more detail by Thayer (1971). It is interesting to note the conclusion given by Thayer, at the end of this article, which reflects his view after further intensive study of this case:

In conclusion, with two highly redundant contacts—the first with ground radar, combined with both ground and airborne visual observers, and the second with airborne radar, an airborne visual observer, and two different ground radars—the Bentwaters-Lakenheath UFO incident represents one of the most significant radar-visual UFO cases. Taking into consideration the high credibility of the information and the cohesiveness and continuity of accounts, combined with a high degree of "strangeness," it is also certainly one of the most disturbing UFO incidents known today.

The other case of special interest is Case 5 listed in the Condon Report rather obscurely as "South-Central, Fall, 1957" (CR, pp. 260–66). This case is reviewed by Craig, who emphasizes that "no report of the incident was found in Blue Book files or in the files of NORAD Headquarters at Ent AFB" (CR, pp. 56–58). (The reason that no report was found is that the project staff had incorrectly dated the event as happening on September 19, 1957, whereas it actually occurred on July 17, 1957.) Craig, in describing the phenomenon, stated:

> It disappeared suddenly and reappeared at a different location both visually and on airborne and ground radars. Since visual and radar observation seemed to coincide, reflection of ground radar did not seem a satisfactory explanation. Other explanations such as airplanes, meteors, and plasma also seem unsatisfactory.

Craig concludes: "If the report is accurate, it describes an unusual, intriguing, and puzzling phenomenon, which, in the absence of additional information, must be listed as unidentified."

The case is also discussed extensively by Thayer in his summary (CR, pp. 136–39). Thayer attempts an explanation in terms of "anomalous propagation" (AP) echoes and an unidentified ground light source, but adds, "'There are many unexplained aspects to this sighting, however, and a solution such as given above, although possible, does not seem highly probable.'" The reader is urged to assess this statement by reviewing the case (CR, pp. 260–66) and the later more extensive account of McDonald (1971), who determined the correct date of this event and so obtained Air Force records that the Condon staff had been unable to track down. McDonald's account is, therefore, more complete and more detailed than the study presented in the Condon Report. McDonald's summary of the case reads:

An Air Force RB-47, equipped with electronic countermeasures (ECM) gear, and manned by six officers, was followed by an unidentified object for a distance of well over 700 mi. and for a time period of 1.5 hr., as it flew from Mississippi, through Louisiana and Texas and into Oklahoma. The object was, at various times, seen visually by the cockpit crew as an intensely luminous light, followed by ground-radar and detected on ECM monitoring gear aboard the RB-47. Of special interest in this case are several instances of simultaneous appearances and disappearances on all three of those physically distinct "channels," and rapidity of maneuvers beyond the prior experience of the air crew.

Another extensive discussion of this case can be found in Clark, *The UFO Encyclopedia* (pp. 761–90).

Condon, in his "Summary of the Study," devotes almost three pages to discussion of radar sightings of UFOs, but his comments on the case studies of the Colorado Project are confined to two short paragraphs. As an evaluation of these case studies, he quotes from Thayer's summary: "there was no case where the meteorological data available tended to negate the anomalous propagation hypothesis." This is, at best, an unfortunate quotation, implying that Thayer regards the anomalous propagation hypothesis as offering a plausible explanation of every case. A more complete quotation of Thayer's remark (CR, p. 172) is the following:

The reader should note that the assignment of cases into the probable AP cause category could have been made on the basis of the observational testimony alone. That is to say, that there was no case where the meteorological data available tended to negate the anomalous propagation hypothesis, thereby causing that case to be assigned to some other category.

In the table to which Thayer is referring (CR, p. 173), we see that for only nineteen of the thirty-five cases does Thayer regard anomalous propagation to be the "most likely or most plausible explanation." Thayer's assessment is perhaps presented more clearly by a later quotation: "Where the observational data pointed to anomalous propagation as the probable cause of an UFO incident, the meteorological data are overwhelmingly in favor of the plausibility of the AP hypothesis" (CR, p. 174). Thayer has clearly concluded that a substantial fraction of radar observations are probably due to anomalous propagation effects; but it is equally clear that he does not ascribe *all* radar observations to this phenomenon. The impression given by Condon's summary concerning radar-visual cases is, therefore, at variance with Thayer's summary and with the cases on which Thayer's summary is based.

Condon's account of radar cases is very similar to his account of photographic evidence: Very little of what he writes makes reference to the work of his staff, and what he does write about his staff's work is misleading.

RADAR DETECTION WITHOUT VISUAL DETECTION

Both Craig and Thayer attach special significance to Case 21, which took place in Colorado Springs, Colorado, on May 13, 1967, in which clear and consistent signals were shown by *two* airport radars, with no corresponding visual observation (CR, pp. 310–16). The abstract of this case, identified only as "South Mountain (Location A), Spring, 1967" (CR, p. 310), reads:

> Operators of two airport radars reported that a target equivalent to an aircraft had followed a commercial flight in, overtaken it, and passed it on one side, and proceeding [*sic*] at about 200 knots until it left the radar field. No corresponding object was visible from the control tower. On the basis of witnesses' reports and weather records, explanations

based on anomalous atmospheric propagation or freak reflection from other objects appear inadequate. The case is not adequately explained despite features that suggest a reflection effect (see Section III, Chapter 6). [Section III, Chapter 6, is devoted to "Visual Observations Made by U.S. Astronauts" and contains nothing relevant to this case.]

Craig, in his summary of "Field Studies," comments further on this case (CR, p. 72): "Of the current cases involving radar observations, one remained particularly puzzling after analysis of the information, since anomalous propagation and other common explanations apparently could not account for the observation."

In his summary of "Optical and Radar Analysis of Field Cases," Thayer devoted two pages (CR, pp. 170–71) to this case. He remarks: "This is a radar-only case, and is of particular interest because the UFO could not be seen, when there was every indication that it should have been seen." He points out that, although no object was seen from the ground, from the landing Braniff plane, or from a following Continental Airlines plane, the UFO followed "precisely the correct procedure for an overtaking aircraft, or one which is practicing an ILS approach but does not actually intend to touch down." In Thayer's opinion, "A ghost echo seems to be ruled out." He concludes that:

This must remain one of the most puzzling radar cases on record, and no conclusion is possible at this time. It seems inconceivable that an anomalous propagation echo would behave in the manner described, particularly with respect to the reported altitude changes, even if AP had been likely at the time. In view of the meteorological situation, it would seem that AP was rather unlikely. Besides, what is the probability that an AP return would appear only

once, and at that time appear to execute a perfect
practice ILS approach?

Condon makes no reference to this case in the section of his
summary dealing with radar sightings of UFOs.

MISCELLANEOUS EVIDENCE

Brief mention only will be made of some of the other types of
evidence considered in the report. Section III, Chapter 6, concerns "Visual Observations Made by U.S. Astronauts" as
studied by Professor Franklin E. Roach (CR, pp. 176–208). The
final paragraph of Roach's "Summary and Evaluation" is the
following:

> The three unexplained sightings, which have been
> gleaned from a great mass of reports, are a challenge
> to the analyst. Especially puzzling is the first one of
> the list, the daytime sighting of an object showing
> details such as arms (antennas?) protruding from a
> body having a noticeable angular extension. If the
> NORAD listing of objects near the GT4 spacecraft
> at the time of the sighting is complete as it presum-
> ably is, we shall have to find a rational explanation,
> or alternatively, keep it on our list of unidentifieds.

Condon, in discussing these observations, quotes Roach's remark that the three sightings are "a challenge to the analyst,"
and goes on to remark that "nothing definite relating to the
ETH aspects of UFOs has been established as a result of these
rather sporadic observations" (CR, pp. 42–43).

Concerning "Direct Physical Evidence," Craig attaches special significance to "metal fragments that purportedly fell to
earth at Ubatuba, São Paulo, Brazil, from an exploding extraterrestrial vehicle. The metal was alleged to be of such extreme
purity that it could not have been produced by earthly tech-

nology" (CR, pp. 94–97). Investigation by the Colorado staff showed that a sample of triply sublimed magnesium, supplied by the Dow Chemical Company, had a smaller impurity level than that of the "Brazil UFO." The analysis, however, showed that the fragments contained traces of both barium and strontium, which are not usual impurities in the production of magnesium; these metals were undetectable in the Dow sample. Craig remarks, "The high content of [strontium] was particularly interesting since [strontium] is not an expected impurity in magnesium made by usual production methods, and Dr. Busk [of Dow Chemical Company] knew of no one who intentionally added strontium to commercial magnesium." It was found that Dow Metallurgical Laboratory had made experimental batches of magnesium alloy containing from 0.1 percent up to 40 percent of strontium, which is to be compared with the level of 500 ± 100 parts per million of strontium in the Brazil sample. Although the lowest value in this range is twice the value found in the Brazil sample, Craig states that Dow had "produced a . . . batch of magnesium containing nominally the same concentration of [strontium] as was continued [*sic*] in the Ubatuba sample."

Craig also remarks: "Metallographic examinations show large, elongated magnesium grains, indicating that the metal had not been worked after solidification from the liquid or vapor state. It seems doubtful, therefore, that this sample had been a part of a fabricated metal object." This is a very curious remark, implying—as it does—that no fabricated object has ever been made of cast metal.

Condon, in his summary, remarks that "the magnesium metal was found to be much less pure than the regular commercial metal produced in 1957 by the Dow Chemical Company . . . [and] therefore it need not have come from an extraterrestrial source."

Once again, Condon's statement does not give an accurate representation of the work of his staff. The staff describes the comparison sample simply as "magnesium produced by known earthly technology" (CR, p. 96). Condon describes it as "regular commercial magnesium." As Craig states, the Dow Chemical Company has "supplied on request samples of triply sublimed magnesium" (CR, p. 95). These samples represented a laboratory production, not "regular commercial magnesium." Furthermore, the samples of triply sublimed magnesium supplied by the Dow Chemical Company had not been annealed (annealing would introduce further impurities), so that their metallurgical properties were grossly different from those of the Brazil magnesium.

However, the most regrettable aspect of the Colorado Project investigation of the Brazil magnesium is that the investigation was confined to a rather limited laboratory analysis of the sample. It is a basic rule of UFO research that one must assess the *total* evidence, which always includes the narrative evidence. According to this rule, another investigator (fluent in Portuguese or accompanied by an interpreter) should have been sent to Brazil to track down any evidence of events that might have been related to the Brazil magnesium sample.

The last category of evidence considered is "Indirect Physical Evidence," which is reviewed by Craig (CR, pp. 97–115). In presenting his conclusions, he states:

> Of all physical effects claimed to be due to the presence of UFOs, the alleged malfunction of automobile motors is perhaps the most puzzling. The claim is frequently made, sometimes in reports which are impressive because they involve multiple independent witnesses. Witnesses seem certain that the function of their cars was affected by the unidentified object, which sometimes reportedly was not seen until after the malfunction was noted. No satisfactory explanation for such effects, if indeed they occurred, is apparent.

The discussion of this evidence, both by Condon and by other members of the project staff, is of special interest. It is argued that, if automobile motors are stopped, it must be attributed to magnetic fields associated with UFOs (CR, pp. 38, 101, 380). For the one case studied by the project, it was determined that the automobile had not been exposed to a strong magnetic field. Craig concludes: "The case, therefore, apparently did not offer probative information regarding UFOs" (CR, p. 380). We shall return to discussion of this argument in the next section.

SCIENTIFIC METHODOLOGY OF THE COLORADO PROJECT

The title of the Condon Report is *Scientific Study of Unidentified Flying Objects*. The great weight attached to this report by scientists, by the public, and perhaps by officers of the federal government, is based on the presumption that the study was, in fact, scientific. This has been disputed by a number of individuals, notably McDonald (1969) and Hynek (1969, 1972), who make specific criticisms of the methodology of the project. These criticisms will not be repeated here. The following comments are more general in nature.

Whether or not there is a well-defined "scientific method" applicable to all scientific problems, the fact is that the practices used by scientists vary from one subject to another. In research areas where the background noise and/or the inherent variability are high, such as epidemiology and meteorology, it is necessary to develop and use appropriate statistical techniques of data analysis. Where the experimental situation is well controlled and where the results are faithfully reproducible, it may suffice and may be desirable to analyze a single experiment in meticulous detail.

Physicists tend to look for an outstanding experiment that, taken in isolation, conclusively proves or disproves some hypothesis. It is perhaps not surprising, therefore, that this is the approach adopted by Condon in appraising the information reported to him by his staff. To some extent, it reflects also the attitude of the scientific staff. For exceptions to this rule, one might cite the above quoted paragraph of Craig (CR, p. 115), concerning "Indirect Physical Evidence," which clearly reflects judgment based on an *accumulation* of evidence. It is also worth pointing out that, if the staff had indeed been searching for one or two cases to prove conclusively one hypothesis or another, it would have been necessary to devote far more time, attention, manpower, and resources to those cases than appears to have been given to any one case.

The UFO problem seems to be closer to astronomy than to physics. No single observation of the position of a single planet establishes Kepler's law. No single observation of the position and magnitude of a single star establishes that the sun is in a disk-shaped galaxy. Nor can data concerning a single star confirm a proposed theory of stellar evolution. In discussing astronomical problems, it is essential to combine evidence derived from many observations. The strength of the observational facts may become significant only when very large numbers of observations are combined.

If one were to adopt astronomical practice as a guide, a crucial first step in the scientific study of UFOs would be the compilation of a catalog. This would have the immediate consequence of drawing upon information already accumulated (in many cases with great effort and great care) by other organizations. For instance, organizations such as APRO (Aerial Phenomena Research Organization), MUFON (Mutual UFO Network), and NICAP (National Investigation Committee for Aerial Phenomena) have compiled extensive files of UFO cases. One valuable collection of data, which the Colorado Project could have used, was that produced by the Battelle Memorial Institute, under contract to the Air Force, and issued as Blue Book Special Report No. 14 (Project Blue Book, 1955). This was certainly available to the project, since it was declassified in 1955. Vallee provided the project with his computer-based catalog in February 1967, but there is no evidence it was ever used.

There is, indeed, great advantage to be derived from using more than one source of data. Data derived from only one source might be spurious, or partly spurious, and the same might be true for another source of data. If both sources of data yield distinct and irreconcilable patterns, one would suspect that at least one has been subject to biased reduction and possibly even to deliberate fabrication. If one of the sources of data is from one's own scientific staff, once might conclude that the fault lies with the other group, or one might choose to check carefully the methods used by one's own team.

On the other hand, patterns that appear *consistently* in data derived from several independent sources are far more significant than a pattern that shows up in only one source. "Strong" facts of this type can be obtained only by careful cataloging of data from as many reliable sources as one can find. After a catalog has been compiled and patterns supported by the weight of evidence in the catalog have been established, one can then begin the comparison of evidence and hypotheses. (An outstanding example of this process is the construction of the Hertzsprung-Russell diagram in astrophysics, which provides the crucial test for any theory of stellar evolution.) This procedure is complex, calling for a careful organization of theoretical work and data reduction.

In assessing a phenomenon, it is essential to "filter" the available evidence. A key filtering procedure is represented by the *definition* of the phenomenon. Condon's definition, which has already been quoted, suffers from the defect that it allows a great deal of "noise" to accompany whatever "signal" there may be in the data. Most students of the UFO phenomenon would adopt a more restrictive definition such as that adopted by Hynek (1972), who recommends that a "UFO report" be defined as "a statement by a person or persons judged responsible and psychologically normal by commonly accepted standards, describing a personal, visual, or instrumentally aided perception of an object or light in the sky or on the ground and/or its assumed physical effects, that does not specify any known physical event, object, or process or any psychological event or process."

However, the definition of the phenomenon is only one filtering procedure. In discussing a complex phenomenon such as the UFO phenomenon, it should be followed by further "filters" that may comprise restrictions on allowable evidence, classification schemes, etc. The staff summaries, indeed, provide a breakdown of evidence into categories, but this is only a rudimentary scheme of analysis.

Another important point of scientific methodology is that, if one is evaluating a hypothesis (such as ETH), it is beneficial to regard this hypothesis as one member of a complete and mutually exclusive set of hypotheses. This point seems to have been clearly recognized by Thayer (CR, p. 116), but it was apparently ignored by Condon and other members of the project staff. It is of little use to argue that the evidence does not support one hypothesis, unless one knows what the surviving hypotheses are. One of Sherlock Holmes's methods was truth by elimination: "How often have I said to you that when you have eliminated the impossible, whatever remains, *however improbable*, must be the truth?" (Doyle, 1994).

Finally, in evaluating a hypothesis, one must avoid procedures of data reduction that depend upon the truth or falseness of that hypothesis. Put another way, one must avoid "theory-dependent" arguments. This requirement, above all, makes the appraisal of the UFO phenomenon very difficult: if we entertain the hypothesis that the phenomenon may be due to an extremely advanced civilization, we must face the possibility that many ideas we accept as simple truths may, in a wider and more sophisticated context, not be as simple and may not even be truths.

As a specific example, we find in the Condon Report the argument that a supersonic UFO should produce a sonic boom (CR, p. 143). This is certainly true of every supersonic object that man has constructed. But we should *not* assume that a more advanced civilization could not find some way of traveling at supersonic speeds without producing a sonic boom. Petit (1986) has paid special attention to this aspect of UFO reports and has proposed a procedure involving magnetohydrodynamic processes whereby the shock wave of a supersonic object would be suppressed.

Although it is simple to state this requirement concerning data reduction, it is by no means simple to put it into effect. It may, indeed, be necessary to proceed by trial and error: Whenever one runs into an impasse, a situation in which it is impossible to reconcile the established data with any explicitly considered hypothesis (including that of ETH), one may need to review the process of data reduction to see if the relaxation of an implicit hypothesis will lead to a situation in which the evidence can be reconciled with at least one explicit hypothesis.

A further example of this type of situation is the discussion of "Automobile Malfunction and Headlight Failure" by Craig (CR, pp. 100–108), which was mentioned previously. As we have noted, the position taken by Condon and other members of the project staff is that, if automobile motors are stopped, this phenomenon must be due to magnetic fields associated with UFOs. Condon and other members of the staff apparently do not consider the possibility that an advanced civilization may know of and use physical processes with which we are now unfamiliar. Yet this possibility is perhaps the most intriguing reason a scientist would be interested in studying the UFO phenomenon! The discussion of sonic booms and of automobile-engine malfunction by the Condon staff provide two prime examples of theory-dependent arguments.

DISCUSSION

The evaluation of evidence by category seems to show that each staff summary is a fair and justifiably cautious accounting of the relevant case material. By contrast, Condon's summary bears little relation to the work, analyses, and summaries of his own staff. Hence, a minimal criticism that one might make is that the efforts of many individuals found no satisfactory integration.* This failing may have been due in part to a faulty initial conception of the nature of the phenomenon. If, as the

---

*When I showed an early version of this analysis to one of the Principal Investigators of the Colorado Project, he remarked, "You should have seen the first draft that Condon wrote. It was much worse. After I pointed out a lot that was wrong with the first draft, Condon rewrote it and improved it considerably."

director may have believed, the phenomenon could be tackled as a straightforward problem of physical science, there might now be little disagreement among the scientific community regarding the validity and conclusions of the report. The UFO phenomenon appears instead to be more akin to some of the enigmatic phenomena of modern astronomy, such as the sources of gamma-ray bursts. Concerning these strange objects, we do not know where they are, we do not know what they are, and we can only speculate on how they function; but these limitations, severe as they are, by no means deter astronomers and astrophysicists from studying them as intensively as possible.

Concerning UFOs, we are not sure whether they are hoaxes, illusions, or real. If real, we do not know whether the reality is of a psychological and sociological nature, or one that belongs in the realm of physics. If the phenomenon has physical reality, we do not know whether it can be understood in terms of present-day physics, or whether it may present us with an example of twenty-first-century (or thirtieth-century) physics in action. If one is, indeed, facing a problem of this magnitude, it is necessary to devote the utmost care to the scientific methodology involved in the project.

In sum, it is my opinion that weaknesses of the Condon Report are an understandable but regrettable consequence of a misapprehension concerning the nature and subtlety of the phenomenon. It is also my opinion that there is much in the Condon Report that supports the proposition that an analysis of the totality of UFO reports would show that a signal emerges from the noise and that the signal is not readily comprehensible in terms of phenomena now well known to science. If this is so, then the report makes a case for the further scientific study of UFO reports.

It appears that this opinion is, in fact, shared by certain members of the Colorado Project staff. For instance, Professor David R. Saunders (who left the project in circumstances to be discussed in Chapter 4) has published a book, *UFOs? Yes!* (Saunders and Harkins, 1968), challenging the findings of the Condon Report. Gordon D. Thayer also has continued his interest in the phenomenon, as is evident from his report on the Lakenheath case (Thayer, 1971).

In conclusion, it is necessary to comment briefly on the review of the Condon Report by the National Academy of Sciences panel (Clemence et al., 1969). This distinguished body reviewed the report and fully endorsed its scope, methodology, and findings. In the section above, "Evaluation of Evidence by Category," we have noted the discrepancies between facts and views advanced by the Colorado Project staff and those advanced by the director. In comparing these with the NAS panel review, it is clear that some of their information is taken from the director's "Summary of the Study," even where the content of this section is contradicted by material presented in Sections III and IV of the report. For instance, discussing photographic cases, the panel asserts that "35 photographic cases were investigated . . . none proved to be real objects with high strangeness." This statement mirrors Condon's discussion of photographic evidence in Section II of the report; but, as we have seen in the "Overview" in this chapter, Condon's statements do not accurately summarize the material presented by Hartmann, who carried out the photographic analysis.

The Condon Report has also been studied by the UFO Subcommittee of the American Institute of Aeronautics and Astronautics (AIAA), as part of their appraisal of the UFO problem, to be discussed in Chapter 4 (Kuettner et al., 1970). The subcommittee states that "not all conclusions contained in the Report itself are fully reflected in Condon's summary." The subcommittee also points out that "Condon's chapter, 'Summary of the Study,' contains more than its title indicates; it discloses many of his personal conclusions."

Condon's most important recommendation was perhaps that concerned with future activity. He states that "further extensive study of UFOs probably cannot be justified in the expectation that science will be advanced thereby" (CR, p. 1). The NAS panel concurred in this recommendation. On the other hand, The AIAA UFO Subcommittee "did not find a basis in the report for his prediction that nothing of scientific value will come of further studies" (Kuettner et al., 1970).

The NAS panel, which was appointed in late 1968, began their initial reading of the report on November 15. The panel convened on December 2 and again on January 6, 1969, to conclude its deliberations and to prepare its findings. Seven weeks is a very short time for panel members to digest a report on what was probably an unfamiliar subject. This is especially true when there are gross discrepancies between the report and its summary, which readers are unlikely to expect. By contrast, the views of the AIAA subcommittee were crystallized late in 1970, allowing more time to appreciate the subtleties of the problem and to digest the massive report.

This reexamination of the Condon Report and my comparatively brief quotations from the reviews by the NAS panel and the AIAA subcommittee may cast doubt on some of the findings of the report and some of the opinions and recommendations of the director.* The following quotation shows that such dissent was foreseen, and even encouraged, by Condon himself:

> Scientists are no respecters of authority. Our conclusion that study of UFO reports is not likely to advance science will not be uncritically accepted by them. Nor should it be, nor do we wish it to be. For scientists, it is our hope that the detailed analytical presentation of what we were able to do, and what we were unable to do, will assist them in deciding whether or not they agree with our conclusions. Our hope is that the details of this report will help other scientists in seeing what the problems are and the difficulties of coping with them. (CR, p. 2)

---

*I have learned from private conversation with one of the members of the NAS panel that, in fact, all of the panelists were not as happy with the Condon Report as the panel report would indicate. He told me that he had had concerns and reservations about the Condon Report but did not press them in the panel discussions because he "did not want to rock the boat."

CHAPTER 4

Aftermath of the Colorado Project

INITIAL RECEPTION OF THE CONDON REPORT

The Condon Report received almost universal praise in the news media when it was published in 1969. The nature of the press coverage was probably set by (*New York Times*) science reporter Walter Sullivan, who had actually prepared an introduction to the published version of the report (CR, v–xiii). Sullivan remarked, in part:

> It was a remarkable fact that, despite the enormous public interest in UFOs, the big guns of science had never been brought to bear on the problem. Now for the first time a full-fledged scientific study has been carried out.

Reviews in scientific journals were mixed. The influential journal *Nature* (1969) described the report as "A Sledgehammer for Nuts." The *Bulletin of the Atomic Scientists* published a critical review by Hynek (1969). The journal *Icarus*, of which Carl Sagan was then editor, evenhandedly published a laudatory review by Dr. Hong-Yee Chiu (1969), then at the NASA Institute for Space Studies in New York, and a critical review by Dr. James E. McDonald (1969), then on the staff of the Institute of Atmospheric Physics at the University of Arizona at Tucson. Hynek (1972) and Jacobs (1975), in their later books on the UFO problem, each devote a chapter to the Condon Report. It is notable that the critical reviews came from those scientists who had actually carried out research in the UFO area, whereas the laudatory reviews came from scientists who had not carried out such research.

As mentioned in the previous chapter, there was and has remained a misperception about the Colorado Project. It is often referred to as the work of the "Condon Committee" (see, for instance, Jacobs). There was no such committee. The "Conclusions and Recommendations" and the "Summary of the Study" appeared over Condon's name, not over the names of all the senior participants of the study. Michael D. Swords (1996), who has carried out an extensive historical research of the project, concluded that "of the fifteen top staff members [of the project], at least twelve . . . definitely disagreed with [Condon]." Indeed, by the time the project was concluded, Condon had fired two members of his staff, David R. Saunders (professor of psychology and one of the principal investigators) and Norman E. Levine, for disclosing material in project files to someone who was not a member of the project. Saunders published a dissenting book in December 1968, just before the Condon Report was published by Bantam Press (Saunders and Harkins, 1968).

Nevertheless, the Condon Report retains crucial significance among the scientific and policy-making communities, since it is believed to be the only unclassified investigation of the UFO phenomenon ever carried out by an established scientific organization under contract to a U.S. federal agency. Condon himself pointed out how important it is that such a study be free from secrecy, writing: "Where secrecy is known to exist, one can never be absolutely sure that he knows the complete truth" (CR, p. 522).

SECRECY AND THE
COLORADO PROJECT

This brings us to perhaps the most curious aspect of the Colorado Project and of the Condon Report. The above remark by Condon was made in relation to the proposition that "some agency of the Government—either within the Air Force, the Central Intelligence Agency, or elsewhere—knows all about UFOs and is keeping the knowledge secret. . . . We decided not to pay special attention to [this hypothesis], but instead to keep alert to any indications that might lead to any evidence that not all of the essential facts known to the government were being given to us. . . . We found no such evidence." It may well be true that Condon and his colleagues found no evidence that any agency of the government "[knew] all about UFOs." However, we learn from the Condon Report that the Air Force was not completely open in its dealings with the project.

The abstract of Case 30 reads: "A civilian employee at an AFB confirmed an earlier report that base personnel had made an UFO sighting, although official sources denied that such an event had occurred" (CR, pp. 341–42). The background reads: "A rumor was relayed to this project by a source considered to be reliable, reporting in the fall, 1967, six UFOs had followed an X-15 flight at the AFB. It was suggested that motion pictures of the event should be available from the Air Force." There follows an account of the investigation that includes the following remarks: "The rumor persisted, however, with indications that official secrecy was associated with the event. . . . Attempts to learn more about the reported event from the PIO [public information officer] were met with apparent evasion from that office. . . . Although it is true that the report of this incident was never more than a rumor, it is also true that project investigators were not able to satisfactorily confirm or deny that an [sic] UFO incident had occurred. Attempts to investigate the rumor were met with evasion and uncooperative responses to our inquiries by base information."

In the late 1970s, the Freedom of Information Act made it

possible to request classified information from federal agencies. On learning that the Central Intelligence Agency had released some information related to the UFO question, I requested copies of this information from the CIA in 1979, and agency staff kindly responded positively to this request (Sturrock, 1987). I learned from CIA documents that the Air Force had made arrangements for the Colorado Project to receive photographic services from the agency's National Photographic Interpretation Center (NPIC). On February 20, 1967, Condon, Low, and Saunders, cleared for at least USAF Secret and accompanied by John Coleman (listed as "ex-director of the National Academy of Sciences"), William Price (Air Force Directorate of Science and Technology), and Dr. Thomas Ratchford of AFOSR (Air Force Office of Scientific Research), visited NPIC, where they met with NPIC Director Dr. Arthur C. Lundahl. It was agreed that NPIC would assist Dr. Condon, on the understanding that the agency's role would not be identified.

It appears that CIA staff provided material assistance to the Colorado Project. During the February 20 meeting, NPIC presented briefings on their analytical capabilities and on their results "on the second UFO project" (presumably a CIA project, but possibly an Air Force project). There followed "a general discussion on UFOs."

On May 1, 1967, the Colorado Project issued a press release calling for "pictures of unidentified flying objects from private citizens," and it gave a set of recommendations to the photographer and a list of items of information the photographer should prepare. This press release is a rewrite of a document prepared for the project by NPIC staff and approved by Lundahl on March 24, 1967.

Condon and his colleagues were again briefed by CIA staff on May 5, 1967. Present at the meeting were Condon, Low, and Hartmann from the Colorado Project; Ratchford from AFOSR; Dr. Charles Reed of the National Research Council; CIA staff; and another person whose name is suppressed in the released documents. This unknown person presented a briefing on photogrammetric analysis that he had carried out on a UFO case, and his briefing impressed Condon and his group very favorably. It was agreed that the unknown person would, through the good offices of the CIA, carry out an analysis of the Zanesville case for the Colorado Project. This unknown person must have been Dr. Everitt Merritt of the Autometrics Division of the Raytheon Company of Alexandria, Virginia, since, in writing about photographic evidence, Condon referred extensively to Merritt and Merritt's analysis of the Zanesville case. Condon did not explain *how* he acquired this information: He simply remarked that he "became acquainted with Everitt Merritt" and "made arrangements with Merritt for his services."

It is indeed curious that, after these secret briefings and analytical support, Condon would write: "Where secrecy is known to exist, one can never be absolutely sure that he knows the complete truth."

CURIOSITY AWAKENED

The reader may wonder how I came to devote so much attention to the Condon Report. By contrast, most of the scientific community paid little attention when the report was published, and none later.

In 1971, I was searching for a scientist with a background in astrophysics, statistics, and computers to assist me with a special project in my astrophysical research. The position had been advertised for only a short time when a soft-spoken Frenchman walked into my office and offered his services. His name was Jacques Vallee. He was exactly the person I was looking for, and he joined my research group almost immediately.

Jacques had been working with me for only a short time when I learned that he had written three books on UFOs. At that time, I had no interest in the subject but, since Jacques was now a colleague, I felt an obligation to learn something of his interests and publications. Reading his books left me with the uneasy feeling that maybe the subject was not ignorable after all.

I had not been looking for a topic that might divert my attention from my astrophysical research, but such a topic was now on my mind. I therefore set myself the assignment of studying the Condon Report, expecting that this would clarify the UFO phenomenon, and enable me to write it off as a "nonproblem," thereby bringing me back into line with my scientific colleagues. Unfortunately, as I have already explained, that did not happen. Quite the contrary. Instead of solving one problem, my study of the Condon Report left me with three. First, the case studies and staff summaries gave me further reason to believe that the UFO problem was nontrivial and unsolved. Second, I was quite unable to understand why Condon's "Conclusions and Recommendations" and "Summary of the Study" bore no relation to the work of the Colorado Project. Third, I found it impossible to publish my evaluation (Sturrock, 1974a) of the Condon Report in a scientific journal. I submitted it to six journals in turn and, in each case, received a polite turndown from the editor, almost by return mail. As I recall, no editor even sent the article out for review.

In the course of my reading, I learned that some positive action had been taken by one professional scientific organization: the American Institute of Aeronautics and Astronautics (AIAA). In 1967, the Board of Directors of the AIAA asked two of its Technical Committees, namely the Atmospheric Environment Committee and the Space and Atmospheric Physics Committee, to form a subcommittee to arrive at an unbiased assessment of the status of the UFO problem. Its chairman was Dr. Joachim P. Kuettner, a distinguished atmospheric scientist at the Environmental Research Laboratories of the National Oceanographic and Atmospheric Administration (NOAA) in Boulder. Kuettner also had the distinction of holding some world records as a glider pilot. The other members of the subcommittee were Jerold Bidwell (Martin Marietta), Glenn A. Cato (TRW Systems), Bernard N. Charles (Hughes Aircraft), Murray Dryer (NOAA Environmental Research Laboratories),

Howard D. Edwards (Georgia Institute of Technology), Paul McCready, Jr. (Meteorology Research Inc.), Andrew J. Masley (McDonnell Douglas Missile and Space Systems), Robert Rados (NASA Goddard Space Flight Center), Donald M. Swingle (U.S. Army Electronics Command), and Vernon J. Zurich (NOAA Environmental Research Laboratories).

The subcommittee addressed the very basic question: Does the UFO problem present a legitimate scientific problem deserving the attention of the scientific and engineering communities? They delved deeply into theoretical and philosophical aspects of the problem and Condon met with the subcommittee more than once. The subcommittee published its report in 1970 in the widely read aerospace journal *Astronautics and Astrophysics* (Kuettner, 1970). Unlike the Condon Report, this *was* a committee report, subscribed to by all members of the subcommittee. The subcommittee also arranged for publication of two notable radar-visual cases that had been considered by the Colorado Project. Articles by Gordon D. Thayer (who had been a member of the Colorado Project) and by McDonald gave more detailed accounts of the 1956 "Lakenheath" case (Thayer, 1971) and the 1957 "RB-47" case (McDonald, 1971), respectively.

In referring to Condon's "Summary of the Study," the Kuettner subcommittee stated that "[we] did not find a basis in the report for his prediction that nothing of scientific value will come of further studies." On the contrary, they found that "a phenomenon with such a high ratio of unexplained cases (about 30%) should arouse sufficient scientific curiosity to continue its study." It was the opinion of the subcommittee that "the only promising approach [would be] a continuing, moderate-level effort with emphasis on improved data collection by objective means and on high-quality scientific analysis."

At about this time, it occurred to me that scientists might be more interested in reports made by other scientists than in reports coming from nonscientists. With the encouragement of Dr. Kuettner, I therefore carried out a survey of the membership of the San Francisco chapter of the AIAA. My report on this survey was subsequently published in the monthly journal of the AIAA (Sturrock, 1974b).

This was a small survey, and it encouraged me to attempt a larger study. The Council of the American Astronomical Society kindly gave me permission to carry out a survey of AAS members concerning the UFO problem. I was pleasantly surprised at the high response rate; about 52 percent of the members actually replied. I was also pleasantly surprised that there were only a few rude remarks about my activity, and many more remarks that were encouraging. It was notable that, in response to my question about whether the UFO problem deserves scientific study, 23 percent replied "certainly," 30 percent "probably," 27 percent "possibly," 17 percent "probably not," and 3 percent "certainly not." Clearly, the response was more positive than negative, contrary to my expectation.

The AAS response to one of my questions had a major influence on my subsequent thinking. As part of my questionnaire, I asked if the reader would like to obtain more information about the UFO problem and, if so, in what form. To my surprise, I found that 75 percent of the respondents wished to obtain more information but (almost unanimously) only in the form of journal articles. The results of my survey were published as a Stanford University report in January 1977 (Sturrock, 1977a) and again in revised form in November 1977 (Sturrock, 1977b).

Since my report on the survey was much longer than the earlier report on the Colorado Project, which I had not been able to publish in a scientific journal, I did not even try submitting it for publication. I had by then learned of other scientists who had submitted articles on the UFO problem, only to have them summarily rejected. It had become clear to me that, if any scientific journal were to meet the need made evident by my survey, it was not going to be a journal then in existence. It would be necessary to start a new one. (The report on my survey was eventually published in 1994 [Sturrock, 1994a, b, c]).

THE SOCIETY FOR SCIENTIFIC EXPLORATION

At about this time, I had the good fortune to meet Robert G. Jahn, Professor of Aeronautics and Dean of the School of Engineering and Applied Sciences at Princeton University. In response to probing questions from an undergraduate student at Princeton, Jahn had begun a series of experiments on consciousness and its possible interaction with the material world. Jahn found that scientific journals were just as resistant to publishing articles in this field of research as they were to publishing articles related to the UFO question. Jahn therefore strongly encouraged me to move forward in organizing a new society and a new journal.

With Jahn's cooperation and good advice, I soon found myself working with a number of scientists in setting up a founding committee for what is now known as the Society for Scientific Exploration. The founding committee comprised George O. Abell (Professor of Astronomy at the University of California at Los Angeles), Bart J. Bok (Professor of Astronomy at the University of Arizona), Robert F. Creegan (Professor of Philosophy at the State University of New York in Albany), Persi Diaconis (Professor of Statistics at Stanford University), Thomas Gold (Professor of Astronomy at Cornell University), Jahn, Roger N. Shepard (Professor of Psychology at Stanford University), George L. Siscoe (Professor of Atmospheric Sciences at the University of California at Los Angeles), Ian Stevenson (Professor of Psychiatry at the University of Virginia), William B. Thompson (Professor of Physics at the University of California at San Diego), James Trefil (Professor of Physics at the University of Virginia), Marcello Truzzi (Professor of Sociology at Eastern Michigan University), and myself. The Society was formally founded in 1982 with Laurence W. Fredrick and Charles R. Tolbert (both Professors of Astronomy at the University of Virginia) as Secretary and Treasurer, respectively; Trefil as Vice President; and myself as President. Since its inception the society has grown to over 250

members and over 500 associates drawn from more than forty
countries. The society has published its journal, *Journal of Scientific Exploration*, since 1987. A recent description of the society includes the following:

> The primary goal of the international Society for
> Scientific Exploration (SSE) is to provide a profes-
> sional forum for presentations, criticism, and debate
> concerning topics which are for various reasons ig-
> nored or studied inadequately within mainstream sci-
> ence. A secondary goal is to promote improved
> understanding of those factors that unnecessarily
> limit the scope of scientific inquiry, such as sociolog-
> ical constraints, restrictive world views, hidden theo-
> retical assumptions, and the temptation to convert
> prevailing theory into prevailing dogma.
>
> Topics under investigation cover a wide spectrum.
> At one end are apparent anomalies in well-established
> disciplines. At the other, we find paradoxical phe-
> nomena that belong to no established discipline and
> therefore may offer the greatest potential for scientific
> advance and the expansion of human knowledge.
>
> The Society encourages such investigations for sev-
> eral reasons that may appeal to different communi-
> ties.
>
> - To the research scientist, we commend the intel-
>   lectual challenge of explaining away an ap-
>   parent anomaly or seizing the new knowledge
>   presented by a new one.
> - To the student scientist, we point out that sci-
>   ence does not begin with textbooks: it begins
>   with the unknown and ends with textbooks.
> - To the nonscientist, we acknowledge that deep
>   public interest in some of these topics calls for
>   unprejudiced evaluation based on objective re-
>   search.
> - To the policy-maker, we point out that today's
>   anomaly may become tomorrow's technology.

The society* has functioned well as a forum for the presentation and debate of research into topics that otherwise are not discussed in scientific societies. However, John Ziman, a physicist at Bristol University in England and a philosopher of science, has pointed out that "the strategy of science is directed towards the creation of a maximum consensus in the public domain" (Ziman, 1978). In other words, science advances in steps: Each step is the general acceptance of a new fact or a new theory. This process can occur fairly rapidly if the new knowledge does not conflict with old knowledge. However, whenever it is necessary to abandon an old fact or theory to make room for its successor, the process can be slow and painful. Perhaps the most pessimistic assessment of these difficulties was made by the great physicist Max Planck, widely regarded as the father of quantum mechanics, who once wrote: "New scientific truth does not triumph by convincing its opponents and making them see the light, but rather because its opponents eventually die, and a new generation grows up that is familiar with it" (Planck, 1950).

---

*For further information about SSE, please check the society web site: *www.scientificexploration.org*.

PART TWO

PRESENTATIONS
AT POCANTICO

CHAPTER 5

Introduction to Pocantico

From 1947 on, UFO reports have continued to pose an unwelcome problem to the Air Force and to the scientific community. On December 17, 1969, acting on Condon's recommendation, Secretary of the Air Force Robert C. Seamans, Jr., announced the termination of Project Blue Book. However, this did not lead to a cessation of UFO reports. They have continued worldwide to the present day. A current catalog of UFO reports (Hatch, 1999) has more than 17,000 entries which is far larger than several catalogs of astronomical objects and events.

The astronomical catalogs receive intense scrutiny; the UFO catalogs do not. The scientific community continues to display remarkably little interest in this topic. This may be due to the fact that there are no public funds to support research into this issue, to the assumption that there are no data worth examining, to the belief that the Colorado Project and the resulting Condon Report had effectively settled the question, and possibly in part to the perception that the topic is in some sense "not respectable." The relative importance of these four causes is unclear, but it seems likely that each has had some impact in dampening the interest of the scientific community in this subject.

When an area that is susceptible to scientific research is in a confused state or at a critical juncture where it is necessary to make hard decisions concerning its future, it may be helpful to hold a panel review in which a number of scientists—some familiar with the field and some comparative outsiders—assess the area, prepare a summary of the state of knowledge, and recommend what steps should be taken to expedite further progress.

Such a review is carried out every ten years by the United States astronomical community. The resulting reports provide the community and funding agencies with expert summaries of each sub-area of astronomy and clear, prioritized recommendations giving the panel's best advice as to what investments should be made in the next ten years. Such an extensive review typically takes a year or more of effort by many scientists and support staff. Although such a review may be supported by federal funds, there is every effort to ensure that the advice is strictly independent of the funding agencies. That is a key requirement for the credibility of such a report.

Not every review lives up to that ideal level of independence. If an agency has an ongoing program, it may need support for that program to ensure that Congress continues to fund it. In that case, a review panel commissioned by the agency may be almost independent—but not quite.

In 1977, it seemed quite likely that a panel review of the UFO question would take place. Frank Press, Science Adviser to President Jimmy Carter, wrote a letter dated July 21, 1977, to NASA Administrator Robert Frosch recommending that NASA organize "a small panel of inquiry . . . to see if there are any significant findings" since the Condon Report. Press remarked that "this is a public relations problem as much as anything else." In his reply to Press dated December 21, 1977, Frosch declined to "mount a research effort . . . or to convene a symposium," citing "[the] absence of physical evidence available for thorough laboratory analysis." However, Frosch added, "If some new element of hard evidence is brought to our attention, in the future, it would be entirely appropriate for a

NASA laboratory to analyze and report upon an otherwise unexplained organic or inorganic sample; we stand ready to respond to any *bona fide* physical evidence from credible sources.
We intend to leave the door open for such a possibility."

Two decades later, in December 1996, Mr. Laurance Rockefeller, a distinguished and influential citizen and chairman of
the LSR Fund, invited me to review with him our understanding of the problem posed by UFO reports. We agreed that
the problem was in a very unsatisfactory state of ignorance and
confusion. I expressed the opinion that the problem will be re-
solved only by extensive and open professional scientific investigation, and that an essential prerequisite for such research is
that more scientists acquire an interest in this topic.

We agreed that the key point determining whether or not the
scientists would take any interest in the subject is the existence
of physical evidence. If there is no relevant physical evidence associated with this problem, then there is very little that scientists can do, and they will continue to do nothing. If, on the
other hand, relevant physical evidence is available, there is a
great deal that can be done, and the problem might be trans-
formed from one that is of no interest to the scientific community into one that is of great interest to the scientific
community—from one in which scientists have an uncomfortable feeling of the existence of a vague and ill-defined problem,
into one in which scientists become aware of the existence of
specific evidence that could be analyzed by known instrumentation and procedures.

Rockefeller and his colleague Mr. Henry Diamond and I
therefore conceived of a meeting at which prominent investigators of UFO reports would meet with a panel of eight or nine
scientists with wide-ranging interests and expertise. The charge
to the investigators would be to present various forms of physical evidence, if such evidence exists. The charge to the panel
would be simply to determine whether further investigation of
such physical evidence would be likely to lead to improved understanding of the UFO problem. It must be emphasized that it
was *not* our intention to ask the panel to "solve" the UFO

problem. It would be unreasonable to expect a few scientists, meeting for only a few days, to solve a problem that remained unsolved after twenty years of study by the Air Force, and two years of study at the University of Colorado!

A panel review requires administrative and financial support, as well as planning and direction. To provide administrative support, it was necessary that some organization have contractual responsibility for the review. This role was filled by the Society for Scientific Exploration. It must be emphasized that the society's role was strictly administrative. The purpose of the society is to encourage research, wherever research may lead. The society had no vested interest in any particular possible outcome from the review. Financial support was provided by the LSR Fund.

In my early discussions with Mr. Rockefeller, I agreed to serve as director. However, I sought and received advice from a small Scientific Steering Committee comprising Dr. Thomas E. Holzer of the High Altitude Observatory at the National Center for Atmospheric Research, Boulder; Dr. Robert Jahn, Professor of Aerospace Engineering at Princeton University; Dr. David E. Pritchard, Professor of Physics at the Massachusetts Institute of Technology; Dr. Harold E. Puthoff, Director of the Institute for Advanced Studies, Austin; Dr. Charles R. Tolbert, Professor of Astronomy at the University of Virginia; and Dr. Yervant Terzian, Professor of Astronomy and Chairman of the Astronomy Department at Cornell University. This committee helped me draw up the general plans and goals of the review, but the details were left in my hands.

Planning the meeting involved several tasks. The first was to persuade a number of experienced UFO investigators to take part in the meeting, with each investigator reviewing a specific category of physical evidence. Each investigator I approached was happy to cooperate. The investigators were Dr. Richard F. Haines of Los Altos, California; Dr. Illobrand von Ludwiger of Feldkirchen-Westerham, Germany; Dr. Mark Rodeghier of the Center for UFO Studies in Chicago; John F. Schuessler of Houston; Dr. Erling Strand of Ostfold, Norway; Dr. Michael

Swords, Professor in the General Studies Science Department at Eastern Michigan University; Dr. Jacques F. Vallee of San Francisco; and Jean-Jacques Velasco of CNES (Centre Nationale d'Études Spatiales, the French counterpart of the U.S. agency NASA, the National Aeronautics and Space Administration).

It was not quite so easy to organize the review panel. It was clear that I needed scientists knowledgeable about atmospheric phenomena, geophysics, astronomy, and some other fields with which I have some familiarity. However, I also needed scientists expert in geology, meteoritics, radiation injuries, photographic analysis, and plant biology, with which I am not familiar. I was able to recruit some colleagues who were well known to me: Dr. Von Eshleman, Emeritus Professor of Electrical Engineering at Stanford University, who is an expert on radiowave propagation and radar operation; Dr. Thomas Holzer, who was a member of the Scientific Steering Committee and who is expert in space science; Dr. J. R. (Randy) Jokipii, Regents' Professor of Planetary Sciences and Astronomy at the University of Arizona in Tucson, who is expert in a wide range of geophysical phenomena; and Dr. Charles Tolbert, also a member of the Scientific Steering Committee, who is expert in a wide range of observational astronomy. Holzer and Tolbert were members of the Society for Scientific Exploration (SSE) and therefore had some exposure to the UFO field, but they were decidedly unsympathetic to much of the material they had seen and heard presented on the subject.

By consulting my scientific colleagues and the directories of some professional societies, and with the help of the Scientific Steering Committee, I was able to arrange for the participation of five scientists whom I had not previously met: Dr. François Louange, Managing Director of Fleximage, Paris, France, an expert in photographic analysis; the geologist Dr. H. J. (Jay) Melosh, Professor of Planetary Science at the University of Arizona in Tucson; Dr. James J. Papike, Head of the Institute of Meteoritics and Professor of Earth and Planetary Sciences at the University of New Mexico in Albuquerque, an expert in upper atmospheric phenomena; Dr. Guenther Reitz of the

German Aerospace Center, Institute for Aerospace Medicine, in Cologne, Germany, an expert in radiation injuries; and Dr. Bernard Veyret of the Bioelectromagnetics Laboratory at the University of Bordeaux, France, an expert in plant biology. Eshleman and Holzer kindly agreed to serve as co-chairs of the review panel.

Panel members had no or little previous involvement with the subject of the meeting, but had opinions nevertheless. It was my view that the meeting in Pocantico would be most instructive if there were a real difference in the attitudes and opinions which investigators and panel members would bring with them to the meeting. I knew that most of the investigators would arrive with the opinion that the UFO phenomenon is real and significant. Not much would be accomplished by presentations to a panel composed of scientists with the same opinion. As I have mentioned already, Holzer and Tolbert had seen articles in the *Journal of Scientific Exploration* and heard some papers presented at society meetings; these articles and presentations had not impressed them. With two exceptions, the other panel members had no previous exposure to the field. Most of them professed themselves to be decidedly skeptical agnostics, who were willing to listen to the presentations with little expectation of being convinced of anything new.

In seeking one panel member to represent a field far from my own, I was told by another panel member that "XXX would be great, as far as his qualifications go, but he has a pretty negative opinion of this field," to which I replied, "Then he is exactly the man that I want!"

Only two of the panel members were not novices. François Louange and Bernard Veyret had both served as consultants to the French UFO research project that was originally named "GEPAN" (pronounced "zhəpõn") and later renamed "SEPRA." This project is described in Chapter 20, "The GEPAN/SEPRA Project.")

Another important requirement was the selection of moderators for the meetings. I needed professional scientists who were very experienced in running meetings, who could follow everything that was being discussed, and who would have the confidence of the investigators and the review panel. It was essential that they would have the skill to control the proceedings without directing them. I was fortunate to be able to recruit, for this task, David Pritchard and Harold Puthoff, who were both members of the Scientific Steering Committee.

The location of the meeting was going to be crucial. We needed a facility with good meeting rooms, in a quiet, pleasant location away from city bustle. Mr. Rockefeller graciously provided such facilities at the Pocantico Conference Center at the Rockefeller estate in Tarrytown, New York.

Since a number of the participants were coming from Europe, my original plan was to conduct all the business of the review within the space of one week. The participants convened at the conference center in the late afternoon of Monday, September 29, 1997. For the next three days the panel listened to presentations by investigators, had extensive discussions with the presenters, and also reviewed the proceeding in executive session. The investigators, panel members, and moderators all participated in all the presentations by investigators. All panel members took part in the executive sessions.

There was initially some tension between the two groups, as was to be expected and was indeed to some extent desirable. The panel members arrived with understandable caution about presenting incredible material to incredulous scientists. Nevertheless, the participants warmed to each other, and a friendly atmosphere prevailed for most of the time.

When the review panel met in executive session on Friday morning, it soon became clear that they were nowhere near a consensus on what would go into their final report. We concluded that a consensus could emerge only from another meeting in executive session. This meeting will be discussed briefly in Chapter 17, "The Review Panel Process," and the final panel report is given in Chapter 18, "Panel's Conclusions and Recommendations." The investigators' presentations at Pocantico, with comments from the review panel, are summarized in Chapters 6 through 16.

CHAPTER 6

Photographic Evidence

Photographic evidence can contribute to a better understanding of the UFO phenomenon if the evidence has sufficiently strong credentials that the possibility of a hoax can be ruled out. Although it is highly desirable that the photographic evidence be accompanied by strong witness testimony, it is very difficult to meet these requirements (as in the case of remotely operated scientific monitoring stations) because of the unpredictable nature of UFO events (events that give rise to UFO reports). In order to be confident of the authenticity and flawless operation of the equipment and acquisition, it is necessary to plan an observational program very carefully. This approach has been adopted by Dr. Erling Strand and is discussed further in Chapter 9, "The Hessdalen Project." However, such equipment must normally be run in an automatic mode so it is unlikely that there will be witness testimony to accompany the data acquisition.

On the other hand, photographic and similar evidence are sometimes acquired in connection with unexpected and incomprehensible UFO events. In these cases, there will normally (but not invariably) be witness testimony but, since the data acquisition was not planned, the equipment, operation, and analysis will probably not be optimal and there may indeed be some question concerning the authenticity of the claimed data.

Dr. Richard Haines presented in some detail one case in which an intriguing photograph was obtained, but the intriguing aspect of the scene was unknown to the photographer at the time the photograph was taken. This event occurred on October 8, 1981, at about 11:00 A.M. Pacific Daylight Time on Vancouver Island, British Columbia, Canada. It has been described in detail elsewhere (Haines, 1987) and is included in Chapter 25, "Two Photographic Cases."

In 1984 Haines received on loan, directly from its owners, two connected frames of 35 mm color negative film. The higher numbered frame shows a child standing in front of a fireplace and the lower numbered frame shows a daytime view of a mountain with evergreen trees on the bottom and a white cloud near the top of the mountain. The intriguing aspect of the latter frame was that it showed a silvery oval-shaped object set against the blue sky. The photographer and her family were making a rest stop in a Canadian provincial park and the exposure was made on impulse because of the beauty of the scene.

Haines and his father, Donald Haines, spent four days with the principals of the case visiting their home and the site where the photograph was taken (north of Campbell River, British Columbia) exactly two years later. Fortunately, the weather conditions were comparable with those of October 8, 1981. Mr. Haines Senior, a registered civil engineer and land surveyor, carried out a land survey of the entire area.

The object appeared to be a disk with the near edge tipped downward, possibly with a rounded "dome" or protuberance on its upper surface. Haines provided detailed information concerning the camera, the lens, and the film. Haines had analyzed the negative using a microdensitometer; the blue sky and cloud were quite bright and the brightest spot on the disk was even brighter. The luminance gradient of the brightness of the disk was measured and found to be consistent with what would be expected for a diffusely reflecting metal object, with a shape similar to that indicated by the photograph and the known position of the sun. The color photograph was also analyzed by making black-and-white enlargements on different wavelength-sensitive papers. The negative was also digitally scanned using a Perkin-Elmer scanning densitometer, using three separate color filters that matched the film's three dye layers.

Haines was especially diligent in looking for evidence of a double exposure, but found no such evidence. He also sought a possible significant linear alignment of pixels or grains that might result from the presence of a thin supporting line or thread, assuming that the object was a small model hanging beneath a balloon, but no such evidence was found. Haines tested for differential edge blur, such as might be produced by linear motion during the exposure, but found no such blur.

Haines also attempted to identify the object in the photograph as something mundane. He considered, in particular, the possibility that a Frisbee had been thrown into the air and photographed. The principals did own a Frisbee, but it was dull black, not shiny, and the principals steadfastly denied having produced the photograph in this way. Haines experimented with several other Frisbees. He attached a dome to the top of one Frisbee and tried to fly it, but it would fly no more than about ten feet before losing lift. Haines also calculated that a Frisbee would have displayed noticeable edge blurring in the photograph.

This case is instructive in showing what detailed analyses of a photograph can be made using modern analytical equipment, but it suffers from the severe drawback that there is no witness testimony to accompany the photograph. While the panel was impressed with Haines's thorough analysis of the evidence he had available, there was some concern that a film defect or blemish may have been introduced during processing, and there was considerable discussion concerning the crucial point that an object that had appeared on the photograph was apparently not seen by the photographer or by her companions. The picture was taken with a single-lens reflex camera, which means that the object must have been in the field of view of the viewing screen as the photograph was being taken. Haines explained that there is published research showing how perceptual "blindness" can occur even when physical objects are clearly present in the environment. Louange also pointed out that an object that is angularly small, stationary, and not expected to be present is not as likely to be noticed as a similar object that is moving.

The panel expressed the opinion that detailed analysis of photographic evidence was by itself unlikely to yield evidence sufficient to convince a neutral scientist of the reality of a new, strange phenomenon unless a number of additional detailed conditions are met (see Chapter 21, "Procedures for Analysis of Photographic Evidence"). They also expressed concern that, now that modern digital techniques are easily available in photo laboratories, it may never be possible to rule out hoaxes without convincing, corroborative eyewitness accounts.

For further information about photographic cases, see Chapter 25, "Two Photographic Cases."

CHAPTER 7

Luminosity Estimates

When witnesses of unidentified aerial objects are debriefed by investigators, some of the most striking statements concern the luminosity of the phenomenon, according to Jacques Vallee. It is not unusual to hear "It lit up the whole landscape" or "Every object in the area stood out, thrown into intense relief," but it is normally difficult to go beyond these subjective statements to obtain reliable quantitative estimates of the luminosity of the phenomenon. Vallee summarized data for six cases of unexplained aerial phenomena that have been reported by qualified observers over a twenty-year period, with a view to making estimates of the optical power output. Vallee's estimates range from a few kilowatts (kW) to many megawatts (MW).

Case No. 1 occurred on August 27, 1956, near McCleod, Alberta, Canada. The witnesses were two Royal Canadian Air Force pilots who were flying in a formation of four F86 Sabre jet aircraft. The planes were flying due west over the Canadian Rockies at 36,000 feet, about one hour before sunset. One of the pilots saw a "bright light which was sharply defined and disk-shaped," that resembled "a shiny silver dollar sitting horizontal," situated below the planes but above a thick layer of clouds. It appeared to be considerably brighter than sunlight reflecting off the clouds. The duration of the sighting was estimated to be between forty-five seconds and three minutes. The first pilot to notice the object reported the observation to the flight leader and then took a photograph on a Kodachrome color slide.

In 1996, this case and this photograph were analyzed by Dr. Bruce Maccabee (1999). Maccabee has presented arguments against the propositions that the phenomenon was due either to reflection of sunlight by the clouds or to lightning. From the available data, Maccabee estimates the luminosity of the object (the power output within the spectral range of the film) to be many megawatts.

Case No. 2 occurred in late September 1965 at Fort-de-France, Martinique. Two French submarines accompanied by a supply vessel were returning to France from Norfolk, Virginia, stopping at Martinique. One evening, according to the report, when there was a dark sky and clear weather, a large, luminous object arrived slowly and silently from the west, flew to the south, made two complete loops in the sky above the vessels, and vanished like a rapidly extinguished lightbulb. The object was observed by a highly qualified helmsman from the deck of one of the submarines. He took six pairs of binoculars to the conning tower and distributed them to his companions. There were in all 300 witnesses, including four officers on the submarine *Junon*, three officers on the submarine *Daphné*, a dozen French sailors, and personnel of the Martinique weather observatory. The appearance of the object suggested either a large ball of light or a disk on edge. Its color was that of a fluorescent tube, and its apparent luminosity was that of the full moon. It moved slowly and horizontally, at a distance estimated to be about ten kilometers, and left a whitish trace in the sky similar to the glow of a television screen. After the object first vanished, the halo remained visible for a full minute. Some time later the halo reappeared and the object then emerged as if "switched on." After further maneuvers, the object flew away.

Based on the descriptions of the witnesses, Vallee estimates that the luminosity of the object was of order 2 MW (megawatts).

Case No. 3, which occurred at Voreppe, France, on November 5, 1976, at 8:10 P.M., was investigated by GEPAN/ SEPRA (GEPAN, 1976). (See Chapter 20, "The GEPAN/ SEPRA Project," for background on the project.) The director of a physics laboratory at the Nuclear Research Center in Grenoble saw a luminous disk in the sky as he was driving. Several other witnesses reported a similar observation on the same day. The main witness, considered to be a reliable scientist, gave a precise description of the position (in front of mountains), size, and speed, as well as of the luminosity of the disk compared to the luminosity of the moon. The illumination of the landscape was reported to have been brighter than the illumination produced by the full moon when it is at the zenith. From this fact, and from the relevant geometrical considerations, the GEPAN/SEPRA investigator estimated the minimum transmitted luminous energy to be 6 kW if the estimated altitude of 500 meters was correct, or 24 kW if the altitude was 1,000 meters.

Case No. 4, which was also investigated by GEPAN/SEPRA, occurred at Gujan-Mestras, France, on June 19, 1978, at about 1 A.M. GEPAN/SEPRA was advised by the gendarmerie that three witnesses had reported seeing a large luminous object that had emitted a loud noise. They also reported that the public lighting in the town had been extinguished for a few minutes as if triggered by morning light. The GEPAN/SEPRA investigators carried out a site investigation and made measurements of the triggering threshold of the photo-cells that controlled the public lighting system. This information led the investigators to an estimated radiated energy in the range of 40 kW to 5 MW.

Vallee reviewed briefly two other cases: Case No. 5 occurred on December 30, 1966, in Haynesville, Louisiana, and Case No. 6 occurred on August 24, 1990, at Greifswald, Germany. Vallee cautioned the panel that the estimates of luminosity presented at the workshop are raw approximations derived from a comparison of the estimated intensity in the visible band with the intensity of known sources, such as the full moon and automobile headlights, and from assumptions concerning the distance and perhaps size of the source.

The panel noted that the human eye is a very poor device for measuring absolute luminosities: The state of dark adaptation of the eye affects the amount of light reaching the retina, and different parts of the retina respond differently to light. Furthermore, the above luminosity estimates were apparently based on the assumption of isotropic emission. This may be a reasonable assumption for a natural phenomenon, but could be inappropriate if a case involves a technological device. For instance, aircraft landing lights are highly anisotropic. A 1 kW source that is beamed with a half-angle of 3.6 degrees has the same intensity as a 1 MW isotropic emitter. Furthermore, the distance estimates may be quite dubious. Hence the power estimates derived for the above cases must be considered quite uncertain. The most promising cases will be those for which some form of physical interference took place (such as an effect on a public lighting system), but these call for detailed investigation by specialists familiar with such systems.

For further information about luminosity estimates, see Chapter 26, "Estimates of Optical Power Output for Six Cases of Unexplained Aerial Objects."

CHAPTER 8

Radar Evidence

Jean-Jacques Velasco presented information on radar cases drawn in part from the files of GEPAN/SEPRA. He pointed out that one catalog of aircraft cases (Weinstein, 1997), now under development at GEPAN/SEPRA with 489 cases in all, contains 101 (21 percent) radar-visual cases (cases that involve both radar detection and visual observation), and the files of the U.S. Air Force Blue Book project contain 363 aircraft cases of which 76 (also 21 percent) are radar-visual cases. Since 1945, reports of aeronautical cases have been collected by order of the French air force chief of staff. From 1977 on, information from civil and military observations made in French airspace have been sent to GEPAN/SEPRA. It should be noted that civil radar information refers only to objects containing a transponder, whereas military radar equipment can detect any object greater than two square meters in radar-equivalent surface area. From 1982 on, twelve French aeronautical cases were reported to GEPAN/SEPRA. Of these, only three or four cases may be considered to be radar-visual cases of the UFO type.

One of these cases is particularly interesting. This case occurred on January 28, 1994, about seventy kilometers southeast of Paris, at a height of 11,700 meters, under excellent meteorological conditions. An object was first noticed by a steward who happened to be in the cockpit, and his observation was then confirmed by the copilot. The captain then saw the object. It was above a thick layer of altocumulus clouds at 10,500 meters. The captain described the object as resembling a gigantic disk (diameter about 1,000 meters, thickness about 100 meters) with slightly fuzzy edges. The witnesses suddenly lost sight of the object when the edges appeared to go out of focus and the object disappeared.

Corresponding radar information was obtained from the military air traffic control (ATC). The object was positively detected by radar for a period of fifty seconds. The apparent speed of the object was measured first as 110 knots, then as 84 knots, and subsequently as zero. The altitude of the object was not recorded by radar. The radar was also tracking a nearby commercial aircraft and appeared to be in good working order. There appears to be good correspondence between the radar measurements and the visual observations.

Von Ludwiger also presented information concerning radar evidence, drawing in part on the results of studies that he had carried out in association with other members of the MUFON Central European Society (MUFON-CES). For a certain period of time, they were able to obtain records from both civil and military ATC radar systems. The Swiss military ATC was particularly cooperative, and provided several hundred hours of radar data over the time period between 1993 and 1996. Radar data were also obtained from Belgian sources through the good offices of Professor A. Messens (SOBEPS, 1991). Military ATC radar systems provide three-dimensional information, whereas civilian ATC radar systems provide only two-dimensional information. Furthermore, the functioning of civilian ATC radar systems depends upon the cooperation of a transponder in the object being tracked. For this reason, civilian ATC radar records are usually not helpful for the study of unidentified objects. Moreover, there is the general problem that ATC systems are designed to register only targets for which the flight characteristics fall within certain parameter ranges. For instance, any object that moves faster than Mach 4, or does not follow a smooth trajectory, will be rejected by the system whether civil or military, and so will not be tracked. A further limitation relevant to the study in hand is that conditions for a good radar record and conditions for a good visual sighting are quite different. An object can best be seen if it is at low altitude, but radar systems normally do not detect objects at low altitude.

In the United States, the Federal Aviation Administration (FAA) radar routinely records on tape all targets, not just aircraft with transponders. Of course, radar systems record only objects that are sufficiently close and have high enough altitude. Although it is unlikely that private investigators will be able to obtain regular access to these records, such access has been granted on occasion. Such data can be very helpful in providing physical evidence for cases that have reliable witness testimony, in which case the records can be compared to witness testimony to determine whether an object seen visually was also recorded on radar, and, if so, to obtain accurate velocity estimates.

According to Dr. Von Ludwiger, there are many events that involve both visual observations and radar responses in Swiss airspace, but the radar records are not publicly available. However, one case for which radar records were released occurred on June 5, 1996, at about 2:30 P.M. Six employees, including radar operators, of the military ATC at Dübendorf, Switzerland, observed from their building in Kloten a large silvery disk apparently at a distance of 1,700 meters. It appeared to be rotating and wobbling at an altitude of 1,300 to 2,000 meters. There was a corresponding recording of a target by three radar devices.

Von Ludwiger also mentioned a number of other cases of radar targets, some of which followed curious trajectories unlike those of conventional aircraft. Recognition of these anomalous trajectories typically came some time after the events when the radar data were analyzed. Von Ludwiger considers this to be one reason why (except for two cases) it was normally not possible to find corresponding visual observations.

Von Ludwiger considers that for many of these cases the most likely explanation involves anomalous atmospheric refraction of the radar signals, but that some cases for which the radar records showed very long connected trajectories may have been produced by real objects.

The panel concludes from these presentations that the analysis of radar records is a very specialized activity that requires the services of radar experts. (See the section on electromagnetic wave ducting in Chapter 22, "Atmospheric Phenomena.") The panel also notes that information from military radar can be obtained only with the cooperation of military authorities, and that most military authorities do not offer this cooperation. Although intriguing cases have been presented by both Velasco and Von Ludwiger, further study of this phenomenon by means of radar-visual cases may not be feasible unless the relevant authorities recognize the mission of an official UFO research organization (as has been done in France) and give the investigators clearance for access to some of the unexploited raw data. It would be necessary for the research organization to help implement adequate software modules that can read and store available data in a mode of operation that does not interfere with the primary mission of the system.

CHAPTER 9

The Hessdalen Project

Dr. Erling Strand summarized the design and operation of the Hessdalen Project. Hessdalen is a valley in central Norway, 120 kilometers south of Trondheim. The valley is 12 kilometers long and a maximum of 5 kilometers wide. The hills to the west and to the east rise to about 1,000 meters above sea level. Most people in the valley live at a height of about 800 meters.

In December 1981 the inhabitants of the Hessdalen Valley began to report seeing strange lights. They were sometimes visible three or four times a day. There were hundreds of reports during the period 1981 to 1985, but the phenomenon began to decrease during 1984, and since 1985 there have been comparatively few sightings. Most observations were on winter nights: there were comparatively few during the summer or during the day.

Witnesses reported observations that seemed to fit into three different categories:

Type 1: A yellow "bullet" with the sharp end pointing down.
Type 2: A strong blue-white light, sometimes flashing, always moving.
Type 3: A pattern comprising many light sources with different colors that moved as if they were physically connected.

In 1983, a small group with five participants set up "Project Hessdalen." They received assistance from the Norwegian Defense Research Establishment, the University of Oslo, and the University of Bergen. They carried out fieldwork in the Hessdalen Valley from January 21, 1984, to February 26, 1984, when up to nineteen investigators were in the field at the same time. The project then involved three stations with observers and their cameras, some cameras fitted with gratings to obtain spectroscopic information. At the principal station, observers used the following equipment: cameras, some fitted with gratings; an infrared viewer; a spectrum analyzer; a seismograph; a flux-gate magnetometer; radar equipment; a laser; and a Geiger counter.

Lights that were recorded to be below the contours of the mountains must have originated in the Hessdalen region, but lights that were recorded to be above the crest line may have originated at a great distance. Without triangulation or other information, it is impossible to determine the distances of the lights. However, some of the events that were seen as lights were tracked also by radar. If taken at face value, the radar measurements would imply speeds up to 30,000 kilometers per hour. (This point is discussed further in the section on electromagnetic wave ducting in Chapter 22, "Atmospheric Phenomena.")

During a period of four days, unknown lights were seen on 10 occasions, and the magnetometer registered 21 pulsations, of which 4 appear to correspond with the observations of lights, suggesting an association between some of the unknown lights and magnetic disturbances. The gratings on the cameras were intended to obtain spectroscopic data; the spectra appear to be continuous, with no indication of either emission lines or absorption lines.

Observations continue to be reported from the Hessdalen Valley; the rate is now about twenty reports per year. An automatic measurement station, for installation in Hessdalen, is now being developed and prepared at Ostfold College (Norway), which is the present base of Project Hessdalen. This station will include a CCD-type camera in the visible region.

The output from the CCD camera will be fed automatically to a computer, which will trigger a video recorder. This automatic station will hopefully prove to be but a first step in the development of a network of stations.

As a result of this presentation, the panel concluded that there would be merit to designing and deploying a not-too-complicated set of instruments. These should be operated according to a strict protocol in regions where the probability of significant sightings appears to be reasonably high. It is recommended that, as a first step, a set of two separate video recorders be equipped with identical wide-angle objective lenses and installed on two distant fixed tripods to help eliminate the possibility that some of the apparent motions detected by video recorders are due to the operators' hand movements or ground vibrations. It would also be useful to set up two identical cameras, one of which is fitted with a grating. However, experience so far at Hessdalen indicates that a grating may not be adequate for obtaining spectroscopic information. In view of the great importance of spectroscopic data, it is highly desirable that special equipment be developed and deployed for obtaining high-resolution spectroscopic data from transient moving sources. This may be a nontrivial problem.

If it proves possible to obtain useful results from a small system, such as that suggested above, one may be able to make the case for the design and implementation of a permanent surveillance network. This should be designed as a multipurpose system so that costs and data can both be shared. This could resemble the Eurociel Project, which was studied in Europe in the 1980s at the request of GEPAN/SEPRA.

The panel notes that in cases that involve repeated, semiregular sightings of lights (such as are said to occur at Hessdalen in Norway and at Marfa in Texas), it is difficult to understand why no rational explanation has been discovered, and it would seem that a small investment in equipment and time should produce useful results.

CHAPTER 10

Vehicle Interference

Dr. Mark Rodeghier reviewed a small but important fraction of UFO reports that are said to involve effects on electric lights, automobiles, and other machines of various sorts. These reports have occurred throughout the modern era of UFO reports (since 1947) and come from all over the world, although (as with all UFO reports) they come primarily from Western nations. Of such reports, those that involve claims of vehicle (mainly automobile) interference have received most attention. One such case is discussed below. A more comprehensive discussion of vehicle interference cases is presented in a report by Rodeghier (1981).

Haines City, Florida, March 20, 1992

Rodeghier presented the following summary of this case, based on his review of the original MUFON report. At about 3:50 A.M. on March 20, 1992, patrolman Luis Delgado in Haines City, Florida, near Orlando, was checking the doors at local businesses. After turning onto 30th Street, he saw a green light in his rearview mirror. Seconds later, the interior of his patrol car was illuminated with a green glow. An object began pacing his car, moving from the right side to the front of the vehicle several times. Delgado called Police Dispatch at 3:52 A.M. and asked for backup, saying "Something is following the vehicle." When the object moved in front of his car for the third time, Delgado pulled off the road. When he did so, the engine, lights, and radio of his patrol car ceased to function.

The object was about fifteen feet long, and thin, with a three-foot-high center area. It was a strange color of green, and the color seemed to "flow over the surface." The object was hovering about ten feet off the ground. As he was stopped, the object shone a bright white light into the interior of his vehicle. At that point Delgado got out of his car and tried to call Police Dispatch on his walkie-talkie, but it would not function. He noticed that the air around him had chilled and he could see his breath fog. According to weather records, the temperature at that time was about 60 degrees Fahrenheit.

Shortly thereafter, the object sped away at a fantastic speed in about two or three seconds, moving low over the ground. Another officer arrived just after the object had departed and found Delgado sitting in his police vehicle with the left door open and one foot on the ground. He was shaking and crying and unable to talk. Eventually he recovered and filed an incident report. The patrol car functioned normally after the event, and Delgado suffered no health problems. Review of the calls to the dispatcher indicate that the duration of the event was in the range of two to three minutes.

Rodeghier pointed out that the Haines City report is typical of many other vehicle-interference reports in the following respects: According to the report, the object was quite close to the witness (a "close encounter" case); the object was of modest size; the object projected a beam of light into the vehicle; the witness did not suffer any injury; the witness did experience an anomalous effect (in this case, the chill in the air); and the object moved at very high speed when it departed.

According to Rodeghier, many such cases have been reported, and he has prepared a catalog of 441 vehicle interference cases. It is noteworthy that vehicles with diesel engines are affected only very rarely (they are involved in less than 1 percent of all vehicle interference reports).

According to Rodeghier, several hypotheses have been advanced to explain these effects:

1. The ignition or other electrical system may have been disrupted by high static electric or magnetic fields.

2. Ignition of the gas-air mixture may have been affected by ionization of the ambient air.

3. Fuel may somehow have been prevented from entering or leaving the carburetor.

4. The engine operation may have been disrupted by electric fields induced by an alternating magnetic field, possibly of low frequency.

Clearly, laboratory tests on automobiles and their engines could be highly informative. Some such tests have in fact been carried out. Staff members of the Colorado Project (Condon and Gillmor, 1969) attempted to determine the effect of a static magnetic field on a simulated automobile ignition system. The staff found that spark plugs continued to operate even in static magnetic fields as high as 20 kilogauss. The Colorado Project staff also investigated the possibility that an automobile involved in such a case might display a change in the pattern of its remanent magnetism (its "magnetic fingerprints"), but they found that this had not occurred for the one case they examined. Rodeghier reported that tests by Australian investigators on vehicles involved in two events (in Adelaide, South Australia, 1977, and Liverpool Creek, Queensland, 1979) also found no changes in remanent magnetism. On the other hand, Randles and Warrington (1979) found a change in magnetism for a vehicle involved in an event that occurred at Thaxted, Essex, England, in 1977.

The panel found these reports to be intriguing. In order to contribute to the analysis of such cases, however, scientists would wish to have available evidence of a variety of types, certainly including narrative accounts, but also involving more concrete information such as radar records, tape recordings, etc.

For further information about vehicle interference cases, see Rodeghier (1981).

CHAPTER 11

Aircraft Equipment Malfunction

At Pocantico, Dr. Richard Haines presented a summary of his extensive research into pilot-UFO sighting reports. He now is compiling a catalog of more than 3,000 pilot reports, of which approximately 4 percent involve transient electromagnetic effects allegedly associated with the presence of strange objects. Another catalog of aircraft-UFO-encounter cases (Weinstein, 1997) referred to by Velasco in Chapter 8, "Radar Evidence," is being compiled by Dominique Weinstein as a GEPAN/SEPRA project; this catalog currently contains several hundred aircraft-UFO encounters.

Haines pointed out some of the reasons that make pilot-UFO sighting reports especially valuable to the UFO investigator:

1. Pilots have received a great deal of relevant specialized training and possess practical flight experience, which better qualify them to report accurately what they see.

2. Pilots are highly motivated, yet they do not overreact during stressful situations.

3. Pilots can change their flight path so as to see the ground behind the object, thereby establishing a maximum slant range to it.

4. Pilots can use their radio to contact ground support for further information or assistance.

5. Aircraft have a wide variety of instruments that react differently to electromagnetic radiation.

Nevertheless, even an experienced pilot can be deceived by some of the unusual phenomena.

Haines focused on cases that appear to involve transient electromagnetic (EM) disturbances that occur only while one or more objects are seen flying near the airplane and return to normal as soon as the object departs (Haines, 1979a, 1983, 1992). Haines has compiled a catalog of 185 such EM events that occurred over a fifty-one-year period (1944–1995), and has developed a taxonomy of electrical-system malfunctions on modern airplanes with which to categorize and better understand them. The largest category of effects is airborne radar contact, while the second largest category is radio interference or complete but temporary radio failure.

Haines discussed two pilot reports in detail, one of which was an interesting case that occurred at 2105 EST on March 12, 1977, between Buffalo and Albany, New York. The incident involved United Airlines flight 94, a nonstop flight from San Francisco to Boston. The DC10 airplane was under the control of autopilot system No. 2 and was flying at 37,000 feet. The entire sky was dark and clear ahead and above the airplane, except for a partial undercast with small clouds extending to about 20 miles ahead. The aircraft was flying at an indicated airspeed of 275 knots (true ground speed 530 knots). The aircraft was about halfway between Buffalo and Albany, and had just changed from contact with the "FROM" VOR (Very-High-Frequency Omnidirectional Radio) signal emanating from Buffalo to the "TO" signal from Albany. The aircraft was just south of Syracuse, New York.

Suddenly and unexpectedly, the airplane began to turn to the left, making a fifteen-degree bank. Within a few seconds, the first officer and the captain looked to the left side of their plane and saw an extremely bright white light at about their own altitude. Subsequently, the flight engineer also saw the light source. It appeared to be perfectly round and its apparent diameter was about three degrees of arc. However, the captain estimated the object to be about 1,000 yards away and about 100 feet in size, which corresponds to an angular size of two degrees. "Its intensity was remarkable—about the intensity of a flashbulb," he remarked. Boston ATC radioed to ask, "United 94, where are you going?" The captain replied, "Well, let me figure this out. I will let you know." He then noticed that the three cockpit compasses (that use sensors in different parts of the plane) were all giving different readings. At this point, the copilot turned off the autopilot and took manual control of the airplane.

Based upon the fact that the object did not move laterally in the cockpit window during the forty-five-degree left heading change and from knowledge of the turn radius of this airplane at its stated velocity, Haines calculated the approximate distance to the object to be about ten nautical miles. If the pilot's angular size estimate for the object is accurate, this suggests that the light source was about 2,000 feet across. The object appeared to stay with the airplane for four to five minutes, after which it departed very rapidly, disappearing within about fifteen seconds behind them to the west. The captain asked ATC if they had any radar traffic in that area and received a negative reply.

The navigation system involves two gyro-suspended compasses, each coupled to a special circuit with a "mismatch annunciator flag." If the readings from the two gyrocompasses differ by three degrees or more, the autopilot should automatically disengage and the mismatch annunciator flag should be displayed (Powell, 1981). This forces the pilot to take manual control of the airplane. However, in this event the readings on the two compasses differed by much more than three degrees, yet the airplane remained on autopilot and the mismatch annunciator flag was not displayed.

Haines reviewed several possible interpretations of this event (c.f. Perry and Geppert, 1997). It seems most probable that the malfunction of the three compasses was due to a transient perturbing magnetic field that disturbed the two primary magnetic compasses, the sensor on the wing tip nearest the object (which was controlling the active autopilot at the time) being disturbed more than the other wing-tip sensor. Upon landing, the compasses were checked and found to be in normal operating condition.

In responding to this presentation, the panel took the position that evidence of interference with aircraft equipment is interesting but, in the absence of corroborative data from flight recorders and other mechanical or electrical recording equipment, the evidence presented must be regarded as anecdotal. It is quite possible that the persons making the report summarized above did indeed see unusual and striking phenomena. It does appear that the airplane departed from its normal flight path, but this could have happened for a variety of reasons. As with reports related to other categories of physical evidence, the evidence summarized in this section should be regarded as suggestive but far from sufficient to establish any actual physical linkage between the reported luminous phenomenon and the airplane's flight deviation. In order to improve our understanding of these phenomena, it will be necessary to establish more definite facts from the casework. To this end, there should be strong efforts to quantify the observations and to obtain multiple measurements of the same event, and investigators should bring a critical attitude to the compilation and analysis of the data.

CHAPTER 12

Apparent Gravitational and/or Inertial Effects

In his presentation, Dr. Michael Swords focused on reports with details that, if true, are difficult to understand in terms of our familiar concepts of gravity and inertia. For instance, a report may describe an object that is stationary yet completely silent and has no visible means of support; there is no rush of air and no roar such as one would expect if the object were being supported by a downward jet of gas. It may be reported that the object makes an abrupt velocity change—a very sudden acceleration or deceleration, or a sudden change of direction, or both—and the witness may describe the event as being completely silent. According to Newton's third law of motion, any sudden change of momentum of an object should be accompanied by an opposite change of momentum of either matter or a field to which the object is coupled. According to reports of the type described by Swords, there is no indication of what force might support the object or what momentum transfer may have occurred.

It is clear that future reports must, if they are to be considered seriously by physical scientists, include very solid physical records, which, unfortunately, present reports do not; most of these cases are anecdotal and therefore very difficult to assess.

One of the better-documented cases occurred at approximately 11:00 P.M. on October 18, 1973, and involved a helicopter of the U.S. Army Reserve. In discussing this case, Swords drew upon an investigation by Ms. Jennie Zeidman on behalf of the Center for UFO Studies. (See Chapter 29, "The Mansfield, Ohio, Case," and Zeidman, 1979 and 1988.) The four-man crew of an army reserve helicopter based in Cleveland, Ohio, flew to Columbus for their regularly scheduled physical examinations. At about 10:00 P.M., after the examinations had been concluded, they left the medical facility, drove back to the airport (a distance of two miles), filed a flight plan, and then took off at approximately 10:30 P.M. The night was clear, calm, starry and moonless, with fifteen-mile visibility. The helicopter was cruising at 90 knots at an altitude of 2,500 feet mean sea level over mixed terrain averaging 1,100 to 1,200 feet elevation.

According to their reports, one of the crewmen saw a single red light off to the left (west), apparently heading south, when they were about seven miles east-southeast of the Mansfield, Ohio, airport. The last altitude the commander noted was the initial altitude of 1,800 feet msl (mean sea level), about 700 feet above ground level. At approximately 11:02 P.M. (about three to four minutes after the above observation), the crew member in the right rear seat noticed a single steady red light on the eastern horizon. It appeared to be pacing the helicopter, and he reported this light to the aircraft commander. The light continued its approach, and the commander took over the controls from his copilot and put the helicopter into a powered descent of approximately 500 fpm (feet per minute). He contacted Mansfield control tower but, after initial radio contact, the radios malfunctioned on both VHF and UHF. The red light increased in intensity and appeared to be on a collision course at a speed estimated to be above 600 knots. The commander increased the rate of descent to 2,000 fpm.

A collision appeared imminent, but the light suddenly decelerated and assumed a hovering relationship above and in front of the helicopter. The crew reported seeing a cigar-shaped gray metallic object that filled the entire windshield. It had a red light at the nose, a white light at the tail, and a distinctive green beam that emanated from the lower part of the object. The green beam swung up over the helicopter nose through the main windshield and into the upper tinted window panels, bathing the cockpit in green light. There was no indication of noise or turbulence from the object. After a few seconds of hovering, the light accelerated and moved off to the west, showing only the white "tail" light. The object made a sharp forty-degree course change during its departure.

While the object was still visible, the crew noted that the altimeter read 3,500 feet with a rate of climb of 1,000 fpm, despite the fact that the collective (the main power control that causes a helicopter to ascend or descend) was still in the full-down position. The commander raised the collective and the helicopter climbed nearly another 300 feet before positive control was regained, at which time the crew felt a slight bump. Radio contact with Akron/Canton was then easily achieved. If these accounts are correct, the helicopter ascended from 1,800 feet to about 3,800 feet even though the helicopter controls were set to cause it to descend.

The Mansfield helicopter case is a particularly puzzling event since it involved not only the testimony of the helicopter crew but also that of independent ground witnesses. These witnesses include a mother, three of her children (ages thirteen, eleven, and ten), and a stepchild (age thirteen). The witnesses were originally driving in the family automobile, then parked it, whereupon two of the children got out of the car for a better view. All the witnesses first saw an unidentifiable pair of lights (one red, one green), and then the encounter between the "object" responsible for the lights and the oncoming helicopter. Their accounts are consistent in their essential elements, the most memorable aspect being the powerful green light that lit up both the ground and the helicopter. This element received further confirmation from another set of witnesses, who were retiring that evening in a nearby house when they were disturbed by the clattering of a helicopter and by a powerful beam of green light that swept over their house and brightly illuminated their son's bedroom. Related evidence comes from an airline pilot who (in the Mansfield area, about an hour and a half before the helicopter event) reported unidentified traffic that had the appearance of a strong blue-green light source traveling at an altitude of about 30,000 feet. Cleveland ATC could not detect any object painting an image on their radar screens and so were unable to identify the object.

According to Swords, there was one item of physical evidence that could have been investigated but apparently was not: the commander reported that the magnetic compass began to spin during the event. The compass continued to spin after the event and it was subsequently removed because it was unserviceable. Swords reported that some years after the event the commander expressed the opinion that his compass, which had not previously malfunctioned, had somehow become demagnetized, but it was not clear whether this opinion was merely a conjecture or whether it was based on laboratory tests.

The panel finds reports of this type quite interesting, but without the existence of any solid physical evidence (such as analysis of the magnetic compass might have provided), it is difficult for a panel composed of physical scientists to draw any conclusions. The panel also found it curious that the commander did not know where to go to report what appears to have been an extraordinary event. He contacted the Federal Aviation Authority chief of operations at Hopkins Field, but this official could not suggest an agency with which the commander should file his report. About a month later, the commander filled out an operational hazard report. Dr. Rodeghier advised the panel that, since the termination of Project Blue Book in late 1969, there has been no official body to receive UFO reports in the United States.

For further information about the Mansfield helicopter case, see Chapter 29, "The Mansfield, Ohio, Case."

CHAPTER 13

Ground Traces

A few of the reports that have been investigated by GEPAN/SEPRA show ground traces that may be associated with the events reported by witnesses. Similar cases have been documented by other investigators. Ted Phillips (1975) prepared a catalog of 561 such cases as a Center for UFO Studies report.

GEPAN/SEPRA has investigated only cases that meet the following conditions:

1. Information concerning the event has come to GEPAN/SEPRA from an official source such as the gendarmerie, local police, etc.
2. The event is recent (a few hours to a few days old).
3. The area has been protected and the traces have been preserved.
4. Sampling and measurements have taken place within a short time after the event.
5. Meteorological conditions have been favorable for preservation of the traces (no rain, etc.).

It is also desirable, but not essential, that the event has multiple independent credible witnesses.

The first steps—to protect the site, to make measurements, and to begin collecting samples—are usually carried out by the gendarmerie, who have received from GEPAN/SEPRA a manual with a complete set of instructions for these responsibilities. GEPAN/SEPRA has also devised procedures to be implemented by specialized laboratories for the collection and analysis of samples. When the services of a specialized laboratory are requested, the laboratory personnel will go to the site for *in situ* sampling.

Soil has the capability of retaining the effects of several processes including mechanical, thermal, magnetic, radioactive, and physico-chemical processes.

Mechanical: A continuous or brief mechanical pressure causes a distortion of the soil. The compression of the soil can be measured by a penetration instrument, for instance.

Thermal: Measurement of the quantity of water in the soil, as compared to nearby control samples, allows determination of the amount of energy required to reduce the water content to that level.

Magnetic: Some soils have a high magnetic remanence. In this case, it is useful to examine the magnetic pattern of the soil with the help of magnetometers either *in situ* or (after sampling) in a laboratory.

Radioactivity: Such measurements may be made *in situ* or carried out on samples in the laboratory.

Physico-chemical: Samples from the trace region and control samples away from the trace region can be analyzed for molecular, atomic, and isotopic composition, etc.

Velasco described in detail their investigation of an event that occurred near Trans-en-Provence, France, on January 8, 1981, at about 5:00 P.M. One weakness of this case is that there was only one witness. The witness was working in his garden when he heard a low whistling sound. Upon turning around, he saw an ovoid object in the sky that approached the terrace at the bottom of the garden and landed. The witness moved forward cautiously to observe the strange phenomenon, but, within a minute, the object rose and moved away in the same direction from which it had arrived. It continued to emit a low whistle. The witness approached the scene of the apparent landing and observed circular depressions, separated by a crown, on the ground.

The Draguignan gendarmerie arrived the next day (January 9) to investigate the report and, following GEPAN/SEPRA instructions, took samples from the ground and from the vegetation. The gendarmerie found two concentric circles, one 2.2 meters in diameter and the other 2.4 meters in diameter. Between the two circles was a raised area 10 centimeters wide. They found, on this raised area, two sectors, diametrically opposite, each about 80 centimeters long, that contained black striations similar to abrasion traces.

A team from GEPAN/SEPRA carried out a site visit on February 17, 1981, forty days after the event. The trace was still visible since there had been very little rainfall since January 8. The arc-shaped area, lighter than the rest of the terrain but with black striations, was still visible. The soil in this region was heavily compacted, forming a crust. Soil samples were taken both on January 9 and on February 17. These samples were then forwarded to various laboratories equipped for physical and chemical analyses. It was found that the compacted soil had a thickness of 6 to 7 millimeters. There was no trace of organic compounds such as one might expect to be produced by combustion. There was some evidence of iron in the form of striations about 1 micron thick, but the iron was not accompanied by chromium, manganese, or nickel, as would be the case for steel. There was some evidence of polymers. Traces of phosphate and zinc were also found. Traces visible as striations seemed to have been produced by a combination of mechanical and thermal effects.

Visual and microscopic examination revealed that, apart from the striations, the soil had been compacted without major heating since the structure of calcium carbonate was not affected. Velasco has made an order-of-magnitude estimate indicating that, to produce the measured compression of the soil, one would need a stationary object weighing about 700 kilograms. On the other hand, the same indentations in the soil could have been made by an object of lower mass if the object were moving at a few meters per second at the time of impact.

The panel was intrigued to learn that ground traces appear to be associated with some UFO reports. These traces could of course be spurious, with no relation whatever to the reported event. They could also be due to hoaxes, or they could in fact be related to a real event. Clearly, it is essential to devise measurement procedures that can distinguish among these three possibilities. For this purpose, it would definitely be helpful to have "baseline" measurements for some likely spurious causes and for hoaxes. The possible spurious causes would of course depend upon the location where the event occurs. For instance, in the Trans-en-Provence case, where the event occurred in a vegetable garden, the trace may have been caused by some piece of gardening equipment such as a metal water barrel. Similarly, someone perpetrating a hoax might have used a standard or manufactured wheeled object. Rather than leave the effects of such spurious causes or hoaxes up to speculation, it would clearly be advantageous to have firm information on which to base a judgment such as could be provided by relevant experiments. The investigators could move a water container to a similar patch of earth, or create a trace with a wheeled, heavily laden object, and then compare measurements from those traces with measurements of the trace associated with the UFO report.

Experiments such as the above could be specific to a particular case, or they could be generic. If such experiments became the rule rather than the exception, it would become possible for an investigator to consult a catalog of spurious causes or of hoaxes as well as a catalog of claimed "real" events.

For further information about the Trans-en-Provence case, see Chapter 28, "The Trans-en-Provence Case."

CHAPTER 14

Injuries to Vegetation

In some cases that involve an apparent disturbance to the soil, there may also be an apparent injury to vegetation. Jean-Jacques Velasco stated that four such cases have been investigated by GEPAN/SEPRA: the "Christelle" case of November 27, 1979; the "Trans-en-Provence" case of January 8, 1981; the "Amarante" case of October 21, 1982; and the "Joe le Taxi" case of September 7, 1987.

In the Christelle case, in which grass was flattened in a uniform direction, plant physiology analysis was subsequently carried out by Professor Touze of the Laboratoire de Physiologie Végétale de l'Université Paul Sabatier (the Center for Plant Physiology, Paul Sabatier University), Toulouse. The Trans-en-Provence case, described in Chapter 13, will also be discussed later in this chapter. In the Amarante case, which took place near Nancy, grass was lifted up, the amaranth leaves withered, and the amaranth fruit seemed to have exploded. The plant physiology was examined by Professor Abravanel, also of the Laboratoire de Physiologie Végétale de l'Université Paul Sabatier. In the Joe le Taxi case, birch leaves were affected by the incident, and a biochemical analysis was carried out by Professor Michael C. L. Bounias of the Biochemistry Laboratory at

INRA (National Institute of Agronomy Research), University
of Avignon.

In the Trans-en-Provence case of January 8, 1981, the gendarmerie took one sample, 1.5 meters from the center of a
ground trace, on January 9, and another sample, 20 meters
from the center, on January 23. On February 17, 1981, investigators from GEPAN/SEPRA visited the site and took a series of
samples beginning at the center of the ground trace and ending
10 meters from the center. Bounias examined the samples in his
laboratory (Bounias, 1990). The principal procedure for biochemical analysis was that of determining the chromatograms
of the pigments. This yielded information for a number of biochemical components (chlorophylides, xanthines, oxychloro-
phylls, lutein, chlorophyll A, chlorophyll B, pheophytins, and
beta-carotene).

In samples taken from the periphery of the ground trace, the
chlorophyll A content had been reduced by 33 percent, the
chlorophyll B content by 28 percent, and the pheophytin content by 31 percent. Bounias also found that the beta-carotene
content had been reduced by 50 to 57 percent and the violax-
anthine content by 80 percent. The above changes, which normally occur as the result of aging of a plant, were found both
in the samples removed by the gendarmerie within one day of
the event and in the samples taken by the GEPAN/SEPRA investigators forty days after the event. Bounias found that the
biochemical changes show a strong correlation with distance
from the center of the event. It appears that the magnitude of
the effect is associated with a specific quantity (the difference in
free enthalpy) associated with the biochemical change. According to Bounias, the glucide and amino-acid content of very
young leaves had been changed to become nearer the content
characteristic of old leaves.

Bounias carried out certain experiments to try to determine
what form of trauma may have been responsible for these biochemical changes. As a toxicologist, Bounias rejected the hypothesis that the changes could have been caused by a
deliberate act involving chemical poisons. Bounias found that

some of the changes could have been caused by powerful microwave radiation. However, microwave radiation by itself would not explain the photosynthetic breakdown or certain other characteristics of the injuries. Bounias found no evidence of effects that one might expect to be produced by ionizing radiation. This is consistent with the fact that there was no trace of radioactivity at the site.

Velasco also reported the GEPAN/SEPRA investigation into the "Amaranthe" case that occurred at Nancy on October 21, 1982. The witness, who is a biologist, reported that an ovoid object descended into his garden but did not descend lower than one meter above the ground. The witness observed the object for twenty minutes before it took off vertically into the sky. The witness did not hear any sound or feel any heat during the encounter, nor were there traces on the ground. However, the witness reported that, just before the object departed, the grass blades stood up straight. Subsequent investigations showed that this phenomenon could be reproduced in the laboratory by using very intense electric fields (several tens of kilovolts per meter).

The GEPAN/SEPRA investigators found that the amaranth plants located near the object had become desiccated, whereas similar plants farther away were in normal condition. The fruit of plants from the vicinity of the object looked as if they had been cooked. Further biochemical analyses of the samples gave results consistent with what one would expect of plants that had been dehydrated.

The panel was impressed by the detailed information that can be obtained by laboratory investigation of samples of vegetation taken from the location of a claimed UFO incident. It appears that a great deal more could be done in the way of laboratory experiments to study the effects of various kinds of radiation and other forms of trauma upon vegetation. One should also examine the effects that could be produced by techniques that might be involved in a hoax, such as chemicals, heat from a blow torch, etc. Such studies would help identify a hoax, if it has been perpetrated, or the studies may lead to the conclusion that a hoax is a very unlikely explanation of the traces. In the latter case, it may or may not be possible to identify the type of technological device that would produce the radiation, or combination of radiations, necessary to cause the identified injuries to the vegetation.

For further information about the Trans-en-Provence case, see Chapter 28, "The Trans-en-Provence Case."

CHAPTER 15

Physiological Effects on Witnesses

UFO reports sometimes include references to physiological effects on witnesses. These effects can range from mild temporary sensations to long-term injuries. Such cases were reviewed by John F. Schuessler.

Among the temporary sensations experienced by witnesses, Schuessler gave the following examples: a strong sensation of heat that was reported in association with an event at Mount Rouge, Quebec, Canada, on September 20, 1972; a "cold" feeling reported by a witness to an event near Eggardon Hill, England, on September 24, 1974; an experience of shock, reported by two witnesses to an event near Tyler, Texas, on November 26, 1976; a sensation like being "hit with a wet blanket" and a very uncomfortable feeling of being unable to move, reported by two witnesses of an event that occurred near Anderson, Indiana, on August 12, 1981; and a tingling sensation, an inability to move, and an experience of having the hair on the neck stand on end, which were all reported by a witness of an event that occurred near Barnsley, Yorkshire, England, on August 15, 1986.

Schuessler also described several cases in which witnesses experienced multiple sensations, including the following: uncontrollable hand motion; eye irritation; difficulty in breathing; an acid taste in the mouth; a sensation of the hair on the arm standing up; loss of consciousness; eye damage so that the witness could barely see; a mark on the hand of a witness where she reported that she had been hit by a beam; a red crust of soft skin on the face that felt sensitive to the touch; and a sensation of heat. Physiological effects were reported that could be long lasting, including the following: burns; temporary deafness; singeing of hair; laceration; swelling; nausea that could continue for months and could lead to weight loss; loss of sight that could take months to overcome; severe itching; memory loss; burn marks; double vision; nose bleeds; and change of urine color. For more information on cases leading to such effects, see Schuessler (1996).

Schuessler gave an extensive account of a notable case that occurred near Dayton, Texas, on December 29, 1980 (Schuessler, 1981, 1988, 1998). This is known as the "Cash-Landrum" case since it involved Betty Cash, then a fifty-one-year-old businesswoman, and Vickie Landrum, a fifty-seven-year-old employee in a restaurant. It also involved Landrum's grandson Colby, who was then seven years old. According to their reports, they encountered a large, diamond-shaped object hovering above the road in front of them. Flames were belching from the bottom of the craft. The interior of the car became hot, forcing them to leave the vehicle. In spite of the heat, Colby and Landrum returned to the vehicle out of fear. Cash remained outside the automobile for seven to ten minutes. The object rose into the night sky and moved away. According to their reports, the object was accompanied by twenty-three helicopters that Cash and Landrum assumed to be military.

The witnesses were initially affected mainly by the heat and the bright light, and they developed headaches. During the night, Colby vomited repeatedly and his skin turned red. The same happened to Landrum. Cash fared even worse: large water blisters formed on her face and head and by morning her eyes had swollen shut. The three witnesses continued to have severe nausea—even drinking a little water would make them vomit—they developed diarrhea, and their health deteriorated severely. Cash was taken to a hospital, where she was treated as a burn patient. This was the first of more than two dozen periods of hospital confinement for Cash.*

Schuessler listed the following medical problems developed by the three witnesses: swollen, painful, and watery eyes; permanent damage to the eyes; stomach pains, vomiting, and diarrhea; sores and scarring of skin, with loss of pigmentation; excessive hair loss over a several-week period, with the new hair having a different texture from the old; loss of appetite, energy, and weight; damage to fingernails and shedding of fingernails; increased susceptibility to disease; and cancer.

As Schuessler pointed out, most witnesses to possible UFO events who suffer from injuries do not tell their physicians about the events that appear to have led to injuries and, if they do, they find that the physicians do not believe them. Follow-up examinations are rare, and investigators usually collect little more than anecdotal data. Nevertheless, some patterns seem to emerge concerning the types of injury that are reported: it appears that burns (and/or sensation of heat) and eye problems are the most frequently reported forms of injury.

The panel members were concerned with these accounts, since it appears that some events related to UFO reports may constitute a public health problem. However, the evidence is weakened by the fact that, in most cases, no unaffected and independent witness is present. The available evidence (which is admittedly sparse) seems to be indicative of microwave, infrared, visible, and ultraviolet radiation, although a few cases seem to point toward high doses of ionizing radiation, such as X-rays or gamma rays. Most of the reported eye problems (sometimes long lasting) may be attributed to strong UV radiation. Superficial burns may be due to UV radiation, but deeper burns may be due to microwaves. It may be noted that injuries

---

*Ms. Betty Cash died on December 29, 1998, after 18 years of continuing and severe health problems that followed the "Cash-Landrum" event.

to vegetation (see Chapter 14), which include desiccation and "aging," also may be due in part to microwave radiation.

Unfortunately, cases that involve injuries to animals and people are usually not well documented, and lack an adequate description of the injuries and of the follow-up investigations (if any). As we have seen, research is also made difficult by the facts that victims typically give no information to the attending physicians and that, when they do, the physicians tend not to believe them. This does not help in the medical diagnosis and treatment. Some cases come to the attention of UFO investigators only years after the event. Nevertheless, it appears that the reported cases involve very uncommon injuries, which have probably been brought about by sources of intense radiation that are usually not accessible to the public.

The Cash-Landrum case seems to be unique in that there is detailed documentation of the injuries (photographs, etc.), and of the subsequent medical treatment. The case seems also to be unique in that it appeared to involve military helicopters, raising the possibility that a secret military operation was in progress.

Schuessler's presentation included an account of the protocols developed by UFO medical experts for the investigation of such cases. Additional relevant tests include tests for radioactive contamination or intake, and also tests for possible chromosomal changes in the lymphocytes that might yield evidence of exposures to ionizing radiation. Investigators and physicians could employ some of the general procedures developed and published by the International Commission on Radiological Protection (ICRP), for responding to emergency and accidental exposures to ionizing radiations.

For the well-being of victims, and for research purposes, it is important that victims receive treatment rapidly. For this to occur, it is necessary that doctors be educated to immediately report cases of unusual injuries, such as those mentioned in this section, to an official organization. For research purposes, it is essential that strong witness testimony supplement that of the victims of the event. Furthermore, it would be helpful if an investigation protocol could be developed for this important category of cases that would guide the investigators as well as the examining physicians.

CHAPTER 16

Analysis of Debris

Jacques Vallee reviewed several cases in which material samples were reported to be associated with unexplained aerial events. Vallee specified four criteria that led to his selection: the documentation of witness testimony; the circumstances surrounding the recovery of the material; evidence linking the material to the reported object; and laboratory analysis of the samples.

Vallee devoted most time to a case that occurred at Council Bluffs, Iowa, on December 17, 1977. Several residents of the town observed a bright flash at 7:45 P.M. The flash was followed by flames eight to ten feet high. When the witnesses reached the scene of the event, they found a large area of a dike at Big Lake Park, on the northern city limits, covered with a mass of molten metal that glowed red-orange and had ignited the grass.

Police and firefighters reached the scene within minutes of the event. One law-enforcement officer described the molten mass as boiling and running down the edges of the levee over an area of about four to six feet in extent. The central part of the material remained warm to the touch for another two hours. There were eleven witnesses in all. Two of the eleven witnesses had observed a lighted object in the sky prior to the falling of the material.

The sample recovered from the event was analyzed at Iowa State University and at the Griffin Pipe Products Company. It was found that the metal was mainly iron with small amounts of alloying materials such as nickel and chromium. The analysts concluded that the material was carbon steel, probably man-made and of a type common in manufacturing.

Concerning the Council Bluffs case, Vallee listed the following four possibilities:

a. An unknown person poured molten metal on the ground as a hoax;

b. An unknown person created molten metal as a hoax by using thermite and ordinary metal;

c. The material came from equipment in an aircraft; or

d. The event was due to a meteoritic impact.

Vallee also discussed the following cases:

Maury Island, Washington, June 21, 1947: Debris that was claimed to be associated with an aerial explosion appeared to be similar to debris from a Tacoma slag mill, leading authorities to conclude that the case was probably a hoax. However, some aspects of the case have never been fully elucidated.

Campinas, Brazil, December 14, 1954: An object, described as disk-like, was said to have wobbled and lost altitude and to have emitted a thin stream of silvery liquid that was subsequently determined to be tin.

Väddö Island, Sweden, November 11, 1956: Witnesses found a shiny "rock," hot to the touch, near the landing site of a strange object. The "rock" was found to be composed of tungsten carbide and cobalt.

Vallee also gave brief mention of the following cases: Aurora, Texas, April 17, 1897; Washington, D.C., 1952; Ubatuba, Brazil, in or before September 1957; Maumee, Ohio, 1967; and an event that occurred in Bogotá, Colombia, in either 1975 or 1976.

The panel found that reports of unusual metallic residue following the observation of an unexplained aerial phenomenon are detailed enough for comparative studies to be undertaken. The Council Bluffs case is notable since the conditions of witness availability and reliability, on-site testimony from law-enforcement officers, and rapid analysis appear to have been satisfied. Some of the other cases, such as the Bogotá case and the Ubatuba case, are sufficiently intriguing to encourage investigators to expand their field investigations.

None of the cases presented offer clear proof of a sample that is outside present scientific knowledge. Nevertheless, the panel encourages the search for further cases for which Vallee's four conditions are met, and urges that the associated material samples be subjected to careful analytical studies of elemental and isotopic compositions, etc.

PART THREE

=

PANEL'S RESPONSE

CHAPTER 17

The Review Panel Process

The value of a panel report rests upon its credibility. The credibility is determined by the intelligence, insight, and integrity of the individual members, and by the independence of the panel from outside influences. I was fortunate to recruit nine scientists who unquestionably met the first set of requirements. I guaranteed and they exercised their independence, and any attempt to restrict that independence would have been immediately rebuffed.

When an agency or organization commissioning a study has a significant stake in the outcome of that study, there may not be complete independence. If the panel is aware that a particular outcome would somehow be beneficial for the sponsor and another outcome would somehow be detrimental to the sponsor, there is a real risk that that knowledge will skew the deliberations and conclusions of the panel. To achieve the greatest independence, the panel should be protected from, and should protect itself from, expressions from the sponsor of what would or would not be in the sponsor's best interests. Reviews carried out by the National Academy of Sciences carry great weight, because of the high intellectual caliber of the members of the academy and also because the academy takes very seriously its role in insulating its review panels from the funding agencies.

In this respect, the Colorado Project is open to doubt. On January 12, 1967, Condon and six of his colleagues in the project, together with Dr. John Coleman, Executive Secretary of the National Academy of Sciences, met with Air Force staff, including Blue Book staff (Colorado Project, 1967). The Project Coordinator, Mr. Robert J. Low, initiated a discussion concerning the appropriate role of the project in making recommendations to the Air Force. It appears that the Air Force representatives had not anticipated this line of discussion, since they declined to respond at that time. But soon thereafter, on January 16, 1967, Lieutenant Colonel Robert R. Hippler sent Condon a letter, which he described as "informal" (Hippler, 1967). Hippler suggested that Condon should "consider the cost of the Air Force program on UFOs, and determine if the taxpayer should support this for the next decade" and added, "If the contract is up before you have laid the proper groundwork for a proper recommendation, an extension of the contract would be less costly than another decade of operating Project Blue Book." Low replied to Hippler on January 27, 1967, taking care to point out that his letter also was unofficial, and that he was "speaking for himself—not for the project" (Low, 1967). Low thanked Hippler for answering "quite directly the question that I had asked," and for indicating "what you believe the Air Force wants of us." The contract was extended and, as we have seen, Condon made a "proper recommendation."

By contrast, there is no reason to believe that the American Institute of Aeronautics and Astronautics exerted any influence upon the Kuettner subcommittee once that body was set up, and no reason to believe that the subcommittee made any efforts to determine what conclusions and recommendations would be most welcome to the AIAA (Kuettner, 1970). Concerning independence, and as far as the relevant facts are known, we may give the Kuettner subcommittee a completely clean bill of health.

With these thoughts in mind, I was ready to protect the review panel from any influence other than the presentations made by the investigators. That was an additional reason why I arranged for the meetings to be held in private with no public announcement. As it turned out, there was no attempt whatever, on anyone's part, to influence the panel. However, this does not mean that the proceedings ran like a well-oiled machine without any friction. Nor did the proceedings move so rapidly that the participants could, at the end of the week, sit down and write the summaries presented in Chapters 6 through 16. Real life is more complicated, and the workshop was a real-life exercise, including crises, of which there were three.

The nine scientists who agreed to serve on the review panel were clearly not closed-minded, or they would never have arrived at Pocantico. They were all curious to learn something about this strange subject that has been in a scientific limbo for fifty years. On the other hand, scientists are human beings, and no human being is free from prejudice. To the best of his or her ability, a scientist must strive to separate his evaluation of evidence from whatever prejudice he may have: this is not always easy, and some scientists are in this respect more successful than others.

I explained earlier that, since it was impossible to recruit scientists with no bias whatever concerning the UFO question, I chose to select scientists whose bias would tend to be the opposite of that of the investigators. The investigators clearly believed that the UFO problem deserved study, or they would not have been investigating it. To the best of my knowledge, no member of the review panel had come to the same conclusion or, indeed, to any relevant conclusion.

The participants arrived at the Pocantico conference center on the afternoon of Monday, September 29, 1997. It is a beautiful, peaceful, and protected estate, and the conference center is run by an efficient and unobtrusive staff. There were a number of residential rooms at the conference center, but not enough to house all participants. Those who could not stay at the conference center were provided accommodation in truly

grand rooms in one of the mansions of the estate, named
Kikuit, a Dutch word meaning "lookout," which has a magnificent view over the Hudson Valley. It seemed more important
for the panel members to stay together in the evenings at the
conference center, since, with only a few exceptions, they were
meeting each other for the first time.

The proceedings began on Tuesday morning. No one knew
quite what to expect. The investigators no doubt hoped for sin-
cere appreciation of the results of their long efforts under difficult circumstances to address a recalcitrant problem. The panel
members probably hoped for clear, crisp presentations as polished as the lectures some of them give each week at their universities. The moderators hoped that they could keep things
moving, while at the same time providing adequate time for discussion. The director hoped that during the exchange each side
would quickly develop an appreciation for and understanding
of the other side, and that the panel members would rapidly as-
similate the information that the investigators planned to
present.

No one got everything he wanted. On the first day, some got
much less than they wanted. The panel members seemed to feel
that the presentations were poorly prepared and poorly presented, and the investigators may have felt that the panel members were overly critical and overly academic. It was not a
match made in heaven.

At the end of the first day, the investigators were invited to
leave the meeting room, so that the panel members could meet
in executive session. This is the normal procedure for a review panel, but unfortunately not everyone knew that. Once
the panel was in executive session, the first crisis occurred. The
panel members could and did speak their minds, and it was immediately very clear that some members were concerned about
what they had gotten themselves into. One or two would
clearly have preferred boarding the next plane out of JFK to
spending another night at Pocantico. Panel members may have
expected the same kind of performance that it is reasonable to
expect of an experienced scientist who has carried out research

with all the logistical and financial support that is usual in mainstream science. Since the time of the Colorado Project, the only UFO research program that has enjoyed any degree of logistical and financial support is the French program GEPAN/SEPRA, and even that has been supported at a very modest level by normal scientific standards. It took considerable discussion for the panel to begin to appreciate these facts and the resulting difficulties involved in UFO research, and to begin to make due allowance for those difficulties.

If every participant at the meeting had then gone off to his own hotel for the evening and night, the second day might have begun on a rather sour note. Fortunately, all the participants spent a very pleasant evening together, and we convened on Wednesday morning somewhat sadder but definitely wiser than we had been when we all arrived on Monday afternoon. No one had bailed out.

The review picked up speed on Wednesday and got into its stride on Thursday. The panel members had probably become somewhat more realistic in their expectations and were beginning to appreciate the complexity of the UFO problem. The investigators had come to realize that they had a tough audience, and they attempted to rise to the challenge. The difference between the earlier sessions and the later sessions was not so much an improved quality of research as it was an improved quality of presentation. Some of the presentations on Wednesday and Thursday came from investigators who had given many lectures and seminars over the course of their careers.

Nevertheless, the second crisis occurred on Friday morning. I had planned that there would be two final presentations at the beginning of the morning, after which the panel would go into executive session for about two hours to formulate their summary and conclusions. That was my mistake. In the first hour of discussion, it became abundantly clear that developing a summary and a set of conclusions would not be accomplished in two hours. We eventually decided that it would take more like two days. The remainder of our time was spent planning when and where those two days would occur.

It was, in retrospect, a remarkable tribute to the dedication of the panel that they were all willing to invest into this project much more of their time than they had originally intended. In planning the review, I took it for granted that the European participants would not want to make more than one round trip across the Atlantic. Events proved me wrong. Every member of the panel was willing to contribute two more days, plus a travel day, to the study. They were also willing to spend many more hours reading draft after draft of the resulting report. The time-demand of this task had not been anticipated.

It would have been difficult to arrange for a second meeting at Pocantico, since the conference center is scheduled many months in advance. We were looking for a meeting in a few weeks' time, not in many months' time. Furthermore, a meeting in New York in winter had much less appeal than a meeting in the fall. We considered several possible locations, with only luke-warm reception, until I mentioned San Francisco. The discussion about location ended abruptly at that point. We found that the only time everyone was free was the weekend immediately following Thanksgiving, which occurred on Thursday, November 27. It was therefore agreed that we would meet at our hotel on Friday afternoon, meet together Friday evening, all day Saturday and Sunday morning, and return home on Sunday afternoon.

Apart from the meetings, the panel did not suffer. We stayed in a small hotel with one of the best restaurants in San Francisco, and we relaxed Saturday evening at a Mandarin Chinese restaurant with a magnificent view of the San Francisco Bay.

Nevertheless, the third crisis occurred at the very beginning of our San Francisco meeting, on Friday evening. The co-chairs of the review panel were Von Eshleman and Tom Holzer. Eshleman set a good example for the panel by appearing at the meeting with two essays he had prepared, one on "electromagnetic wave ducting," which can explain some peculiar radar observations, and the other on the relationship between UFO research and the SETI (search for extraterrestrial intelligence) program. These essays, with other essays later prepared by panel members, are included in Part Four.

Holzer was in the chair for the meetings in San Francisco, and controlled the proceedings with skill, humor, and good grace. In order to provide the meeting with a definite agenda, Holzer had asked me to outline an executive summary that I thought reflected the panel discussions in Pocantico. He suggested that the proceedings would move along more rapidly if there were something to attack. The attack came immediately from panel members who were highly critical of the presentations in Pocantico. One of the advocates of this negative position worked late into the night, and came to the meeting on Saturday morning with a draft executive summary that forcefully articulated that position.

There were other pressures that influenced the proceedings. One member took the position that the main task of the panel was to point out where it agreed with the Condon Report and where it disagreed with that report. Another member thought that the nature of the UFO problem could be clarified by seeking historical parallels with topics that were, in their time, widely reported by the public but were discounted by the scholars of the day. All day Saturday, and all of Sunday morning, the panel went over each item of the summary, line by line and word by word. Well over one hundred man-hours went into the preparation of just two pages of text.

No one could have predicted just how the executive summary would turn out. Each sentence was debated. For each clause of each sentence, there would initially be two or three very different proposals. But eventually someone would formulate a version that everyone could agree to. At the end of Friday evening, November 28, there had been the very real prospect that there would be not one report, but two: a majority report and a minority report. This had been the unfortunate outcome of the Colorado Project, which led to both the official report (the Condon Report) and an unofficial minority report (Saunders and Harkins, 1968). If this had occurred in San Francisco, I would have considered that the study had failed. It is a great tribute to the panel members that they were able to talk to each other, listen to each other, and understand each other sufficiently well that they could all finally come together behind one document. The summary, here presented as Chapter 18, may read easily, but it was not written easily.

It was my expectation that the investigators, when they finally read the executive summary, would be very disappointed, but I was wrong there, too. They realized that the key point of the summary was the second item in the panel's itemized list: "Whenever there are unexplained observations, there is the possibility that scientists will learn something new by studying those observations." That one sentence, modest though it may seem, made many months of preparation, and days of strenuous meetings, seem worthwhile.

However, the review really did not end in San Francisco on Sunday, November 30, 1997. The executive summary had been written, but nothing else. In planning the study, I had expected that papers prepared by the investigators would be sufficiently coherent and sufficiently consistent in style that they could be used to provide the necessary base for the executive summary. This proved to be wishful thinking. The eight investigators came from four different countries—five, if we go by countries of birth. The working papers of the study were written in eight different styles, with widely divergent levels of detail. As working papers, they had been useful. The panel recognized all of this, and pointed out to me that someone would need to rewrite everything, and that I, as director, should be that someone.

The next week I began the long process of drafting the complete report. Twenty years ago, there would have been a very slow process of sending packages of paper around the world and waiting for the return of the marked-up copy. Fortunately, we live in an age of instant communication. As soon as a section had been drafted, it was sent electronically to all the investigators and all the panel members for their comments and correction and, eventually, for their approval. Each section was circulated several times, and the process went on until April 27, 1998, when the report was finally sent to the editorial office of the *Journal of Scientific Exploration.*

It was something of a surprise, and certainly a great relief, to find that these seventeen people, spread over two continents, with a wide spectrum in skills, knowledge, culture, and temperament, could all eventually agree on one document concerning such an ill-defined topic as the UFO problem. Chapter 18 comprises the panel's conclusions and recommendations. Chapter 19 is my attempt to summarize various ideas, drawn from the panel and other sources, of how the recommendations could be implemented.

CHAPTER 18

Panel's Conclusions and Recommendations

SUMMARY REPORT OF THE SCIENTIFIC REVIEW PANEL:
Von R. Eshleman, Thomas E. Holzer, J. R. Jokipii, François Louange, H. J. Melosh, James J. Papike, Guenther Reitz, Charles R. Tobert, and Bernard Veyret

From September 30 to October 3, 1997, a workshop was convened at the Pocantico Conference Center in Tarrytown, New York, in which this scientific review panel met with the investigators. The panel and the workshop director, Peter Sturrock, also met in San Francisco from November 28 to November 30, 1997. The participants addressed the problem of understanding the cause or causes of UFO reports, which have continued worldwide for at least fifty years. The investigators were asked to present their strongest data to the review panel. The thrust of these presentations was that at least some of the phenomena are not easily explainable. The panel focused on incidents involving some form of physical evidence, with clear recognition of the dangers of relying wholly on the testimony of witnesses and of the importance of physical measurements for distinguishing among hypotheses.

It was clear that at least a few reported incidents might have involved rare but significant phenomena such as electrical activity high above thunderstorms (e.g., sprites) or rare cases of radar ducting. On the other hand, the review panel was not convinced that any of the evidence involved currently unknown physical processes or pointed to the involvement of an extraterrestrial intelligence. A few cases may have their origins in secret military activities.

The history of earth science includes several examples of the final acceptance of phenomena originally dismissed as folk tales: two centuries ago, meteorites (then regarded as stones falling from the sky) were in this category. The reality of ephemeral phenomena such as ball lightning and sprites was questioned until quite recently.

It may therefore be valuable to carefully evaluate UFO reports to extract information about unusual phenomena currently unknown to science. However, to be credible to the scientific community, such evaluations must take place with a spirit of objectivity and a willingness to evaluate rival hypotheses.

It appears that most current UFO investigations are carried out at a level of rigor that is not consistent with prevailing standards of scientific research. However, the panel acknowledged the initiative and dedication of those investigators who made presentations at this workshop, both for their efforts to apply the tools of science to a complex problem long neglected by the academic community, and for their diligence in archiving and analyzing relevant observational data.

The panel concluded that further analysis of the evidence presented at the workshop is unlikely to elucidate the cause or causes of the reports. However, the panel considers that new data, scientifically acquired and analyzed (especially of well-documented, recurrent events), could yield useful information. In this case, physical scientists would have an opportunity to contribute to the resolution of the UFO problem.

The panel made the following observations:

- The UFO problem is not a simple one, and it is unlikely that there is any simple universal answer.
- Whenever there are unexplained observations, there is the possibility that scientists will learn something new by studying those observations.
- Studies should concentrate on cases which include as much independent physical evidence as possible and strong witness testimony.
- Some form of formal regular contact between the UFO community and physical scientists could be productive.
- It is desirable that there be institutional support for research in this area.
- The GEPAN/SEPRA project of CNES (Centre National d'Études Spatiales—the National Center for Space Research) in France has since 1977 provided a valuable model for a modest but effective organization for collecting and analyzing UFO observations and related data.
- Reflecting on evidence presented at the workshop that some witnesses of UFO events have suffered radiation-type injuries, the panel draws the attention of the medical community to a possible health risk associated with UFO events.

The panel also reviewed some of the conclusions advanced in 1968 by Dr. Edward U. Condon, director of the Colorado Project. He asserted that "nothing has come from the study of UFOs in the past 21 years that has added to scientific knowledge," and that "further extensive study of UFOs probably cannot be justified in the expectation that science will be advanced thereby." While agreeing with the first conclusion and its extension to the present, the panel considers that there always exists the possibility that investigation of an unexplained phenomenon may lead to an advance in scientific knowledge.

The panel considers that the chances of such an advance are greater now than they were in 1967 because of the advances in scientific knowledge and technical capabilities, and in view of the GEPAN/SEPRA model for data acquisition.

CHAPTER 19

Panel Recommendations Concerning Implementation

The purpose of this section is to summarize ideas of what might be done to implement the panel's suggestions, presented in Chapter 18, "Panel's Conclusions and Recommendations." The panel's observations and recommendations may perhaps be summarized very briefly as follows: The UFO problem is not simple and should receive more attention, with an emphasis on physical evidence; regular contact between UFO investigators and the scientific community would be helpful, as also would institutional support; and the possibility of health risks associated with UFO events should not be ignored.

The panel was greatly impressed by work reported from GEPAN/SEPRA, the French project originally named GEPAN and now known as SEPRA (see Chapter 20, "The GEPAN/SEPRA Project"), and there is no doubt that the best prospect for real advance in our understanding of the UFO problem would be the creation of similar projects in other countries, for the following reasons:

1. Such a project could be mandated to obtain access to relevant data such as police records, radar records, etc.

2. The project could organize and draw upon a network of laboratories and consultants.

3. The project could set up and maintain a central database.

4. The project could construct and operate one or more mobile "observatories" that would include a number of cameras and other detectors, including, as a minimum, optical, infrared, spectroscopic, acoustic, magnetic, and radiation instruments.

5. New cases could be investigated from the outset purely on the basis of data collected through official channels and procedures.

6. If there is indeed a health hazard associated with some events related to the UFO problem, some government office should offer a response to this hazard.

Even the most speculative hypotheses could be evaluated by a well-conceived and well-supported project. For instance, an analysis of the isotopic composition of material specimens could provide evidence that a specimen is probably of extraterrestrial origin, and analysis of the spectra of stationary objects, if it were to yield evidence of red-shifts or blue-shifts corresponding to a fraction of the speed of light, could indicate that some extraordinary physical process is involved. However, material specimens are rare, and it would take special equipment (which does not now exist) to obtain high-resolution spectra of transient and unpredictable sources.

We realize that not every country could duplicate GEPAN/SEPRA, since not every country has a police force similar to the French gendarmerie. Furthermore, the creation of any such project would represent a political act that can be taken only by a national government for its own reasons or in response to public pressure.

For these reasons, it is necessary to be realistic and look for more modest approaches that could be initiated without government action. It would appear that progress is most likely to come about through incremental changes in institutional support and incremental changes in level of interest, these changes occurring symbiotically. We therefore inquire into what small positive changes could be made by scientists and by private institutions such as societies, journals, universities, and foundations.

The most important change that could be made by scientists is to become curious. In view of the fact that modern UFO reports began in 1947, in view of the emergence of clear patterns in UFO reports (as was established some time ago by Poher [1973], among others), and in view of great public interest, it is remarkable that the scientific community has exhibited so little curiosity in the past.

There is no doubt that this lack of curiosity is due in part to a lack of reliable and accessible information. When Sturrock carried out a survey of members of the American Astronomical Society in 1975, he asked if members would like to obtain more information about the UFO problem, and most respondents replied that they would (Sturrock, 1994 a, b, c). Sturrock also asked whether members would like to acquire this information from lectures, symposia, books, or journal articles; most respondents wanted only journal articles. At that time, most editors of most scientific journals would not consider accepting an article on the UFO problem. Since that time, the Society for Scientific Exploration has been founded, and its journal is now in its thirteenth year of publication. However, the journal can be found in only a few university libraries. Hence the situation persists that it is not easy for scientists to obtain information about the UFO problem by the normal process of going to the library and looking up journal articles.

Clearly, there is a need for a change in policy on the part of journal editors. The scientific community would become much better informed if the major multidisciplinary scientific journals were to carry occasional review articles that could guide readers to the specialized journals where more detailed information could be found.

Similarly, it would be very helpful if the major scientific societies were occasionally to include a review lecture or a review session containing several lectures devoted to the UFO problem. Specialized societies could also play an important role. For instance, a meteorological society could review those meteorological phenomena that are most likely to be responsible for UFO reports.

It is likely that more scientists at universities would take an interest in this problem if they felt that their activities would receive the same recognition and level of support as their more conventional research. Moreover, students would become better informed if there were occasional lectures or seminars on this subject. Investigators could help this process by developing resource material for such seminars.

However, even without waiting for such a change in policy of journals, societies, and universities, scientists could exhibit a great deal more curiosity than they do now. Of course, it must be professional curiosity if it is to lead to professional results. It is not enough for a scientist to occasionally pick up a tabloid at the supermarket checkout stand. To become at all knowledgeable about the subject, a scientist should read the Condon Report (Condon and Gillmor, 1969), the report of the UFO Subcommittee of the American Institute of Aeronautics and Astronautics (Kuettner, 1970) and its supporting articles (McDonald, 1971; and Thayer, 1971), and obtain as much information as possible about government-sponsored studies such as U.S. Air Force Projects Sign (1949), Grudge (1949), and Blue Book (1955). Jacobs (1975) remains an excellent introduction to the history of this topic. He or she would then be well advised to read some of the reports of GEPAN/SEPRA, the French official study group.

Study of the material mentioned in the preceding paragraph may arouse sufficient interest that a scientist would wish to become involved in actual research. Unfortunately, it would be far more difficult for a scientist to plan effective research on the UFO problem than in his or her main research area. The scientist would therefore be well advised to collaborate with one or more investigators with experience in fieldwork or some other aspect of UFO research. Such collaboration would be greatly facilitated if, as the panel recommended, there were "some form of formal regular contact between the UFO community and physical scientists." Such contact could help acquaint a broader spectrum of UFO investigators with the normal procedures, protocols, and standards of scientific research.

The proposed further contact could take the form of workshops similar to that held at Pocantico. Such workshops could focus on some more limited aspect of physical evidence, or they could deal with quite different aspects of UFO research. The panel recognized the importance of "strong witness testimony," but of course physical scientists have no expertise relevant to that aspect of the problem. It might therefore be very helpful to hold a workshop dedicated to the collection and evaluation of witness testimony.

In the absence of government funding for UFO research, foundations and corporations can play an important role. It is likely that great progress would be made if funds were to be made available for the support of (a) further workshops similar to the Pocantico workshop, (b) a few research projects that might be identified during the workshops, and (c) one or more symposia at which the results of these research projects would be presented and discussed.

The UFO problem is very complex, and it is quite impossible to predict what might emerge from research into this area. But the same is true of any really innovative and exciting area of scientific research. As the panel remarked, "Whenever there are unexplained observations, there is the possibility that scientists will learn something new by studying those observations." What is learned may bear no relation to the concepts that were entertained when the research was undertaken. We venture to hope that more scientists will take an interest in this curious subject so that there will be more progress in the second half century than there has been in the first half century. There could hardly be less.

PART FOUR

———

POST-
POCANTICO
REFLECTIONS

INTRODUCTION

As I mentioned in Chapter 17, Von Eshleman arrived at the panel meeting in San Francisco with two interesting essays: one on "electromagnetic wave ducting," a process that can give rise to spurious signals on the radar screen, and the other on the relationship between UFO studies and the SETI (search for extraterrestrial intelligence) Project. This initiative stimulated other panel members to prepare additional essays. François Louange also prepared an essay on the relationship between UFO studies and the SETI Project.

In the course of our discussions, we realized that we were referring quite frequently to GEPAN/SEPRA and Louange agreed to prepare a short account of that project, drawing upon the assistance of investigator Jean-Jacques Velasco. Louange also prepared a detailed set of recommendations for the analysis of photographic evidence. These contributions, specially prepared by panel members for this review of physical evidence, are given in Chapters 20, 21, 22, and 23. These chapters are followed by my own review of the state of UFO research (Chapter 24), as viewed from the perspective of this panel review, and my thoughts about what could occur in the next fifty years of the UFO phenomenon.

CHAPTER 20

THE GEPAN/SEPRA PROJECT

By François Louange and Jean-Jacques Velasco

For more than twenty years, the French space agency has conducted a nonmilitary but official investigation into UFO reports. In its first phase, the project was named GEPAN and its focus was primarily on UFO reports. Subsequently, the project was renamed SEPRA and was assigned a more general responsibility for studying all atmospheric reentry phenomena. In the body of the report, we have for convenience referred to the project as "GEPAN/SEPRA." This chapter gives a brief summary of the history, mission, operations, and achievements of this project.

The French space agency is known as CNES (Centre National d'Études Spatiales). It was founded in 1962 to conduct French space activities on a national basis and also in the context of the European Space Agency (ESA) and other international collaborations. CNES currently has 2,500 employees. The CNES headquarters are in Paris, but its technical center is in Toulouse.

GEPAN (Groupe d'Étude des Phénomènes Aérospatiaux Nonidentifiés—Study Group for Unidentified Aerospace Phenomena) was established as a department of CNES in Toulouse in 1977. At that time, its head was Dr. Claude Poher, who had already performed statistical analyses of files containing over a thousand observations worldwide (Poher, 1973). CNES set up a scientific advisory board comprising astronomers, physicists, legal experts, and other eminent citizens to monitor and guide GEPAN's activities.

The first tasks undertaken by GEPAN were:

- To establish data collection procedures in conjunction with the Air Force, civil aviation authorities, the gendarmerie (French internal police), meteorological offices, the national police, etc.
- To conduct statistical analyses of eyewitness reports.
- To investigate previously reported cases.

These initial studies led to the following conclusions:

- Those events that remain unexplained after careful analysis are neither numerous nor frequent.
- The appearance of some reported phenomena cannot readily be interpreted in terms of conventional physical, psychological, or psychosocial models.
- The existence of a physical component of these phenomena seems highly likely.

Following these initial steps, GEPAN undertook to develop a more theoretical but rigorous approach to these studies. It was clear at the outset that it would be necessary to consider both the physical nature and the psychological nature of the phenomenon. In order to fully understand a witness's narrative account, it was necessary to consider not only the account but the psychology and personality of the witness, the physical environment in which the event occurred, and the witness's psychosocial environment.

GEPAN negotiated agreements with the Gendarmerie Nationale, the Air Force, the Navy, the meteorological offices, police, etc. These negotiations led to procedures by which these organizations provided GEPAN with relevant reports, videotapes, films, etc., which were then processed and analyzed either by GEPAN or by associated laboratories. However, from 1979 on, GEPAN worked mainly with reports from the gendarmerie, since these reports proved to be best suited for GEPAN's purposes.

GEPAN developed a classification system to reflect the level of difficulty in understanding the reports:

Type A: The phenomenon is fully and unambiguously identified.

Type B: The nature of the phenomenon has probably been identified, but some doubt remains.

Type C: The report cannot be analyzed since it lacks precision, so no opinion can be formed.

Type D: The witness testimony is consistent and accurate but cannot be interpreted in terms of conventional phenomena.

Reports of Type A and Type B were further subdivided into astronomical, aeronautical, space, miscellaneous, and identified. GEPAN carried out statistical analyses aimed at classifying cases according to sets of physical characteristics.

Two types of investigations were carried out on individual reports:

- Mini-investigations, which were applied to cases of limited significance, and
- Full investigations, which were applied to unexplained cases (Type D), where an effort was made to obtain as much information as possible, including gathering and analyzing physical and biological evidence.

During the GEPAN phase, the project initiated several lines of research involving other laboratories and consultants. These were aimed at seeking a possible basis for modeling unexplained aspects of UFO reports, as well as seeking new techniques for the more active investigation of UFO events by the development of detection systems. These research topics included:

- Research on possible magnetohydrodynamic propulsion systems;
- Study of facilities to collect data concerning unexpected atmospheric phenomena on a worldwide basis, that led to the proposal of the Eurociel Project to develop a network of ground stations equipped with wide-angle observation systems and powerful real-time processing algorithms;
- Methodology for image analysis (photographs, videos, etc.); and
- Study of aeronautical cases, especially radar-visual cases.

In 1988, GEPAN was replaced by SEPRA (Service d'Expertise des Phénomènes de Rentrées Atmosphériques—Atmospheric Re-entry Phenomena Expertise Department). J.-J. Velasco, who had been a member of GEPAN since the very beginning, took charge of this new project, which was then assigned a wider mission. This new project was called upon to investigate all reentry phenomena, including debris from satellites, launches, etc. However, the budget was drastically reduced so that research into UFO reports could not be maintained at the earlier level. Nevertheless, all existing official procedures concerning data collection have been maintained to ensure continuity in receiving reports.

After twenty-one years of activity, the GEPAN/SEPRA files now contain about 3,000 UFO reports supplied by the gendarmerie. About 100 of these reports were found to justify specific investigations. Of this number, only a few cases remain unexplained today.

There have been attempts by SEPRA to increase the scope of the project at least to a European level, but this has not yet been successful. One of these attempts was the Eurociel Project: The basic concept was to implement two sets of wide-angle optical detection stations, sited some tens of miles apart following a parallel of latitude, each station to be equipped with CCD-type cameras, with a minimum of one in the visible part of the spectrum and one in the infrared. The output from these cameras would feed data into a microcomputer that triggers recording of the data when the computer determines that a change has suddenly occurred. The data from all these stations would be stored in a central facility to permit the calculation of trajectories. Such a system could detect lightning, meteors, unknown satellites, and other known or unknown phenomena.

During the GEPAN phase, the project produced many reports and investigations and technical documents concerning topics related to the study of UFO events. These reports were made publicly available. These reports are no longer being disseminated, but some information can still be requested from CNES.

CHAPTER 21

Procedures for Analysis of Photographic Evidence

By François Louange

The panel recommends that, given a new alleged UFO photograph, the decision to invest effort into its investigation should be taken only if both of the following conditions are fulfilled:

a. The original documentation (negative, slide, videotape) is available, and

b. There is at least one other independent source of information—either witness testimony or some other physical record.

If, after visual examination, the displayed object has not been identified (planet, balloon, cloud, etc.), investigation should be performed in two steps:

Step 1 consists of establishing or rejecting the authenticity of the photograph (or other record), taking into account evidence of unintentional false operation of equipment and various spurious phenomena that may affect the recording equipment. However, this concept of authenticity is at best relative, since in this area of investigation only negative conclusions may be considered as final, so that authenticity can never be demonstrated absolutely.

Step 2, if warranted, consists of extracting as much information as possible from the photograph or other record, so as to obtain as much information as possible about the object of interest (size, shape, distance, albedo, emitted energy, spectrum, etc.).

When the original film is available and analysis seems justified, all technical data concerning the site, viewing conditions, camera, film, processing, etc., must be collected. If the camera is available (in an ideal case still loaded with the original film), it must be used to perform the following calibrations:

a. Photos of density patterns for relative photometry;

b. Photos of sources calibrated in intensity, in various positions in the frame (for absolute photometry);

c. Photos of spatial frequency patterns, to determine the modulation transfer function (MTF);

d. Photos taken at the same site as the original, eventually with models to simulate the object.

The film should be processed under rigorously controlled conditions (if it has not already been processed commercially). If the camera is available but empty, the same operations should be conducted with a film of the same type as the original.

The investigator should visit the original site and make measurements concerning the three-dimensional geometry of the observed landscape, or this information should be extracted from detailed maps. If the photograph has been acquired at nighttime, an astronomical map of the sky at the time of acquisition will be necessary. The investigator should determine the meteorological conditions from the official offices or air bases in the neighborhood with particular attention to the horizontal visibility. The investigator should also take into account all quantified or quantifiable elements of the witness testimony, including the estimated shape, angular size, velocity, color, etc.

For analysis of the photograph, it is essential to work from the original negative. This should be carefully washed and examined under a microscope to look for possible telltale artifacts and scratches, and to check the regularity of the grain structure so as to detect multiple exposures. The negative should be analyzed by conventional photographic instruments (enlarger, projector, etc.) and the information on the negative should be digitized by a microdensitometer.

Once digitized, the image may be analyzed by computer analysis, using the classical tools of contrast enhancement, noise suppression, contour detection, restoration, etc., and more specialized techniques such as maximum-entropy analysis, which may be used to remove the effects of target motion and/or camera motion. Such analysis will assist in the detection of a possible hoax. For instance, a suspension thread may be brought into evidence through standard differential operations. Also, one may estimate the distance (hence the size) of the object through MTF computations, based on an analysis of atmospheric diffusion and contour blurring. If there are black areas on the object, it is possible to obtain estimates of the distance by comparing the luminance of such regions with other identified black parts of the scenery. If the object is nearer than the minimum depth of field, one should be able to detect geometrical distortions in the image. If the operator had made a slight movement while taking the picture, analysis of the corresponding blur on the object and on other elements of the landscape might allow the calculation of a possible range for the distance of the object.

In the case of a color photograph, one should carry out the above procedures in three steps, using three appropriate color filters for scanning.

If an event is recorded on a cine camera, each frame may be analyzed as above. However, it is now possible to obtain additional information by combining and comparing the sequence of images.

In principle, images recorded by video cameras may be subjected to comparable analyses. However, video records suffer from one very important weakness: since the basic data is in electronic form, it could have been modified by the use of suitable electronic equipment, so that the authenticity of a video record will depend even more critically upon the credibility of the witness testimony.

CHAPTER 22

Atmospheric Phenomena

INTRODUCTION

There was typically a very lively discussion following each presentation at Pocantico. There was keen questioning of material being presented, and there were also many suggestions of possible interpretations of some of the case material. Two of the proposals advanced by Dr. Von Eshleman are presented in this chapter. D. H. Menzel, some years ago, drew attention to the possibility that some "UFO reports" may be due to meteorological phenomena (Menzel, 1953; Menzel and Boyd, 1963; Menzel and Taves, 1977). Eshleman continued that theme at Pocantico.

Events in the Hessdalen area, which were reported by Strand (Chapter 9, "The Hessdalen Project"), were especially interesting in this respect; since the surrounding area is mountainous, some of the events seemed to occur over mountain tops, and some seemed to be related to distant thunderstorm activity. Eshleman pointed out that some peculiar radar observations in mountainous regions may be due to a process called "ducting," and that some optical displays may be related to a phenomenon known as "sprites," which has been discovered only recently. These ideas are covered briefly in the following two sections of this chapter.

Dr. Eshleman discussed also the interesting phenomenon of "formation flying," and described one of his personal experiences when a bright white light flew for minutes in perfect formation between his aircraft and the ground, with the air above and below being transparently clear. This event proved to be due to a "subsun," due to flat, hexagonal ice crystals falling in a very stable manner so that they were always horizontal. They were sufficiently few in number that the air appeared to be clear in every direction, but there were enough of them to produce a bright reflection of the sun. These and many other curious meteorological phenomena are explained by Greenler (1980).

ELECTROMAGNETIC WAVE DUCTING
(by Von R. Eshleman)

It is possible that some of the radar cases presented to the panel have a natural explanation. It seems likely that some possible natural explanations could be investigated without cooperation or assistance from the controlling military authorities except for a time record of unidentified traces that occur during designated test periods.

Some of the observations suggest that time-variable atmospheric ducting may on occasion result in echoes being obtained from distant ground locations as a result of refraction. Some of the accounts described (a) groups or swarms of echoes that persist for some time in the same general location; (b) apparent trajectories of echo sources that exhibit sudden changes in the vertical and/or horizontal positions; and, in particular, (c) the tendency of apparent echo sources to concentrate over mountain tops. These are all characteristics to be expected of ducting conditions due to weather. These effects can come and go over long periods of time and they can also lead to scintillation or other changes over short time periods (Hall and Barklay, 1989).

An atmosphere is said to be "super-refractive" when a horizontal light or radio ray curves downward with a radius of curvature that is less than the distance to the center of the planet. The atmosphere of the planet Venus is at all times globally super-refractive below an altitude of about thirty kilometers. In principle, echoes could be obtained from every area of the spherical surface of Venus from a radar system located at any position on the surface. If the air of Venus were perfectly clear, an observer would see all areas of the surface, all areas repeating in range to indefinite distances. In the four giant planets also, the large gradients of refractivity (or density) in their atmospheres produce super-refractive conditions.

The Earth's atmosphere is normally not super-refractive. However, common weather effects (in particular thermal inversions, where the air temperature increases with altitude, and/or the water-vapor content decreases with altitude) can and do produce regions of super-refraction that are localized geographically and in height. As a result, atmospheric ducts (channels that trap and conduct radar waves) can form, which carry the signals far beyond the normal horizon. Such ducts can bend rays down to a distant surface area, or, more easily, to a distant mountain top. Back scattering of the radar energy from the ground or from discrete objects on the ground then results in echoes that appear to the radar to be due to a target that is far away and (if the angle of elevation of the returning energy is measured) high in the atmosphere. A similar transient ducting of sound can produce the experience of hearing the whistle of only one particular train out of the many that originate at difference times from a busy track in the next valley.

As is well known, atmospheric ducting is the explanation for certain optical mirages, and in particular the arctic illusion called "fata morgana" where distant ocean or surface ice, which is essentially flat, appears to the viewer in the form of vertical columns and spires, or as "castles in the air."

People often assume that mirages occur only rarely. This may be true of optical mirages, but conditions for radar mirages are more common, due to the role played by water vapor, which strongly affects the atmospheric refractivity in relation to radio waves. Since clouds are closely associated with high levels of water vapor, optical mirages due to water vapor are often rendered undetectable by the accompanying opaque cloud. On the other hand, radar propagation is essentially unaffected by the water droplets of the cloud so that changes in water vapor content with altitude are very effective in producing atmospheric ducting and radar mirages.

With regard to "impossible" flight paths that may appear to be indicated by some of the echoes obtained by military radars, it is important to note that the records presented to the panel are based on measured time delays and measured elevation and azimuth angles-of-arrival of the reflected energy from the echoing object. As presented, certain target positions were plotted as height versus time. But height is computed from two parameters: (1) the measured time delay, which is a very good indication of range; and (2) the measured vertical angle of arrival, which may not be a valid representation of the vertical direction to the target. In particular, when ducting occurs, reflections from distant and distinct surface targets (buildings, bridges, trucks, etc.) may be received at elevation angles of several degrees, so that a ground target at a range of 100 kilometers, for example, would appear to represent an object at a height of several kilometers. Atmospheric turbulence would distort the duct and could cause sudden changes in angle of perhaps a few tenths of a degree, which would be interpreted as a sudden change in altitude of the order of half a kilometer. The angle of arrival would also be affected by turbulence, adding to the chaotic character of the apparent flight path.

Ducting to and from distant mountain tops requires less refractive bending than echoes to and from lower surface areas, and should therefore be more common. This may explain the concentration of apparent targets over mountains. A test of this hypothesis would be to place a radio receiver, tuned to the radar frequency, on or near the top of a mountain associated with unidentified targets. It should be connected to an antenna that has its unobstructed receiving lobe centered in the azimuthal direction of the radar and its vertical pattern extending from zero to at least several degrees in elevation. If ducting does in fact occur, the occurrence of unidentified radar echoes would be found to be correlated with major increases in the strengths of the radar signals measured by this receiver.

SPRITES
(by Von R. Eshleman)

One of the optical displays reported by Dr. Strand may be of special significance as a tentative bridge across the wide gulf that exists between the UFO and scientific communities.

Two women reported an unusual, colored, intermittent light display that slowly moved over two hours of observation made from a remote cabin in Norway in the post-midnight hours of August 3, 1991. The sky was clear until the end of the observation period, when a few clouds moved in. The key point about this display is that while there was no local thunderstorm activity, there was an electrical storm in the direction of the display, but the storm was 120 kilometers away. For decades, it has been conventional scientific wisdom that all of the visible electrical activity of such storms is within and below the clouds, which in this case would have been below the observers' horizon.

However, recent developments in the observations and theory of electrical activity in the high atmosphere (mesosphere and low ionosphere) demonstrate that this conventional wisdom is in error (Pasko et al., 1996; Sentman and Wescott, 1995). Some of the reports of observations in the Hessdalen area could be related to phenomena that occur *above* storms, up to an altitude of nearly 100 kilometers, well above the observers' horizon. This electrical activity goes by the names of "blue jets," "red sprites," and "short-lived elves." There have in fact been sporadic reports of these phenomena decades ago, but these reports were dismissed by the "experts." Now these events have been captured on film and video.

This example can serve to remind us of the continual development and change that occurs in all fields of scientific knowledge, and of the potential advantages of open communication between the purported experts and interested amateur observers.

CHAPTER 23

SETI and UFO Investigations

INTRODUCTION

Since, at least in public perception, the UFO phenomenon is related to extraterrestrial visitation and since the scientific community has given careful thought to the possibility of communicating with extraterrestrial civilizations, it is natural to compare these two fields of investigation. They both fundamentally have a severe signal-to-noise problem. In the case of SETI, the noise is that typically found in radio astronomy, and it is basically well understood. In the case of UFO research, the "noise" is more complex, and inevitably involves the uncertainty and variability of witness testimony. The latter is not familiar to most scientists, and we do not yet have well-established protocols for extracting a "signal" from this type of noise.

The SETI (search for extraterrestrial intelligence) enterprise was not discussed during the formal meetings at Pocantico, but it was discussed informally. After the Pocantico meeting, Von Eshleman and François Louange each prepared an essay setting out their thoughts on the relationship between these two fields, which they shared with other panel members at the time of the San Francisco follow-up meeting. These essays are reproduced in this chapter. I present my own further thoughts on this topic in Chapter 24.

SETI AND UFO INVESTIGATIONS COMPARED
(by Von R. Eshleman)

My perception is that the SETI and UFO studies of a decade ago shared positions beyond the pale of "respectable" science. They no doubt still do, in the view of many scientists. However, there have been several fundamental advances during the past few years that indirectly provide some increase in plausibility for both areas, and the SETI community seems to be responding with renewed vigor. It may be useful for our panel to consider some UFO-SETI comparisons, and the different cultures of their respective participants. These are my personal and incomplete thoughts on this subject.

There have been recent advances concerning the question of the possible existence and state of extraterrestrial life (ETL). Knowledge that there is such life would increase the presumptive probability of extraterrestrial intelligent life (ETIL). SETI investigators search for the latter mainly by examining the radio spectrum for telltale electromagnetic signals that may be purposely sent or inadvertently leaked from a technological society. UFO investigators may invoke visitation by ETIL as a fallback or default explanation of an apparition or event that they believe cannot be explained any other way. There are huge gaps in our knowledge that must be filled in before we can pretend to understand either of these subjects.

With regard to the first question, the existence and possible abode of ETL, three major recent developments are of particular note:

1. It is only in the last few years that we have finally obtained direct evidence of the existence of a planetary-sized body

orbiting a star other than our sun. We now have evidence for several (of order of 10), and more are being discovered as the Doppler observational technique is being improved. There are billions of stars in our galaxy alone, and these results suggest that stars may quite generally be accompanied by planets. One may expect that conditions on these planets would vary over a wide range, at least as wide as the range covered by the planets of our solar system (Cosmovici et al., 1997).

2. Life that is fundamentally different from nearly all near-surface life on Earth has been found deep in terrestrial rock and in the deep ocean, where it exists under conditions long assumed to be so hostile as to be sterile. It would appear that near-surface and subterranean life-forms are essentially independent and that either could exist without the other. It is also possible that life started several different times on Earth after epochs of total extinction caused by asteroidal and cometary impacts. These new findings suggest that life might have started independently at two levels on Earth, or that life can adapt to extraordinarily different environments. The development of life, under conditions that are thought to be favorable and under conditions that we previously thought to be unfavorable, may be the rule rather than the exception for the innumerable planets that probably exist in our galaxy.

3. A meteorite found in Antarctica and known to have come from Mars (from isotopic "fingerprinting" of its elements) has several detailed internal characteristics (both structural and elemental) that are thought to be best explained as being due to ancient microscopic life indigenous to Mars. Several other Mars meteorites are currently being investigated (McKay et al., 1996).

These subjects are currently being investigated widely and were featured among the many areas discussed at an international meeting in July 1996 held in Capri, Italy, titled Astronomical and Biochemical Origins and the Search for Life in the Universe. About 200 astronomers, biologists, chemists, physicists, and other scientists from 27 countries met for this Fifth International Conference on Bioastronomy and Colloquium No. 161 of the International Astronomical Union. This meeting was supported by international and national scientific organizations, including the International Astronomical Union, the International Scientific Radio Union, the National Aeronautics and Space Administration, the European Space Agency, the Consiglio Nazionale delle Richerche, and other Italian organizations. Clearly, this was a mainstream scientific meeting. The SETI community was very visibly represented in all aspects of the conference, but the problem posed by UFO reports was never mentioned.

However, the UFO and SETI communities share defining attributes, including a surfeit of putative evidence that remains unidentified and the lack of a single example that can be unequivocally verified, repeated, understood, or captured. That is, both are subject areas of investigation that totally lack identified objects. Then why is one moving into the mainstream of acceptable science while the other is not?

It may not be generally realized that the several different groups of SETI observers have received and tabulated an appreciable number of URS, or unidentified radio signals, in the course of listening to billions of radio channels for hundreds of thousands of hours, looking in tens of thousands of directions. They measure signals that are noise and signals that range up to many times stronger than can be explained in terms of natural noise. They identify nearly all of the strong signals as coming from radio and TV stations, from military radars and various kinds of communications systems, from satellites and deep-space probes launched by various national and international organizations, and from many kinds of equipment that leak electromagnetic energy over broad spectral bands. After very thoughtful and vigorous winnowing, there has been a residual number of strong signals received by every group that are, and will no doubt remain, unidentified. But these are not described and released to the media as something unusual or mysterious. This is because they could not be verified by other observers or by repeat observations at the same frequency and

in the same direction in the sky. Improved techniques and protocols are being developed to markedly reduce the frequency of
URS (even to the point where there may be concern that a real
ETI signal could be discarded). Nevertheless, it is to be expected that continuing URS will persist in the SETI endeavor,
and will remain unidentified and undiscussed.

The SETI participants include a large fraction of scientifically trained radio astronomers, and they employ complex and
expensive equipment that includes the largest antennas and
most sensitive electronic and digital systems in the world. The
UFO community is much broader and diverse, and cannot
bring to bear the instrumental firepower that is routine in SETI
research. In fact, no equipment is involved in most UFO case
studies. The nature of UFO phenomena is such that it would be
unreasonable to demand repeat observations of the same kind
of incident and independent confirmation of events by different
observers.

However, the status of UFO studies may be improved if we
can find a way to move in a direction where independent confirmation and repeatability could be realized and become routine. Where some level of repeatability exists but explanations
are incomplete (e.g., in the Hessdalen Project), more investigative resources are clearly required. Open channels of communication between UFO investigators and a broader scientific
group may lead to natural explanations of many observations
and thereby winnow the numerous reports to a few notable examples to which intense cooperative efforts could be applied.

FURTHER THOUGHTS ON SETI AND UFO INVESTIGATIONS
(by François Louange)

The SETI and UFO problems may or may not be related to each
other. As there does not so far exist any proof concerning this
question, it seems wise to keep those two problems apart and

not to confuse them. The questions raised by the UFO and SETI problems are not at all comparable, and the strategies for their research are drastically different. The SETI problem corresponds to a one-bit theoretical question: Does there exist, elsewhere in the universe, any form of intelligence that has reached the technological level of transmitting intelligent electromagnetic signals that humans could detect and identify? Although this question is undoubtedly exciting and justified by existing probabilistic computations about the existence of planets, the appearance of life, the duration of a civilization, etc., the final answer is theoretically yes or no. However, only a yes answer will be final, since a no answer may be revised in view of technical improvements of detection techniques.

The UFO problem arises from the verified existence of a very large and coherent set of testimonies worldwide. Its approach is bound to be in three steps:

Step 1: Try by all means to identify the stimulus that has led to the report: the report may be due to inadequate information, misinterpretation of a familiar phenomenon or device, an unusual astronomical or atmospheric phenomenon, an unusual technological device, or a hoax (perpetrated by the reporter or on the reporter).

Step 2: If Step 1 has not yielded an explanation of the report, try to characterize the event that led to the report and compare it with other case descriptions

Step 3: For any case that is strong in testimony and rich in detail, one should try to define a model. In this activity, we are clearly not dealing with a simple question with a yes/no (one-bit) answer. Different cases require analyses with different levels of complexity.

The SETI and UFO problems also involve different approaches. Scientists may pursue the SETI project and remain in a very familiar environment: the relevant technological area is clearly identified, and one may follow a predefined strategy by specifying the frequency search band, the required receiver sensitivity, the intrinsic properties of an intelligent signal, etc. On the other hand, research on the UFO problem is necessarily complex, multidisciplinary, unpredictable, and must be expected to evolve as research progresses. The basic detection is usually carried out by unprepared human beings, and analysis may call upon a wide range of disciplines, including human perception, psychology, astronomy, image processing, physics, chemistry, etc. Moreover, effective research in this field must be conducted with an open mind.

Although in public opinion the UFO and SETI projects are closely associated, they should be kept clearly separated as far as serious research is concerned. The questions being addressed are quite different in nature: the SETI project aims at a simple yes/no answer to the question of the existence of extraterrestrial intelligence, whereas research into the UFO project must be pursued with a completely open mind as to the questions that need to be posed and answered. Moreover, the respective technical strategies have nothing in common: SETI research is carried out primarily within the established framework of radio astronomy, whereas UFO research is necessarily multidisciplinary and innovative.

CHAPTER 24

The Next Fifty Years

In trying to look ahead to what might happen in the next fifty years, it is of course instructive to reflect on what has happened over the last fifty years. UFO reports have continued world-wide, and hundreds of investigators have evaluated thousands of cases. Working without institutional support and sometimes in a hostile environment, these investigators have built up an impressive body of evidence that deserves careful study by the scientific community. The presentations at Pocantico represent only a glimpse of that evidence.

The UFO problem continues to attract enormous public interest, and now has a very extensive literature, including three encyclopedias. ("A Brief Guide to UFO Literature" may be found at the end of this book.) The term "UFO" has entered the public consciousness all over the world, and is now incorporated in many foreign languages. Every child knows what a UFO is supposed to look like. For all this, the subject remains a profound mystery.

As we noted in Chapter 5, "Introduction to Pocantico," the scientific community has given very little attention to this topic, so that there is no informed consensus based on scientific study. The contributing factors that we considered were:

a. There are no public funds to support research into this issue;

b. There may be an assumption that there are no data worth examining;

c. There may be a belief that the Colorado Project and the Condon Report effectively settled this question; and

d. The topic may be perceived as being in some sense "not respectable."

The review panel disagreed with point (b), and indeed recommended that future studies should concentrate on cases that include as much independent physical evidence as possible, together with strong witness testimony.

In view of the Kuettner report and in view of material presented in Chapter 3, "The Colorado Project and the Condon Report," point (c) must be rejected. This leaves us with points (a) and (d), and possibly some other factors not previously listed.

Point (a) is indeed valid: There are no public funds to support research into the UFO area. Despite this fact, it has been possible for a few scientists to carry out small-scale individual research projects, as we saw from the presentations at Pocantico. As we noted in Chapter 20, "The GEPAN/SEPRA Project," some public funds have been invested into UFO research in France, and the Norwegian project described in Chapter 9, "The Hessdalen Project," has received some public financial support. More recently, a small official research activity has been initiated in Chile. However, it appears that the funding and staff levels are quite modest, so there is no comparison between the level of support of UFO research and even a sub-area of astronomy or geophysics.

For comparison, let us consider one or two topics in astronomy. It is interesting to note that quasars were first discovered by astronomers Professor Maarten Schmidt and Professor Jesse Greenstein at the Palomar Observatory of the California Institute of Technology in 1963, sixteen years after the Arnold sighting. These fascinating objects have been subjected to intense research, including observations by optical observatories, radio observatories, and space-borne observatories, and also to intense theoretical effort. This has led to enormous progress in our understanding of these strange objects, and there is now a clear consensus that a quasar is a galaxy with a massive black hole at its center.

We may also consider pulsars. These strange objects were discovered in 1967, while the Colorado Project was in progress and twenty years after the Arnold sighting, by radio astronomers Ms. Jocelyn Bell and Dr. (now Professor) Antony Hewish at the Mullard Radio Observatory in Cambridge, England. I understand that when the first regular radio signals from pulsars were discovered, the Cambridge scientists seriously considered that they might have come from an extraterrestrial civilization. They debated this possibility and decided that, if this proved to be correct, they could not make a public announcement without checking with higher authorities. There was even some discussion about whether it might not be in the best interests of mankind to destroy the evidence and forget it! However, the radio astronomers soon realized that this was not the case, and they made light of that factor by whimsically labeling the sources "LGM 1," "LGM 2," etc., the term "LGM" standing, of course, for "Little Green Men"!

Pulsars have been studied intensively not only by means of radio observations, but also by optical, X-ray, and gamma-ray observations. They have also been subjected to intensive theoretical research, and there is now a consensus on this topic also. Pulsars are now known to be rapidly spinning neutron stars with extremely strong magnetic fields. Pulsars have even been used to make other important discoveries: Observations of the behavior of an orbiting pair of neutron stars has provided the best test of general relativity to date. Our understanding has advanced so far and so rapidly that the discovery of pulsars led to Professor Hewish receiving a Nobel Prize (jointly with Professor Sir Martin Ryle) in 1974, and the application of pulsars as a test of general relativity led to the award of a Nobel Prize to Professor Joseph H. Taylor and Dr. Russell A. Hulse, both of

Princeton University, in 1993. There are many readable books on astronomy that provide more details about these fascinating scientific topics and human events.

These two examples show how much progress can be made, and how rapidly, when the scientific community bears in upon a problem with institutional (including government) support. What would have happened if a lone amateur astronomer had detected pulsed radio signals in 1967 with a home radio kit and announced his discovery in his local newspaper? There is a real risk that the claimed discovery might have been dismissed by radio astronomers as preposterous and never investigated.

A significant scientific advance (such as discovering and understanding pulsars or quasars) typically involves the *collective* efforts of a large number of scientists working with sophisticated equipment and sophisticated theories. Why has this not happened with the UFO question? We come back to the remaining two possibilities: that it is due to the lack of institutional support, and that it is a result of the perception that the topic is in some sense "not respectable." (Of course, these factors are not independent—they are mutually supportive.)

The lack of financial support is something that an agency or Congress could change. If the Air Force were to announce plans to make available, say, $50 million per year for ten years for UFO research, it is quite likely that the subject would begin to look somewhat more interesting and somewhat less disreputable. A wide range of scientists—from psychologists to astronomers—might take a second look at the problem. However, an agency is unlikely to initiate a program at any level until scientists are supportive of such an initiative. We see that there is a chicken-and-egg problem. It would be more sensible, and more acceptable to the scientific community, if research were to begin at a low level.

The O'Brien Committee recommended that the Air Force should fund research programs at "a few" universities (see Condon and Gillmor, 1969, p. 811). This was a good plan. Typically, a field will advance faster if a given investment is divided among a few groups than it would if the entire sum went to a single group. Science also needs checks and balances.

It is notable that, despite his negative conclusions and despite his negative recommendations to the Air Force, Condon was quite open to the possibility that other scientists might at a later date come up with good plans for UFO research and advocated that, if this were to occur, such plans should be funded. Condon even mentioned the possibility that a new agency might be required for effective research. He wrote (on page 2 of the report):

> Scientists are no respecters of authority. Our conclusions that study of UFO reports is not likely to advance science will not be uncritically accepted by them. Nor should it be, nor do we wish it to be. . . . Although we conclude after nearly two years of intensive study, that we do not see any fruitful lines of advance from the study of UFO reports, we believe that any scientist with adequate training and credentials who does come up with a clearly defined, specific proposal for study should be supported. . . . Just as individual scientists may make errors of judgement about fruitful directions for scientific effort, so also any administrator or committee which is charged with deciding on financial support for research proposals may also make an error of judgement. This possibility is minimized by the existence of parallel channels, for consideration by more than one group, of proposals for research projects. . . . Therefore we think that all of the agencies of the federal government, and the private foundations as well, ought to be willing to consider UFO research proposals along with others submitted to them on an open-minded, unprejudiced basis. . . . We do not think that at this time the federal government ought to set up a major new agency, as some have suggested, for the scientific study of UFOs. This conclu-

sion may not be true for all time. If, by the progress of research based on new ideas in this field, it then appears worthwhile to create such an agency, the decision to do so may be taken at that time.

The Kuettner Report (1970) contains more modest recommendations:

> There is . . . little hope to expect a solution of this extremely complex problem by the efforts of a single individual. The Subcommittee sees the only promising approach as a continuing, moderate-level effort with emphasis on improved data collection by objective means and on high-quality scientific analysis. This would eliminate the difficult problem of witness credibility. . . . The financial support should be kept at a moderately low level . . . until reevaluation of the situation allows another assessment. Without such an effort the controversy can be expected to suffer further polarization and confusion. . . . The approach recommended by this committee requires not only the attention of the scientist and engineer, but also a readiness of government agencies to consider sound proposals in this field without bias or fear of ridicule and repercussion. . . . This perhaps is our most important conclusion.

The Kuettner committee's comments on polarization were prophetic. The naive reader might imagine that, since it has repeatedly been suggested that UFO reports might have something to do with extraterrestrial life, and in view of the formation and development of the SETI Project (the search for extraterrestrial intelligence, mainly by searching for radio signals), there would be a strong overlap of interest between the UFO community and the SETI community. Such is not the case. For whatever reasons (and some of the differences between the SETI and UFO projects are explored by Eshleman and Louange in Chapter 23, "SETI and UFO Investigations"), there is an unfortunate polarization between the two fields.

As far as observations are concerned, SETI scientists discuss in great detail and with great ingenuity the observational requirements and observational strategy of searching for signals from extraterrestrial civilizations, but there has been no comparably careful and extensive study of the nature and significance of UFO reports by the SETI community.

As far as theory is concerned, SETI scientists have long realized that there may be physical laws, yet unknown to us, that could influence communications technology. These considerations figured prominently in discussions at an early SETI conference held in Byurakan, Armenia, in 1971. Dr. Carl Sagan, who was chairman of the U.S. organizing committee for that conference, made the following remarks:

> I would like to return to the question of possible new or alternative laws of physics. . . . [Maybe] there are new laws of nature to be found even under familiar circumstances. I think it is a kind of intellectual chauvinism to assume that all of the laws of physics have been discovered by the year of our meeting. Had we held this meeting twenty or forty years ago, we would perhaps have erroneously drawn the same conclusion. The reason this is important is that if we imagine civilizations substantially in advance of ourselves, they may have discovered hypothetical new laws of physics about which we can only dimly guess. (Sagan, 1973, p. 206)

The great Russian physicist Dr. V. L. Ginzburg, of the Lebedev Physics Institute in Moscow, added:

> Science of course never ends. There will always be new laws and clarifications. When we say some law of physics is valid, we always bear in mind that it is

true within certain limits of applicability. (Sagan, 1973, p. 207)

Part of the problem, as Ginzburg and Sagan both realized, is that the term *law of physics* is somewhat misleading in that it implies an unwarranted permanence. Perhaps we should use the term *bylaw of physics* to remind ourselves that today's law may be tomorrow's history.

At the same conference, Dr. George Marx of the Department of Physics at Budapest University presented a thorough and influential paper analyzing possible scenarios for interstellar space travel. Marx took into account "all possibilities not forbidden by the laws of physics," and concluded that the consequent constraints on the energy and time requirements of interstellar travel are so severe that such travel is virtually impossible. Neither Sagan nor Ginzburg raised the point that new laws of physics might have an impact on interstellar travel, as well as on interstellar communication.

We may review the present state of this continuing polarization by studying a collection of interviews titled *SETI Pioneers* compiled by Dr. David W. Swift (1990), Professor of Sociology at the University of Hawaii. Among other questions, Swift asked SETI scientists to express their thoughts about UFO reports. Astronomer Professor Frank D. Drake (Swift, 1990, p. 83) gives one of the few responses that indicates any interest whatever in UFO evidence:

I've given it a lot of study. UFOs are, in my opinion, in most cases natural phenomena misinterpreted. . . . A substantial fraction of UFOs are frauds and hoaxes. We run into a lot of those. Since no UFO has ever left an artifact, there's no evidence that any of them are spacecraft from another world. . . . My conclusion is that there is no evidence that any UFO is the product of another intelligent civilization.

It appears, from this response, that Drake has had sufficient interest to actually examine a few UFO cases, all of which he found to be frauds and hoaxes. Although UFO investigators do come across some frauds and hoaxes, these do not by any means represent the majority of their cases. It would therefore be interesting to understand the difference between Drake's casework and that of experienced UFO investigators. They may have different evaluation criteria, or they may have different selection criteria.

The more typical response of SETI scientists—and indeed of many other scientists—is to interpret the UFO question theoretically and then give a theoretical reason for dismissing it. Drake himself presented such an argument during his Bunyan Lecture given at Stanford University on February 11, 1998: If UFO reports are real, they must be due to extraterrestrial spacecraft; however, interstellar travel is impossible; hence, UFO reports may be discounted. Reduced to its essentials, this line of argument is "It cannot happen, therefore it does not happen." Such reasoning is used by scientists only in dealing with uncomfortable problems that they would prefer not to give serious attention to. In normal scientific research, observational evidence takes precedence over theory, as expressed very concisely by the great physicist Professor Robert Leighton of the California Institute of Technology: "If it does happen, it can happen."

Some of the SETI scientists interviewed by Swift pointed to political rather than scientific factors. Dr. John Billingham, at one time head of the SETI program at the NASA Ames Research Center, made the following remarks concerning the SETI project and its relationship to UFO research (Swift, 1990, p. 256):

> It is politically quite sensitive. One always runs the risk of being classified with the far-out, fringe communities. Establishment figures tend to look upon anything new in that way, and SETI in particular, so we have to deal with that. There is the perennial issue of wasting government money on far-

out ludicrous projects. Indeed, we got a Golden
Fleece Award back in 1979. . . . Last but not least,
we have to deal with the UFO. "How are you guys
related to UFOs?" "Are you looking for UFOs?" To
which our answer is very clear, "We are not related
to it. We do not have anything to do with UFOs at
all." . . . We deal with three constituencies: the general public, the scientific community, and the Washington political community. The general public is
much the easiest; the other two are very difficult.
The political community want to know first of all
whether the scientific community endorses the thing.
That is usually the first question, which I think is a
good way to operate. . . . It has been our experience
that the public is a good deal more enthusiastic
[about the SETI program] than scientists are. Scientists, by and large, are very conservative people and
want to be very sure before they embark on something.

Political considerations are understandably more significant
for the SETI community than for most scientific communities,
since their field has achieved political recognition only recently,
but political considerations are—or should be—secondary. If
there is ever convincing evidence that UFO reports have something to do with extraterrestrial life, it is likely that SETI scientists will be among the first in line to examine the evidence.

Most scientists are curious, and most scientists do not need
to pay too much attention to political considerations. As evidence, I can cite the fact that I experienced little difficulty in re-
cruiting nine very active scientists for this panel review. It has
always been the case that scientists are quite willing to look into
the UFO problem if they are asked to do so. In 1952, General
Samford instructed Project Blue Book to enlist the aid of top-
ranking scientists. To judge from Ruppelt's account, the project
had no difficulty in getting the support it needed (Ruppelt,
1956). In 1952, the Central Intelligence Agency persuaded five

distinguished scientists, led by Professor H. P. Robertson of the California Institute of Technology, to spend several days debating this topic (Jacobs, 1975, pp. 89–107).

Nevertheless, one should also recognize that it has always made the recruitment of scientific effort somewhat easier if the consultation is quiet and unpublicized, and very much easier if the request comes from official quarters and if the consultation is held in secret. Ruppelt has written about his experience (Ruppelt, 1956, p. 191) when, as the head of Blue Book, he had occasion to consult scientists:

> Normally scientists are a cautious lot and stick to proven facts, keeping their personal opinions confined to small groups of friends, but when it is known that there is a sign on a door that says "Classified Briefing in Progress," inhibitions collapse like the theories that explain all the UFOs away. People say just what they think. I talked to plenty of [scientists] who believe that flying saucers are for real, and who are absolutely convinced that other planets or other bodies in the universe are inhabited.

From the very beginning, the biggest obstacle to scientific research into the UFO problem has been the absence—or at least the paucity—of physical evidence. As early as 1949, the staff of Project Sign (1949) were writing:

> Reporting agencies should be impressed with the necessity for getting more factual evidence on sightings, such as photographs, physical evidence, radar sightings, and data on size and shape.

The staff of the Colorado Project made every effort to collect and examine physical evidence such as photographs and movie films, radar records and material specimens and, as we noted earlier in this chapter, the Kuettner committee recommended "data collection by objective means" (Kuettner et al., 1970).

We pointed out in Chapter 5, "Introduction to Pocantico," that if there is no relevant physical evidence, physical scientists cannot become involved in research, and it is then hard to see how very much progress can be made. If, on the other hand, there is physical evidence, there is a great deal that physical scientists can do. Our scientific review panel advocated that future research should aim at the acquisition of new cases with both physical evidence and strong witness testimony.

If such research were to be initiated, what form might it take? A very basic requirement of scientific research is that it be carefully compartmentalized. A scientist may report new experimental findings, or a new theoretical development, and get respectful attention from his colleagues. But if he reports both new experimental findings *and* a new theory to explain those findings, his colleagues are going to be suspicious of both contributions.

UFO research is not a laboratory science. It is more complicated, and this field will therefore require more careful compartmentalization. It is my view that, as a minimum, there should be the following distinct activities:

a. Field investigations leading to case documentation and the measurement or retrieval of physical evidence

b. Laboratory analysis of physical evidence

c. The systematic compilation of case reports into catalogs

d. The analysis of compilations of data (descriptive and physical) to look for patterns and so extract significant facts

e. The development of theories and the evaluation of these theories on the basis of the facts.

Theoretical research, and the evaluation of theories on the basis of the relevant evidence, will require very careful planning and execution. In view of the complexities and uncertainties— what some would call the "softness"—of the field, it is my own view that it would be helpful to go back to fundamentals, and structure this part of the research program on the rules and procedures of scientific inference (Sturrock, 1994d). This is a formalism that has been developed to represent what is called "inductive" thinking, which is the basis of science. It does not deal with absolutes such as "true" or "false," but with relatives such as "more likely" and "less likely," and their representation in terms of probabilities. It gives rules for assessing the probability that some hypothesis is true, based on one's initial prejudice and on new evidence, and it provides a valuable procedure for separating the influence of prejudice from the evaluation of evidence. Two scientists may differ greatly in their initial prejudices, but they should be able to agree on the weight of new evidence.

A theory is an analysis of a hypothesis, but the rules of scientific inference tell us that we should deal with a complete set of hypotheses, not with just one hypothesis. We could, for instance, list the possibilities for the explanation of any one event as follows:

a. Hoax
b. Some well-developed phenomenon or device
c. Some established but unfamiliar natural phenomenon
d. Some unfamiliar terrestrial technological device
e. Some hitherto unknown natural phenomenon
f. A technological device not of terrestrial origin
g. Some other cause not covered by the above possibilities.

In principle, we can prove a hypothesis not only by finding strong evidence in its favor, but also by finding strong evidence against every other possibility. We have already quoted Sherlock Holmes (Doyle, 1994): "How often have I said to you that when you have eliminated the impossible, whatever remains, *however improbable*, must be the truth?"

The weight of evidence can be measured in "db" or "decibels," a unit that originated in electrical engineering: 10 db means a factor of 10; 20 db means a factor of 100, etc. (Photographers will recognize this as being related to the enigmatic "DIN" concept used in Europe to quantify the sensitivity of film.) If someone betting on a race receives a tip that in his mind increases the odds on a certain horse winning by a factor of 10, say from one chance in ten to even odds, we would say that the weight of the new information is 10 db. If some other information takes the odds back to one in ten, the weight of that evidence would be –10 db. These two pieces of evidence would just cancel out. It seems likely that research in a difficult subject such as the UFO problem could proceed much more smoothly and perhaps more rapidly if we were to seek only to quantify the weight of relevant evidence, rather than demand absolute proof of one hypothesis or another. We would then be asking scientists to change their minds, one way or the other, little by little, not all at once.

Two scientists may differ greatly in their initial prejudices, and it can only be helpful for them to understand those differences at the outset. Their initial or "prior" assessments may be expressed in terms of db. If a scientist considers, at the outset, that a hypothesis is just as likely to be true as to be false, this prior assessment may be expressed as 0 db. If he considers at the outset that the odds are 100 to 1 in favor of the hypothesis, he gives it 20 db. Another scientist may, at the outset, estimate the odds to be 1,000 to 1 against the hypothesis, that is equivalent to –30 db. His prior odds may be large, but according to the rules of scientific inference, they may not be infinite: he may not say that a hypothesis is certainly true, or certainly false.

If both scientists receive new information that has a weight of evidence of 10 db (weak evidence in favor of the hypothesis), then the first scientist will revise his estimate to 30 db (odds of 1,000 to 1 in favor), while the second scientist will revise his estimate to –20 db (odds of 100 to 1 against). But given sufficiently strong evidence one way or the other, they will, in the end, agree either that the hypothesis is more likely to be true than false, or vice versa.

Carl Sagan frequently remarked that "extraordinary claims require extraordinary evidence." This is quite true, but the extraordinary evidence (worth, say, 60 db, which would change the odds by a factor of 1 million) may come from one remarkable event, or from six comparatively unspectacular events, each of which is worth only 10 db, provided of course that these events are truly independent.

The collection, screening, and combining of evidence will all be essential for the future of UFO research. Concerning the collection of evidence, the panel recognized that witness testimony will remain crucial in this field. However, the skills required to assess witness credibility are quite different from the skills required to analyze a photograph or a piece of metal, and recommendations along these lines must come from relevant experts such as lawyers, forensic investigators, and police inspectors.

Since the combination of evidence is critical, the compilation and analysis of catalogs will play an important role. If one event yields one piece of physical evidence, it will be difficult to assess its significance for the field as a whole. If, on the other hand, one can identify a pattern that recurs in ten or one hundred cases with physical evidence, that may be regarded as a "fact" that any theory should explain.

Probably the first computerized catalog of UFO cases was one developed by Dr. Jacques Vallee in the 1960s. Since that time, other catalogs have been developed: UFOCAT is a catalog that Dr. David Saunders began to compile as part of his work for the Colorado Project, and then continued to develop on behalf of CUFOS; UNICAT, compiled by Dr. Willy Smith; AIRCAT, a catalog of aircraft cases compiled by Dr. Richard F. Haines; another catalog of aircraft cases has been compiled by Dominique Weinstein in France; and the *U* Database has been compiled by and is available from Larry Hatch (Hatch, 1999).

Of course, not all patterns are significant. Some patterns are due to the way the evidence is acquired. If an investigator begins with the fixed idea that only red lights are important and investigates only reports of red lights, it is neither surprising nor significant that he can produce evidence that all UFO events involve red lights. It will be necessary to pay very careful attention to the selection criteria that influence data collection.

Nevertheless, if a large amount of relevant data can be acquired, with due controls of the selection criteria and other sound scientific procedure, one should be able to draw much more secure conclusions than one could from any one case. Indeed, one may be able to obtain information that could never be obtained from any single case. To clarify this, I can point out that it is possible for an astronomer to image a star or other astronomical object that is so faint in comparison with the night sky that it cannot be seen by eye. The measurement is made by integrating the light from that area of the sky for a very long time. Light comes in tiny packets called photons, and modern instrumentation makes it possible to register individual photons. If we were to inspect the photons one at a time, we would discard every one of them, because each photon is more likely to come from the sky background than from the source of interest. But by accumulating a very large number of photons for each point of the image, the astronomer can extract a picture of a source that is invisible to the eye.

Engineers refer to this as the "signal-to-noise" issue. In order to detect a very faint source, it is necessary to reduce the noise level as much as possible, and also to continue the observations for as long as possible.

Physical evidence need not be restricted to data acquired by observations of UFO events. It can also include the results of planned experiments. Such experiments could help to determine whether apparent physical effects associated with a case are due to a hoax. For instance, ground traces may have been caused by someone rolling a metal barrel over the ground rather than by the landing of an extraterrestrial spacecraft or of an advanced military vehicle. This hypothesis could be tested by trying to duplicate this suspected hoax. If it proves to be easy to reproduce the essential features of the ground traces, that makes the hoax hypothesis much more likely and we add a few db to that hypothesis. If, on the other hand, it proves to be virtually impossible to reproduce those features, then the hoax hypothesis becomes much less likely and we subtract a few db.

As a result of these and similar research activities, scientists may eventually conclude that all UFO reports brought to their attention can be satisfactorily explained by known natural phenomenon, known terrestrial devices, or hoaxes. On the other hand, they may conclude that the evidence points to a new natural phenomenon with properties that they can specify, or to an unknown technological device with certain properties and capabilities. Any one of these conclusions would be an enormous advance in our understanding of the UFO problem.

We are left with the puzzle of how the necessary level of professional scientific research, comparable—or even faintly comparable—with the level of any other scientific problem of similar complexity, could come about. The scientific community would no doubt respond to a request to engage in such research, as they have done in the past, but it is highly unlikely that scientists will initiate organized research. There is no incentive—and there is perhaps a disincentive—for federal agencies or Congress to become involved. This, in a sense, leaves the public disenfranchised. The public has strong interest in the UFO problem, and in the end it is the public that pays for all federally financed scientific research.

It is of course possible for the public to exert pressure on Congress. Indeed, as we saw in Chapter 2, "UFO History: 1947 to 1967," it was public pressure that led to the Rivers hearings that led in turn to the Colorado Project, but this is a cumbersome process. The public would be better served if there were some simpler process, continuously available, to draw the attention of the scientific community to topics that are of widespread interest and that are susceptible to scientific research, but for whatever reason are not being subjected to such research. If this need were recognized, either by the funding agencies or by Congress, one or two half-day meetings involving a few scientists and a few administrators would no doubt lead to several workable plans by which this need could be met.

Unless there is some event that galvanizes the scientific community into action, or some new initiative that permits a modest but effective level of scientific research, it is likely that the problem will remain an enigma—perhaps for another fifty years. In the meantime, we may well reflect once more on the first two observations of the scientific review panel:

1. The UFO problem is not a simple one, and it is unlikely that there is any simple universal answer.
2. Whenever there are unexplained observations, there is the possibility that scientists will learn something new by studying those observations.

The panel's final observation was:

> Reflecting on evidence presented at the workshop that some witnesses of UFO events have suffered radiation-type injuries, the panel draws the attention of the medical community to a possible health risk associated with UFO events.

PART FIVE

===

CASE
MATERIAL

INTRODUCTION

During their presentations at Pocantico, the investigators were drawing upon a great deal of case material, primarily their own research, but some derived from the published case material of other investigators. Some of this material is presented in the next five chapters. Chapters 25 and 28, dealing with two photographic cases and the Trans-en-Provence case, contain material published in the *Journal of Scientific Exploration* (*JSE*) by investigators Richard Haines, Jacques Vallee, Jean-Jacques Velasco, and their collaborator Dr. Michel Bounias. Chapters 26 and 27, dealing with luminosity and physical traces, were prepared by Jacques Vallee specially for presentation at Pocantico and subsequently published in *JSE*. Chapter 29 represents an extensive case study, by Ms. Jennie Zeidman, of the Mansfield, Ohio, helicopter case that was discussed by Michael Swords at Pocantico. This has not previously been published, except as a report of the Center for UFO Studies.

These chapters will give the reader some idea of what goes into the investigation of a UFO report. Chapter 29 is especially interesting, since it contains a great deal of dialogue between the investigators (Ms. Jennie Zeidman and Dr. J. Allen Hynek) and the witnesses of this remarkable event.

CHAPTER 25

Two Photographic Cases

ANALYSIS OF A UFO PHOTOGRAPH
(by Richard F. Haines)

INTRODUCTION

Contrary to common belief, there are many photographs of alleged UFOs. Of course the problem lies not so much with the details of the photograph and its negative as with the photographer and the equipment used. It is for this reason that one must be careful to fully document seemingly unimportant details concerning the person taking the photograph, the social situation that surrounded the photograph(s), the camera-lens-film data, the developing-printing-enlarging activities, and the manner in which the photograph came to the attention of the investigator. Since such a photograph image is only as credible as the photographer who took it, one must exercise "due diligence" in each of the above areas. Many older UFO photographs remain useless artifacts of the UFO enigma because the investigator did not or could not obtain all of the relevant background information. As will be made clear, the author attempted to consider all of the above factors. Length restrictions of this paper impose certain practical limits upon the depth to which these facts can be documented, however.

The remainder of this report will cover the following topics: (a) the photograph and negative, (b) the camera and lens, (c) the film and its processing, (d) the results of image analysis, (e) the site visit results, (f) the credibility of the photographer, and (g) a brief review of Frisbee characteristics.

THE PHOTOGRAPH AND NEGATIVE

The author received a color negative strip of two frames. The higher-numbered frame showed a small child standing in front of a fireplace inside a home. The lower-numbered frame showed a mountain whose top was very nearly centered within the frame. The foreground detail was in sharp focus, indicating that either a fairly high shutter speed had been used or the camera had been stabilized, or both. Figure 25-1 is an enlargement of the full negative reproduced as a positive print. A sharply focused disk-like object is seen above and to the right of the mountain top. The tip of the mountain was located close to the geometric center of the 35mm frame. This tends to support the statement made by the photographer that she was intent upon photographing the mountains and never saw the aerial object. The presence of a cloud directly illuminated by sunlight through extremely clear air provides a useful upper exposure limit for later densitometry measurements. Dark shadows seen within a stand of trees in the left foreground provide a lower end to the exposure. Thus, a maximum of 12,500 footlambert (ft-L) is assumed for the luminance of the cloud and approximately one ft-L for the shadow area. The atmospheric clarity makes it almost impossible to judge the separation distance between the camera and object by means of an extinction coefficient calculation.

Figure 25-1. Photograph of mountain and disk.

The negative measured 36 x 24 mm. A photographic enlargement of the disk image provided for linear measurements. Its
major axis on this print was 5.70 cm while its minor axis was
1.60 cm, for a width/height ratio of 3.56. The width of the
"dome" protruding from the upper surface was 1.3 cm and its
height about 0.7 cm (ratio of 1.86). Finally, the disk-to-dome
width ratio was 4.38 and the dome-to-disk height ratio was
2.29. While these ratios are a function of the viewing aspect
angle, they may, in general, be compared with corresponding
values given elsewhere (Haines, 1978, 1979b) of similarly
shaped aerial objects of unknown origin that have been reported over the years. This previous work shows that the present photographic image of a disk is not uncommon; there is a
large context of drawings of purported UFOs into which this
object fits.

The *hyperfocal distance* is the nearest distance from an object being photographed to the camera at which the object is in sharp focus when the lens is focused on infinity. Since the mountain is in sharp focus and the photographer said that she took great care to manually focus the camera, it is possible to determine the hyperfocal distance by also knowing the focal length of the lens and its aperture (Neblette, 1965). For a 50 mm focal length lens and f-11 aperture, the hyperfocal distance is 15 feet. Corresponding distances for f-8 and f-16 apertures are 20 and 10 feet, respectively. Thus, the airborne object in question must have been farther than 10 feet (and probably farther than 20 feet) from the camera, since it also was in sharp focus.

The actual camera settings used can only be inferred. A film with an ASA 100 exposure index (as this was) and a lens with the optical quality of this one would have very likely automatically preset a shutter speed of 1/125th second at an aperture of f-11 for the ambient scene luminance that was present.

Finally, the negative was in very good condition and did not have any visible scratches, major blemishes, or other defects. An invisible vertical scratch was noted in one of the dye layers, as will be described later. However, this scratch was well away from the disk image.

THE CAMERA AND LENS

The camera was a Mamiya, model 528AL, single-lens reflex (SLR) type with permanently attached Mamiya/Sekor 48 mm lens with aperture f-2.8. The serial number on the lens was M197535. The camera is of the automatic exposure type, meaning that all one needs to do to take a photograph is insert the film, preset the correct ASA number for the film used on the camera, aim and manually focus the lens for the best focus, and press the shutter release. Both shutter speed and aperture adjust automatically for "best" exposure. The shutter actuation lever is of the standard top-mounted type, which requires a downward finger depression. Once the shutter has opened and closed, another exposure cannot be taken without first advancing the film to the next frame. The author borrowed this camera and took a series of photographs with it under closely similar sun angle, sky brightness, and other conditions to check for possible lens- and/or shutter-related image artifacts. None were found. The lens was coated with the standard antiscattering material. No scratches or other flaws could be seen in the lens elements or surface coatings.

THE FILM AND ITS PROCESSING

The film used was Kodak Safety Film 5035, 35 mm, commonly known as Kodacolor II. Its ASA rating is 100. The photograph is question was located at frame 11. The so-called "characteristic curve" (i.e., exposure versus optical density) modulation transfer function, and spectral sensitivity for this film, are presented in Figure 25-2 (a), (b), and (c), respectively (Eastman Kodak, 1980).

The concepts of "graininess" and "granularity" of photographic film are important here. Graininess is defined as the subjective sensation one gets when viewing an enlargement of a photograph of a random pattern of variations in texture, color, or both in regions of homogeneous luminance and color exposure. Granularity is the result of an objective measurement of the film using an instrument known as a densitometer, which measures the local density variations that give rise to the sensation of graininess (Eastman Kodak, 1973). Most silver halide crystals that make up photographic film are dispersed in a gelatin and coated in thin layers on a supporting base (paper, etc.). These crystals vary in size, shape, and sensitivity to light energy. In general, they are also randomly distributed. As the Kodak manual states, "Within an area of uniform exposure, *some* [Haines's italics] of the crystals will be made developable by exposure; others will not. The location of the developable crystals is random."

One result of this random distribution of light-sensitive crys-

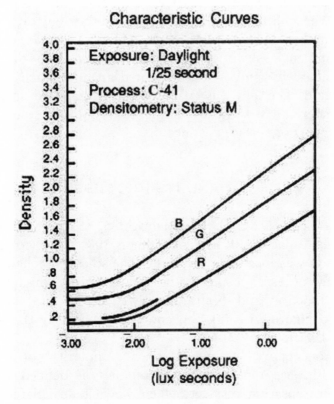

Figure 25-2. Kodacolor 11 film characteristics.
(a) Characteristic curves.

tals (grains) is that patterns can be produced that have nothing
to do with the object that was originally photographed. If such
a pattern is perceived as having a recognized shape, it is possible to conclude that the shape represents an object somehow
related to the primary object when, in fact, there is no func-
tional correlation with the object.

The diameter of the film's crystals is also important. The
Kodak film manual indicates that a typical crystal diameter
ranges from 0.2 to 2.0 micrometers. At a normal viewing distance of 25 to 35 cm, the human eye can just discriminate a
crystal (grain) of the order of 0.05 mm diameter. Normally the

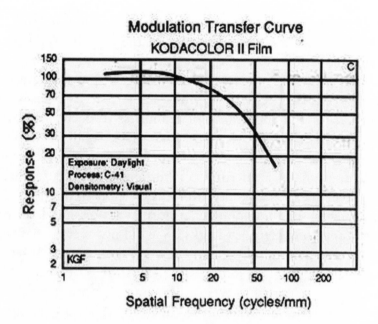

Figure 25-2.
(b) Modulation transfer curve.

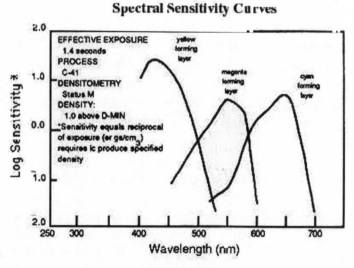

Figure 25-2.
(c) Spectral sensitivity curves.

eye does not perceive the granular structure at low magnifications. The finer the mean diameter of the crystals, the higher the magnification must be before graininess is noticed. It is the random nature of the exposed crystals, each possessing a different spectral reflectivity in white light, that is a necessary condition for the appearance of graininess to occur. Also, the mean diameter of film crystals becomes a significant factor when deciding on a diameter for a scanning digitizer's entrance aperture. A 6 micron diameter aperture was used here.

The roll of exposed Kodak film was developed commercially. According to the photographer, a normal processing delay occurred (approximately 1.5 weeks). She did not specify that special development or any enlargements were desired. A set of color positive prints ("jumbo size") and the developed color negatives, cut apart into sets of two frames, were received by the photographer on or about October 26, 1981. Inspection of the attached second frame to the one in question by the author showed that it was of a child standing inside a home. This child was the daughter of the couple who owned the camera; the scene was confirmed to have been taken inside their home in Campbell River, British Columbia. This fact agreed with the story told by the couple concerning the sequence of events of their automobile trip to the north end of Vancouver Island and return and the photographs they remembered taking.

It was not until the couple had received the set of color prints from the Vancouver processing laboratory that they noticed the strange aerial disk in the clear blue sky near the mountain top.

IMAGE ANALYSIS RESULTS

My analysis of the negative (and also first-generation positive black-and-white and color prints) included the following steps: (a) linear and angular measurements, (b) micro-densitometry scans to establish optical density range, (c) black-and-white photographic enlargements using papers having different spectral sensitivities, and (d) computer-based contrast enhancements.

Linear and Angular Image Measurements

Selected linear measurements of the disk's image on the enlarged print are given earlier in this chapter (see "The Photograph and Negative"). The angular measurements shown in Figure 25-3 were determined on the basis of the linear measurements of the image, the camera lens's focal length, and an on-site survey, which is described below. Referring to Figure 25-3 it may be pointed out that the photograph's center was elevated about 9 degrees of arc above the horizontal and the tip of the mountain was very close to the geometric center of the photograph. The disk subtended 1.3 degrees of arc. Elevation angles from the local horizontal were measured with a surveyor's transit to the top of the mountain, the location of the photographer, and the sun. These latter measurements were obtained at the same time of day, day of the year, and location as

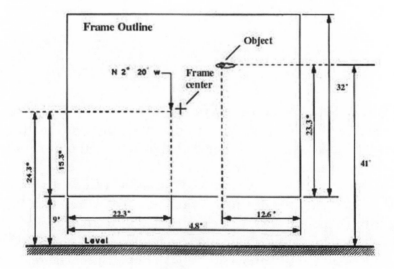

Figure 25-3. Horizontal and vertical angles in the photograph.

that of the original photograph, but two years later. These results are presented in Figure 25-4, with the disk shown in side
view. The exact outline of the disk is not known; also, the
dome-like protuberance is not shown here.

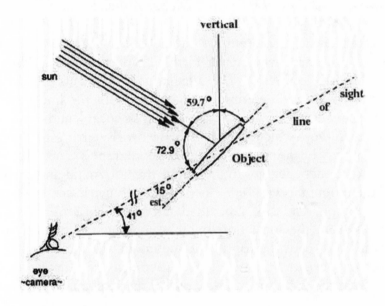

Figure 25-4. Summary of elevation angles.

Micro-densitometry Scan

A Joyce Loebl Recording Micro-densitometer with x20 power
objective, 50:1 linear magnification ratio, slit width of 0.02
inches, and vertical-slit height of 1 mm was used on the original negative.

Density calibration was carried out using a Kodak ND step
wedge spanning the densities on the negative. Greatest optical
density (brightest positive image) was approximately 0.65 to
0.7 density units ($\log_{10}ND$) and was found on the sunlit cloud.
This is equivalent to about 12,500 ft-L luminance. Figure 25-5
is a vertical scan through the disk's two brightest areas using
the micro-densitometer. The tracing peak marked T represents

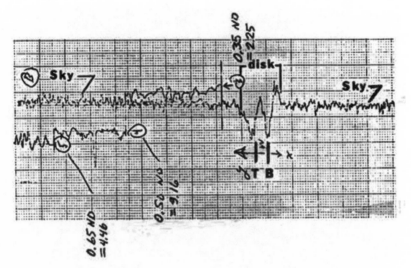

Figure 25-5. Micro-densitometer vertical scan through the disk image.

the upper-most (dome) bright area and B represents the lower area of brightness on the front edge of the disk. This scan line is shown in Figure 25-6, which is an enlargement of the disk's image. Points T and B both have optical densities of about 0.55 to 0.6 density units.

The optical density of the blue sky on the negative is shown in Figure 25-5 and has a value of approximately 0.4 density units. The gradual slope of this densitometry tracing is due to the progressive sky brightness increase from the zenith to the horizon, while the smaller amplitude deviations are due to single and grouped film grains.

Of particular note is the fact that the brightest area on the disk was of lower brightness than the cloud by approximately 0.15 density units. According to a physics handbook (Allen, 1963), a smooth, polished silver surface reflects (within the visible spectrum) increasingly higher percentages of incident radiation with increasing wavelength. An average reflectance value of about 90 percent is found. Polished aluminum reflects about 85 percent regardless of wavelength of the incident radiation;

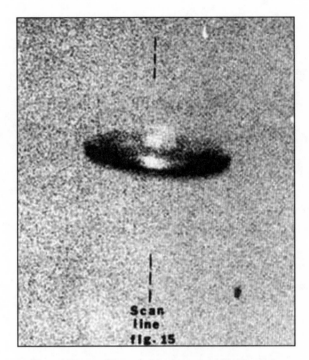

Figure 25-6. Photo enlargement of the disk.

this is also true for nickel (reflectance of about 60 percent), silicon (about 30 percent), and steel (about 54 percent). This comparison of dark areas on the negative suggests that the surface of the disk is very likely not a polished surface of any of the above metals. Direct sunlight has a brightness of about 750,000 ft-L, and if a 90 percent reflectance is assumed for the disk's surface, the brightest area should produce a brightness of about 675,000 ft-L, which is more than an order of magnitude greater than what was found on the negative.

A horizontal scan using the micro-densitometer was also made to see if there was any evidence of a double exposure. A double exposure might be indicated by the presence of double edges if the film registration is not precisely the same during a manual rewind. No such evidence was found. In addition, this camera could not take double exposures due to its frame-locking mechanism.

Black-and-White Enlargements on Different Wavelength-Sensitive Papers

The disk area of the negative was enlarged and printed on panchromatic paper which provided a relatively complete and undistorted translation of the three primary colors in the negative into shades of gray. This is shown in Figure 25-7(a). The top "dome" protuberance is clearly visible. The same area on the negative also was printed at the same enlargement using blue-green sensitive paper, which significantly reduces the contribution of the red emulsion layer to the final black-and-white print. This is shown in Figure 25-7(b). The blue-green sensitive paper

Figure 25-7. Black-and-white image enlargement.

 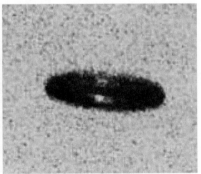

(a) Panchromatic paper.   (b) Blue-green sensitive paper.

increases the overall brightness of the sky and causes the "dome" area on the disk to almost disappear. Apparently, the dome is not reflecting or emitting radiation in the red end of the spectrum.

Computer-Based Contrast Enhancement

The negative was digitized using a Perkin-Elmer scanning densitometer set to 6 microns diameter entrance aperture. Optical density was measured to 16-bit resolution. The negative was scanned and digitized three times; each scan was made using a color filter having approximately the same spectral distribution as the dye layers in the negative.* The system output was recorded on 0.5-inch magnetic tape at 1,600 bits per inch density for processing and display by a digital computer. The region studied was only slightly larger than that of the disk in order to conserve memory and processing time. The range of optical densities found within this image area ranged from 5 to 400. Since the optical densities extended only from about 200 to 400 for the disk's image, the computational range was truncated by dropping the top 8 bits. Thus, the 8 bits from zero to 255 levels of density are presented in all of the following computer color enhancements.

Figures 25-8 and 25-9 are enhancements obtained using only the blue filter scan; that is, there is almost no contribution to this image from green or red wavelengths. A very high contrast color enhancement is shown in Figure 25-8 using blue picture elements (pixels) on the cathode ray tube monitor to represent film densities associated with the image of the disk, and orange and red pixels to represent film densities characteristic of the surrounding sky density. It must be emphasized that there is no particular significance to the colors seen in these computer-enhanced photographs.

---

*The film's yellow forming layer, magenta layer, and cyan layer peaked in sensitivity at 425, 545, and 650 nanometers (nm), respectively. This technique permitted the information content in each layer to be analyzed separately.

Figure 25-8. Black-and-white image formed from a color enhancement of disk image using a blue filter.

Figure 25-9 shows a black-and-white enhancement using an undistorted contrast. Much of the top surface detail becomes invisible in both Figures 25-8 and 25-9. Presumably this is due to the particular range of wavelengths that are being reflected or emitted by the disk. Both of these figures show that the sky is fairly homogeneous, and the film's crystals (each possessing different sensitivity to light) are approximately random in their spatial distribution, as expected. Also shown is a sharply defined bottom edge of the disk relative to its upper edge. The shadow seen under the disk's lower edge in Figure 25-6 is barely evident here.

Figure 25-10 presents an enhancement made using a green filter where purples and blues are assigned to densities that predominate within the image of the disk, and yellows are assigned to densities characterizing the background sky. A long vertical scratch exists to the left of the disk's image within this particular

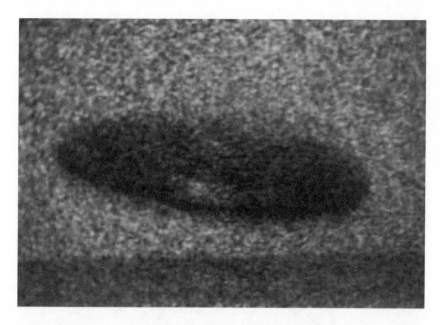

Figure 25-9. Black-and-white enhancement with undistorted contrast.

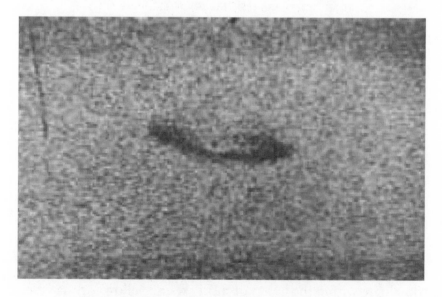

Figure 25-10. Black-and-white image formed from a color enhancement of disk image using a green filter.

emulsion layer. Not only is the sky fairly homogeneous in its density, but the two regions of greater brightness on the disk become much more apparent. The overall shape of the disk is symmetrical but has more pointed ends. The significance of this is unclear.

A red filter was used to generate the enhancement shown in Figure 25-11. As was noted in enhancements using a green filter, the dome is missing in this enhancement, suggesting that the protuberance on top of the disk is reflecting or emitting wavelengths mainly in the blue-green portion of the spectrum.

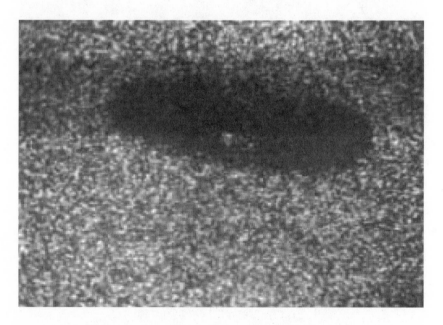

Figure 25-11. Black-and-white image formed from a color enhancement of disk image using a red filter.

Finally, a three-color composite enhancement including blue, green, and red wavelengths was made. Figure 25-12 presents one such enhancement to illustrate the homogeneity of the sky as well as the emulsion flaw and highlights on the image of the

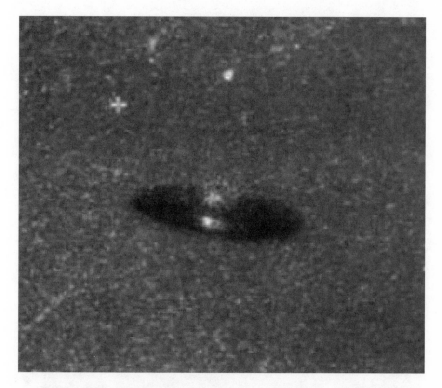

Figure 25-12. Black-and-white image formed from a three-color enhancement of disk image.

disk. None of the above enhancements shows any evidence for a suspension line or thread above the disk.

SITE VISIT RESULTS

A comprehensive site visit was made by the author on October 7–8, 1983.* Photographs, measurements, and general inspections were made of the entire vicinity of the provincial park

*I am greatly indebted to Donald H. Haines, my father and a registered civil engineer, who accompanied me and who performed the survey of the site. I am also grateful to the Fund for UFO Research, in Maryland, which supported a part of the travel costs to British Columbia from California.

where the photograph had been taken. Figure 25-13 is a topographic chart of the area with the mountain darkened. This location is just east of Highway 19 at the Eve River bridge, about forty-nine miles west-northwest of Campbell River, British Columbia, on Vancouver Island. Area X on this chart marks the approximate location of the photographer. This spot is located at 126° 14' west and 50° 19.4' north. The photographer and her family had stopped at this park for a rest when the photograph was taken. The rectangular area marked with a C is property operated by the McMillan-Bloedel Lumber Co., Ltd., camp, which was unoccupied when the author was there. The clearing in the forested area was gravel covered with a few

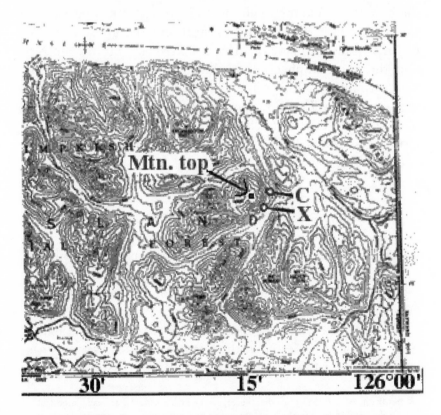

Figure 25-13. Topographic chart of photographic site on northern Vancouver Island, British Columbia.

buildings, fuel pumps, a dynamite shack, and vehicles of various kinds. Intense white yard lights illuminated the area at night (in 1983). A registered civil engineer (see footnote on page 190) conducted a site survey and determined that the photographer stood approximately 4,240 feet north of Highway 19 (within the provincial park) and faced 3° 18' north by west toward the peak of the mountain. The slant distance to the mountain peak was 7,580 feet, for an elevation angle of 24° 17'. The height of the mountain from the local horizontal was 3,117 feet, while the elevation of the photographer's position was 984 feet above mean sea level.

Although the provincial park was located within an area cleared of evergreen trees, second-growth timber extended from the base of the mountain almost to its top. After inspecting the site, it was clear that there was sufficient flat ground to have flown a model airplane or thrown a Frisbee* into the air. Neither the photographer nor her husband admit to doing this. Apart from the buildings in the lumber yard, there are no buildings or stores within a radius of fifteen miles of this spot. The photographer does not remember passing any vehicles on the morning she took the photo, other than a few logging trucks with loads of logs.

CREDIBILITY OF THE PHOTOGRAPHER

In cases such as this it is essential to establish the credibility of the persons involved. Mrs. D. M. (age twenty-six) was the photographer. She was accompanied by her husband (age approximately thirty), their eighteen-month-old daughter, and the family dog. They were on their way to visit the photographer's sister at Holberg, located at the northwest tip of Vancouver Island. Mrs. D. M. was an outgoing, pleasant person with a ca-

---

*Both Mr. and Mrs. D. M. stated that the large open area afforded a wide and unobstructed view of the surrounding terrain. They noticed no other persons at the provincial park when they were arriving, leaving, or at the campsite. They also stated they heard no sounds from the direction of the mountain while they were at the campsite.

sual interest in UFOs. Inspection of their home did not indicate any interest at all in the occult, the psychic realm, or related subjects. Mr. D. M. worked at the lumber mill in Campbell River. Neither person claimed to have read any books specifically on UFOs, but had seen the movie *Close Encounters of the Third Kind*. The husband was an avid science fiction fan in earlier years.

When asked what they had done immediately after noticing the disk on the photograph (some eighteen days later, on October 26, 1981), Mrs. D. M. replied, "Well, we didn't know what to do. Eventually we showed it to our neighbors and Mr. and Mrs. M. Sr. [husband's parents]." Mrs. D. M. phoned the Canadian Forces Base at Comox in mid-November 1981 concerning their possible interest in seeing the photograph. She "just wanted to see if they were interested in it and if they knew anything about what the object could be." An Air Force representative (allegedly) said they were not interested in viewing it, but did take her name and address. It was not until the summer of 1982 that the family traveled to Vancouver, B.C., bringing one four-by-five-inch color print with them. They visited the Vancouver Planetarium and spoke with the director, David Dodge, who called in David Powell, who was interested in UFO phenomena. The couple were persuaded to lend the original negative to them to make enlarged copies. The negatives were delivered to Mr. Powell in June 1982 and were returned to Mr. and Mrs. D. M. on January 28, 1983. These dates may be significant since they suggest that the photographer was willing to wait a long time before pursuing an explanation for the disklike image on her photograph. If this event had been a deliberate hoax it is more likely that some overt action to capitalize on it might have been taken soon after the disk had been discovered, and not almost a year later. Of course this is not a conclusive argument to support this contention.*

* While it is true that Mr. and Mrs. D. M. have had color enlargements made of their photograph and have sold some, this was done as a courtesy to their friends and to others who wrote asking for copies. Almost no profit has been made from the sale of these photographs.

The author found the photographer and her husband to be middle-class, hardworking people. Their property was well kept. Nothing could be found that pointed to a deliberate hoax. Both displayed genuine puzzlement about the origin of the disk on the photograph. Mr. and Mrs. D. M. were not defensive, nor did they ever attempt to cover up anything as far as could be determined. For example, when asked if he owned a Frisbee, Mr. D. M. said yes and located it immediately for the author's inspection. It was a nine-inch-diameter, dull black, Professional FIFI Model. He claimed to have been proficient in throwing it in the past, but had not done so in some time. There was no indication that some type of dome-like structure had been attached to it. The suspicion lingered throughout the investigation that a Frisbee or other similar object had merely been tossed up into the air and photographed. It became important to learn more about Frisbees and their "flight" qualities.

A REVIEW OF FRISBEE CHARACTERISTICS

Three topics are briefly reviewed here: (a) surface characteristics, (b) flight records in competition, and (c) subtended angles and related distances. The author [Haines] consulted with a person[*] who had previously worked for a well-known manufacturer of Frisbees. He explained the necessity of having a smoothly curved leading edge at the circumference of the disk and tiny microgrooves in the top surface in order to create a lifting force during its spinning flight. He suggested that the addition of a dome-like structure to the top would probably reduce or destroy this aerodynamic lift. The author later proved that this was indeed true. The author also contacted various toy stores to inspect various Frisbee models. A total of seven different models were inspected. All possessed a glossy (specular) outer surface. Most had reflectances of about 80 percent or

[*] I wish to thank Mr. Gordon Holt for his professional assistance in this phase of the analysis.

less. Of the six models produced before 1981, only two had paper labels; the other four had colorful embossed drawings centered across the top surface.

Men's and women's world records for throwing Frisbees were obtained from the International Frisbee Association (IFA). This organization has hosted tournaments, which have become qualifying events for the World Frisbee Championship. It was discovered that the men's outdoor distance record is 166 meters (540 feet) and the women's record is 122 meters (397 feet). These records were set in 1983 and 1980, respectively, and are meant only to indicate the general range of human capability for this skilled activity. The men's world record for maximum time aloft is 15.5 seconds (1981); the women's record is 11.4 seconds (1980).

The linear width of the disk's image on the negative was 0.98 mm. The width of the 36 mm frame was equivalent to a horizontal angle of 48 degrees. From these data, we calculate that the angle subtended by the disk was 1.307 degrees. Hence, we find that if W is the width of the object and D is the distance of the object from the camera, W/D = 0.0228. Hence, if (for a possible Frisbee) W = 9 inches, we find that D = 32.88 feet, which exceeds the hyperfocal distance. If the object instead had a diameter W = 10 or 50 feet, then the distance D would have been 438 feet or 2,192 feet, respectively. If the disk had been directly over the mountain, then the distance would have been 7,580 feet, and the width of the object would have been 173 feet.

Assuming that the camera shutter speed was 1/125th second and the disk image was produced by a typical Frisbee traveling at 10 feet per second, a 9-inch-diameter disk moving normal to the line of sight would move 0.96 inches in this duration. Approximately 9.3 percent of the Frisbee's diameter would show up as a blur on the leading and trailing edge of the Frisbee's photographic image. There is virtually no blur visible on the photograph in question, which strongly argues that the disk was not traveling normal to the line of sight. If it was motionless, it would be more difficult for the photographer to perceive, particularly if the photographer (a) was looking through the camera, and (b) was not expecting to see anything hanging motionless in the air.

It is highly unlikely that the object photographed was a commercially available Frisbee. There are significant top-surface-contour differences between a Frisbee and the photographed disk. This was shown by a careful comparison of photographs of a Frisbee model with a dome oriented the same as the photographed disk and illuminated by sunlight under the same angular conditions. The surface reflections were markedly different in each case. In addition, the presence of the tiny, concentric microgrooves on all Frisbees would not be expected to yield a sharp contrast gradient as is seen in Figures 25-7(b), 25-8, and 25-9.

When the author attached a lightweight dome to a Frisbee, it would not fly very far nor very high. It is problematical whether another person could have achieved such a feat. The author inspected the frame immediately following the frame in question and found that it had been taken at home in Campbell River following the trip north. The immediately preceding frame was also located. It showed Mr. D. M. and their daughter standing in front of a small pond at the provincial park on the day the photograph had been taken, exactly as stated by the photographer. If someone had tossed a model up into the air in order to photograph it, only one photo was taken. It would be remarkable for such a clearly focused image to be obtained on the first try, if this is what happened. Furthermore, this explanation does not stand up under scrutiny of the author's in-depth interviews and site visit.

The fact that the photographer stated that she was taking a photograph of the mountain (and not of a UFO disk or model) is further supported by the fact that the top of the mountain is well centered in the photograph. The object was not centered. The lack of any image blur suggests that the disk was nearly motionless, which would make it more difficult to see, other factors being equal.

In summary, this investigation has shown that a mature adult with high credibility and little or no interest in UFO phenomena, obtained a single, colored, sharp-imaged photograph of an unidentified aerial disk-like object. Her subsequent reactions to seeing the disk's image on her photograph produced surprise and dismay as well as the normal array of "answer-seeking" behavior. She has not capitalized on having such a photo and still acts somewhat embarrassed at having taken it without seeing the disk. The disk's identity has not been established to date.

PHOTO ANALYSIS OF AN AERIAL DISK OVER COSTA RICA
(by Richard F. Haines and Jacques F. Vallee)

BACKGROUND

On September 4, 1971, a mapping aircraft of the government of Costa Rica with a crew of four recorded an unusual disk-shaped image as it was flying over the region of Arenal. It took several years for this photograph to find its way into the hands of a Costa Rican investigator, Mr. Ricardo Vilchez, who (along with his brother Eduardo) runs a civilian research group in San Jose. In 1980 Mr. Vilchez met in person with Sergio L.V., the specialist in aerial photography who was aboard the aircraft that day. They discussed the circumstances surrounding the flight and the photograph without reaching a conclusion regarding the nature of the object. One of the authors saw the photograph while attending a meeting in Costa Rica in 1985, and Mr. Vilchez was kind enough to provide a second-generation negative to be taken back to the United States for analysis. Later we requested and obtained detailed maps of the area in question, as well as copies of prints from the immediately preceding and following frame numbers 299 and 301. These photographs did not show the disk that was present on frame number 300.

In spite of the lack of a first-generation negative, we felt several unusual factors justified a detailed analysis of this photograph, if only to refine our methodology in dealing with such evidence: (a) It was taken by a high-quality professional camera; (b) the camera was looking down, which gives a maximum distance, hence a maximum size for the object; (c) the disk was seen against a reasonably uniform dark background of a body of water; and (d) the image was large, in focus, and provided significant detail.

LOCATION

The disk was located about 3 miles north of the town of Arenal and some 25 miles south of the border with Nicaragua. The precise site was at latitude 10.583 degrees north and longitude 84.916 degrees west in the province of Alajuela above a small lake called "Lago de Cote" measuring approximately 1,800 by 1,600 meters. The lake level is about 640 meters above sea level, and the surrounding countryside consists of rolling and sharp hills rising several hundred meters above the valley floor. The region is densely wooded, with some broad, grassy patches. A dirt road, which is passable only in summer, runs along the southern edge of the lake. It connects the small town of Cabanga to the northeast with Aguacate to the southwest. When the photograph is carefully examined, a few houses or other structures can be seen along this road, as well as animals in the fields.

The location of the disk was about 800 meters due north of the boundary between the province of Alajuela and the province of Guanacaste.

Figure 25-14 is a black-and-white contact positive print of most of the aerial negative.

Figure 25-15 is a copy of the 1:50,000 chart in the region of Lago de Cote above which the disk was located.

Figure 25-14. A black-and-white contact positive print of most of the aerial negative.

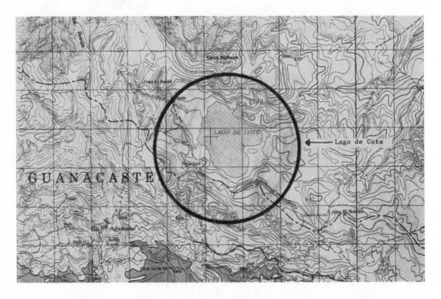

Figure 25-15. Detail from the 1:50,000 chart in the region of Lago de Cote above which the disk was located.

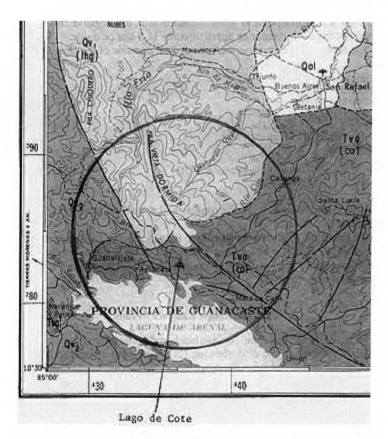

Lago de Cote

Figure 25-16. Detail from the geological chart with an arrow
pointing to the Lago de Cote.

Figure 25-16 is a copy of a geological chart with an arrow
pointing to the Lago de Cote. A heavy, long, dashed line labeled
"Fila Vieja Dormida" is seen passing almost directly through
the location where the disk was recorded. This line represents a
geological fault. The legend on the chart indicates that the dark
areas are of volcanic origin.

PARAMETERS OF THE PHOTOGRAPH

According to Mr. Vilchez, the camera used was an R-M-K 15/23. The lens would have featured a fixed focus and a 6-inch focal length. The shutter speed was 1/500 second at f-5.6. The intervallometer was set at 20 seconds between successive exposures.

The film used was black-and-white emulsion with an ASA speed of 80. This fine-grain film produces a high-resolution negative given a stable film plane and camera and sufficiently fast shutter speed.

The negative was printed on Kodak Safety aerial film, type 3665. The image measured 23 cm by 23 cm (529 square centimeters), while the film base measured 25.3 cm by 23.8 cm. Comparing the image area with the reduced-scale topographical chart indicated that the negative included a region of the Earth measuring approximately 11.5 km on a side.

The following information was recorded on one side of the film:

> Frame counter: 909
> Altimeter: 10,000 feet
> Bubble level: Approx. level
>   C = 152.44
>   Nr21186
> Clock: 08:25 am local time
> Notations: ARENAL
>   10,000 feet
>   4-9-71 (September 4, 1971)
>   R. L. B.

Handwritten between the frame counter and the above information is the notation: 300 L-11 M-13.

On board the aircraft were four men, namely: Sergio L.V., specialist in aerial photography; Omar A., pilot; Juan B.C., geographer; and Francisco R.R., topographer. No member of the crew observed anything unusual during the flight.

THE DISK IMAGE: ANALYSIS RESULTS

Figure 25-17 is a photographic positive black-and-white enlargement of intermediate contrast of the disk, showing (a) a dark edge across the top and upper-right corner, which is the edge of the frame, and fiduciary mark included for measurement purposes; (b) the shoreline, also for measurement purposes; and (c) the ellipsoidal disk. This figure is oriented with true north facing up.

A number of features are worthy of note on Figure 25-17.

First, the disk image appears to possess light/dark shading that is typical of a three-dimensional object that is illuminated by sunlight. At this time and location, the sun's azimuth was

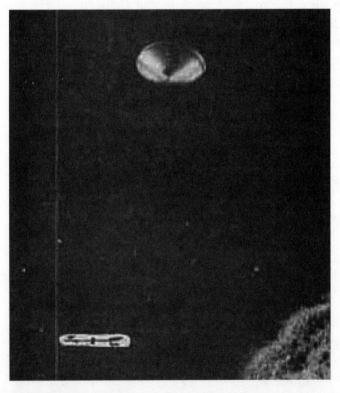

Figure 25-17. A photographic positive black-and-white enlargement of intermediate contrast of the disk.

85.4 degrees (clockwise from true north) and altitude was 16.7 degrees, which explains the lateral displacement of the cloud shadows from the cloud locations.

Second, the generally triangular dark region on the right-hand side of the disk cannot be a solar shadow cast by the (assumed) opaque disk from the right-hand side. If the disk is an opaque, flat conical section of revolution (the dark spot being the tip of the cone) and if the right side is tipped upward, then the entire surface of the disk should be dark. It is more likely that the light and dark regions are surface markings.

Figure 25-18 shows measured and calculated parameters for this image. The longitudinal axis of the disk was 7 degrees

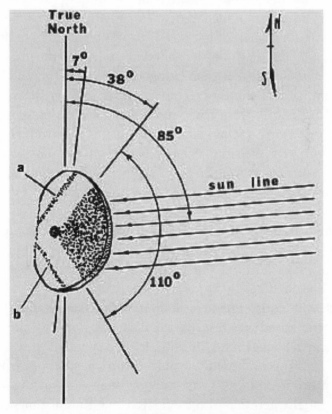

Figure 25-18. illustration of the measured and calculated parameters of the image.

clockwise (CW) from true north. The total included angle of the dark triangular region was about 110 degrees arc with the most northerly edge of this shadow 38 degrees from true north. The approximate centerline of the triangular shadow region was 93 degrees CW from true north.

Third, the finite thickness of the disk is suggested by the curved thin dark line parallel to the right-hand side of the disk (facing east). Two straight, thin dark lines (a, b) are also visible spanning the top of the disk diagonally and pointed toward the west. Each line is generally parallel with an edge of the triangular darker shadow area.

Fourth, while the right-hand edge of the disk image is in very sharp focus, the left-hand edge is diffuse and appears to be an irregular boundary which almost transits the light of the background in a transparent manner. It is of interest to note that the general orientation of this left-hand boundary of the image runs north and south rather than being parallel with the visible longitudinal axis of the disk. This irregular edge is shown more clearly in the following computer enhancement photographs.

The top (north-facing) edge of the disk is in extremely sharp focus with not even the grain structure of the film being apparent, whereas the entire top "surface" of the disk shows a mottled graininess, which could be representative of a diffusely reflecting surface.

If the disk image was of a real object traveling at a high rate of speed relative to the film plane, then one would expect a blurred image on both the leading and the trailing edge. This did not occur here.

Fifth, the entire image is in sharp focus suggesting that (a) the shutter speed was fast, (b) the disk was not moving relative to the Earth background, or both. It is known that the exposure lasted 1/500 second, which would "stop" a slowly moving object but not necessarily a fast-moving one.

Of equal interest is the calculated maximum dimension of the disk if it was located at the Earth's surface, 10,000 feet away from the camera. The object cannot be farther away than this. The 4.2 mm length of the image is equivalent to an object 210 m in length, or 683 feet.

Figure 25-19 is a photographic enlargement of the negative contrast in which the film's grain structure is apparent. In this regard, there is no distortion of the grain anywhere around the disk's image, which suggests that the image was not the result of a double exposure. Nor is there any obvious indication of heat-produced atmospheric distortion around the object. There

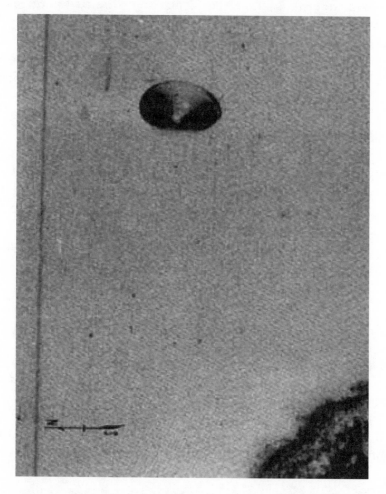

Figure 25-19. A photographic enlargement of the negative contrast in which the film's grain structure is apparent.

are no visible lines to or from the disk. The magnification is
identical to that of Figure 25-17. It is noted that the finite thickness of the disk is apparent, as is the edge sharpness on its right
and diffuseness on the left.

GROUND SHADOWS

All available photographic evidence was studied for the existence of a shadow of the disk. Since the lighting geometry is
known, the existence of a shadow would make it possible to
calculate the linear size of the disk. The sun line extending from
the disk's location was traced on the negative, positive prints,
and digital enhancements, and any evidence for an approximately symmetrical shadow was sought. None was found. In
this regard it may be pointed out that the atmosphere was relatively clear (between the clouds) so that the solar-collimation
angle (32 minutes of arc) should produce a sharply defined
shadow on the ground. Of course, the greater the altitude of the
disk above the ground, the more diffuse would be the shadow
edge due to light scatter/diffusion effects. It should also be emphasized that if the disk was at or close to the Earth's surface,
one would not expect to find a significant shadow.

DIGITAL ENHANCEMENT

This negative was also subjected to digital enhancement. A region measuring 13 by 13 mm centered on the disk was digitized
using an aperture of approximately 1 micrometer diameter and
16 bit resolution. A number of color assignments to the density
distribution were made to emphasize different features. Unfortunately, the following four figures are printed in black and
white and do not show all of this rich detail.

Figure 25-20 is a high reverse-contrast image to illustrate
two features. First, the density gradient on the left-hand side of

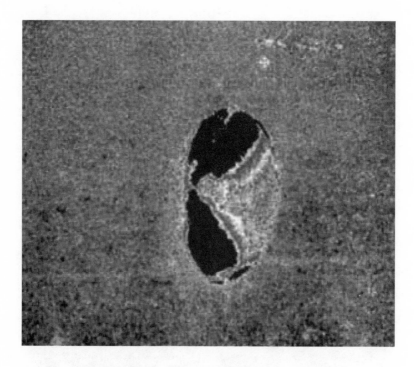

Figure 25-20. A high reverse-contrast image
(f = 4, t = 1/8 sec.).

the disk is not visible on the photographic prints (Figures 25-17 and 25-19). The same density was found on the left and right sides of the disk. The left side of the disk is not a circular extension of the rest of the disk but is flattened to some unknown extent. Second, the brightness of the lake behind the disk varies regularly from the top of the photograph to the bottom, which is consistent with its reflection of collimated sunlight over the range of angles involved.

In Figure 25-21 the original densities of 100 to 125 were mapped or expanded to 1 to 256 levels of gray to demonstrate extremely subtle optical density changes, mainly in the area of the disk's dark regions and edge.

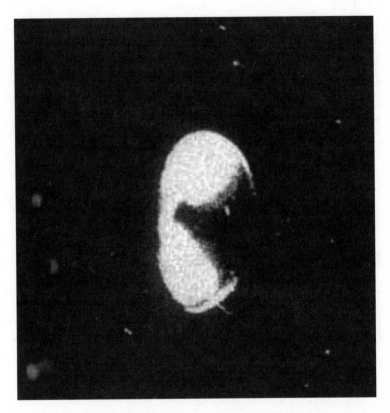

Figure 25-21. The original densities of 100 to 125 were
mapped or expanded to 1 to 256 levels of gray
(f = 4, t = 1/8 sec.).

In Figure 25-22 the original densities of 175 to 200 were
mapped to 1 to 256 levels of gray. The dark and light regions
on top of the disk become more evident here, as does the apparent third dimension of the object.

In Figure 25-23 a wider variety of colors was used to better
emphasize the disk's surface density differences as well as the
lake's luminance distribution. Located above the disk is a generally oval shaped region of higher density (darker). However,
it cannot be the shadow of the disk on the water's surface because it is in the wrong position relative to the sun.

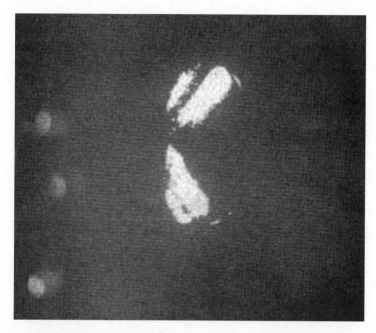

Figure 25-22. The original densities of 175 to 200 were mapped to 1 to 256 levels of gray (f = 4, t = 1/8 sec.).

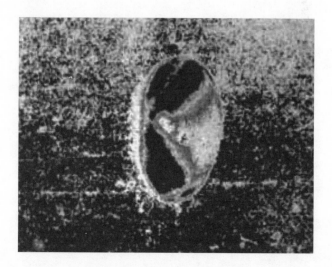

Figure 25-23. Emphasis on the disk's surface density differences as well as the lake's luminance (f = 2.8, t = 1/8 sec.).

SUBSEQUENT GROUND SIGHTINGS

On October 25, 1986, about fifteen years later, at about 9:00
A.M., by clear weather, two men saw an object at the surface of
the Lago de Cote. They are Joaquin U.A., forty years old, a
farm manager, and Ronald-Alberto L.A., a twenty-three-year-
old farmer. This sketch of what they saw is presented as Figure
25-24.

When interviewed at the site by Ricardo and Carlos Vilchez
two weeks after the observation, they gave a detailed description of the events. First they saw, about 1,800 feet away, a row
of three or four post-like cylinders rising to about 3 feet above

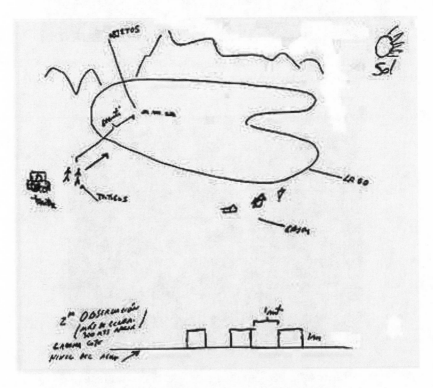

Figure 25-24. Sketch by the witnesses.

the surface of the lake, which was quiet and flat as a mirror. These cylinders appeared to be attached to a structure that remained submerged. Later they again saw a series of objects sticking out about 3 feet above the water and 3 feet apart. By then they had driven their tractor much closer to the lake, and they could clearly observe the cylinders, which were of a dark hue, either gray or coffee-colored.

After five or ten minutes these objects disappeared, the emerged portions again tilting together as if they were attached to a single submerged structure, and the whole object disappeared back into the lake with significant turmoil and waves.

It should be noted that such observations of submerged objects, although rare, are not unknown in the UFO literature. For example, on October 27, 1978, at 6:40 P.M., two Italian fishermen in Falcone (Piombino) saw a luminous, bell-shaped object come out of the sea with a metallic sound and fly to within 150 feet of their location (Cappa and Winter, 1979).

A number of questions are raised by this analysis. In particular, we have not been able to provide an interpretation for the fact that the disk's image has a sharply defined edge on the sun's (right) side and a fuzzy edge on the opposite side. The possible significance of the proximity of a geologic fault line is unknown. There is no indication that the image is the product of a double exposure or a deliberate fabrication.

Computer enhancement (see Figures 25-20 and 25-23) emphasizes extremely small variations in background brightness. Several horizontal lines are most likely printing artifacts rather than real, environment-related effects. Another feature of interest has to do with the edge of the dark triangular region on the disk's right-hand side. Figures 25-20 through 25-23 all show that the top edge of this dark region is more convex than is its lower edge, as would be expected if the disk presented a generally conical surface of revolution.

In summary, our analyses have suggested that an unidentified, opaque, aerial object was captured on film at a maximum distance of 10,000 feet. There are no visible means of lift or propulsion and no surface markings other than darker regions that appear to be nonrandom. This case must remain "open" until further information becomes available.

PHOTO ANALYSIS OF AN AERIAL DISK OVER COSTA RICA: NEW EVIDENCE (by Richard F. Haines and Jacques F. Vallee)

In responses to the comments of a referee, Dr. Marilyn Bruner, on our report "Photo Analysis of an Aerial Disk over Costa Rica," we made further efforts to obtain the original negative of the unidentified object, photographed by chance during an aerial mapping mission, for further study. Indeed, we were concerned that some of our reviewer's suggestions might require stricter tests than we could carry out on a second-generation negative. We are pleased to state that through the efforts of Peter Sturrock, Jacques Vallee, and Ricardo Vilchez in San Jose, Costa Rica, we received three connected frames (Nos. 299–301) of the original black-and-white negative on February 11, 1990.

As one would expect, there is more fine detail visible on the original negative than on the copy, and this detail is highly interesting. Several points deserve further comment based on careful unaided and magnified visual inspection of this new negative and different contrast positive print enlargements that were made. Figure 25-25 is a high-contrast enlargement of the disk made from the original negative.

a. The oval disk image is present in the same relative location on frame 300 as already described in our first article. Also, the entire film plane on frames 299, 300, and 301 is flat, with absolutely no protrusions or depressions anywhere.

b. The emulsion side of frames 299 and 301 possessed several small, irregularly shaped developer stains, which only affected the specular reflectivity of the emulsion but did not in any way influence the transmissivity of the film. These stains were completely invisible except when the film was viewed

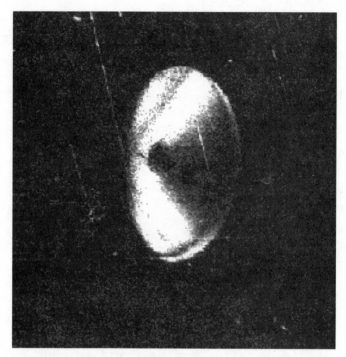

Figure 25-25. Enlarged positive print of disk from
original negative.

against a diffuse, glancing, reflecting light source. No stains
were found at any place on frame 300, the frame on which the
image of the disk was located.

c. There are a number of long linear scratches (mostly on the
non-emulsion side) running parallel to the edge labeled with the
Kodak Safety Film markings running east-west. It is apparent
that the negative has received rough usage over the years. There
are three very thin parallel scratches running through the image
of the disk as well that are visible in Figure 25-25.

d. The individual film grains were somewhat more apparent
on this original negative throughout all three frames as compared with the second generation negative, as would be expected. They appeared to be randomly spaced and possessed
random diameters as well.

e. Our examination of the original negative confirms our initial speculation that the image of the disk is not the result of a double exposure, a reflection, a deliberate paste-up, or other kind of hoax.

f. There appears to be a very interesting obliquely oriented micro- and macrostructure detail on the image of the object itself. Figure 25-26 is a drawing of the disk that indicates the location of this detail.

Referring to Figure 25-26, the left-hand edge (L) consists of dozens of thin, parallel fingers of light that originate in the "body" of the object and fade off into the background luminance. The tips of these fingers end approximately along a curved line that corresponds to the oval-shaped outline of the disk's form. The right-hand edge (R) possesses a much more regular (smooth) contour than the left but also possesses many very short jagged lines of light, each of which is oriented in the same direction as the longer fingers discussed above. The line labeled X-Y is the orientation of all of this microstructure just described. There are even some very short jagged lines with this orientation, found along the inner edge labeled (z).

Three other details having this same orientation are also of note. They are: (a) the upper and lower edges of the disk, labeled (d') and (d), respectively; (b) a relatively long, thin, dark line that originates at the central dark region, which is labeled (n); and (c) the alignment of the two dark regions near the middle of the disk. We have no clear understanding of the origin or meaning of this oblique orientation effect seen in so many of its surface details.

On the basis of a very careful examination of the preceding and following frame, under different levels of magnification, it is clear that a second image of this aerial disk is not present in either one (unless it is concealed behind a dense cloud). Therefore, it must have flown into and then out of the field of view of frame 300 in 20 seconds or otherwise become invisible. These considerations lead us to estimate that the object must have been traveling at a speed of at least 2,000 miles per hour.

g. We examined frames 299 and 301 under various magnifi-

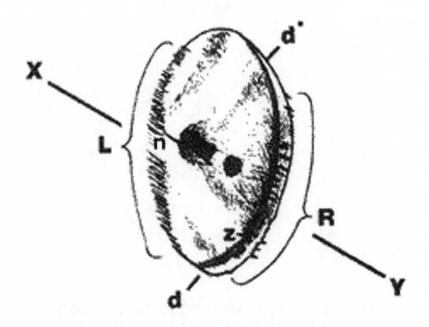

Figure 25-26. Drawing of fine surface details based on
original negative.

cations in the same region of the lake where the disk is found.
We were looking for any kind of disturbance to the surface of
the water. There was none.

In summary, our good fortune in obtaining the original negative for frames 299–301 has resulted in confirmation of our
earlier speculation that the aerial disk is certainly anomalous.
While it may not be inexplicable, it remains unidentified.

CHAPTER 26

Luminosity

ESTIMATES OF OPTICAL POWER OUTPUT FOR SIX CASES OF UNEXPLAINED AERIAL OBJECTS
(by Jacques F. Vallee)

INTRODUCTION

Some of the most striking statements made by witnesses of unusual aerial objects during their debriefing by investigators have to do with the luminosity of the phenomenon. They frequently use expressions like "It lit up the whole landscape" or "Every object in the area stood out, intensely thrown into relief." Beyond these subjective statements (which could be affected by physiological and psychological factors), it is difficult to obtain reliable quantitative data on the power output of the observed objects. Typically, the witnesses are surprised by the phenomenon, and it is rare for them to have any basis of comparison or calibration. A few such cases do exist, however, and a special effort has been made here to derive estimates from the data.

Obvious cautions are immediately raised by this exercise. By definition the source of the luminosity is an unknown phenomenon. We do not know if the light is a primary manifestation of its internal physical state (as would be the case for the sun) or a secondary one, as would be the case for the moon or an automobile headlight. We do not even know if most of the electromagnetic energy is released in the visible domain to which human witnesses and most cameras react.

Given these cautions one can, at best, hope to bracket a physical range to characterize the phenomenon in question. More relevant than the actual numerical values obtained in a few cases is the methodology involved in acquiring and processing such parameters.

Case Studies

The cases that follow have been extracted from a larger sample where luminosity or power output data could be obtained. We have excluded some extreme cases (such as the Tunguska explosion of 1908 in Siberia) and all cases involving a single observer, leaving six adequately documented and researched incidents with multiple witnesses. In Cases No. 2 and 3 the primary witnesses are known to the author, who has interviewed them personally. In Case No. 4 the author has visited the site. In other cases we rely on the data assembled by qualified investigators, all of whom are known to us.*

Case No. 1: August 27, 1956.
McCleod, Alberta, Canada

The witnesses in this case are Royal Canadian Air Force pilots who were flying in a formation of four F-86 Sabre jet aircraft

*The author [Vallee] is particularly indebted to Dr. Claude Poher, Dr. Bruce Maccabee, Dr. Illobrand Von Ludwiger, and Jean-Jacques Velasco, who made investigation reports available for this study.

Figure 26-1. Childerhose was flying west in the second position
(left side) of a formation of four F-86 Sabre jets of the
Royal Canadian Air Force.

(Figure 26-1). The planes were flying at 36,000 feet (about 11 km), headed due west over the Canadian Rockies, about an hour before sunset (Childerhose, 1958). As they were approaching a large thunderhead, R. J. Childerhose, the pilot in the second position (left side of the formation) saw a "bright light which was sharply defined and disc-shaped" or "like a shiny silver dollar sitting horizontal," far below the planes but above the lower layer of clouds. It appeared to be "considerably brighter than the sunlight" (Figure 26-2).

The sighting duration was variously quoted at 45 seconds (Childerhose, 1958) to three minutes. The pilot reported the observation to the flight leader, then took a photograph of it. That photograph, a Kodachrome color slide, was subsequently analyzed by Dr. Bruce Maccabee, who considered the hypotheses that the object was a cloud, a plasma phenomenon, or

Figure 26-2. Photograph of an unidentified high-altitude bright light source. Picture taken by Royal Canadian Air Force pilot R. J. Childerhose on August 27, 1956, from an altitude of approximately 11 kilometers. The object was higher than approximately 4 kilometers and was observed for more than 45 seconds. If acting as an isotropic Lambertian radiator, the power output within the spectral range of the film would have been in excess of 10^9 watts.

ball lightning (kugelblitz). We refer the reader to his recent article (Maccabee, 1999) while presenting here only a summary of his arguments.

The cloud hypothesis was contradicted by two facts, namely the equal brightness of the object on both sides as opposed to the darker appearance of clouds away from the sunlight, and the fact that portions of the object were brighter than the brightest clouds.

The plasma or ball-lightning hypothesis was mentioned by Philip Klass (1968) and by Martin D. Altschuler (1968). It is contradicted by the radiance of the object and the duration of the observation. Maccabee derives the radiance L by solving the standard photographic equation, corrected for the effects of atmospheric attenuation:

$$L = 4Ef^2 \ exp[(b-a)/cos\theta]/Tcos^4\o \qquad \text{(Eq. 26-1)}$$

where

$$E = H/t. \qquad \text{(Eq. 26-2)}$$

H is the film exposure level in J/cm^2 and t is the shutter time in seconds. L is the radiance of the object in the direction to the camera in W/sr cm^2, E is the irradiance on the focal plane of the camera in W/cm^2 and f is the ratio of the focal length to the diameter, as set by the operator of the camera. The factor $exp \ [(b-a)/cos\theta]$ corrects for atmospheric attenuation, b being the optical thickness of the atmosphere from the ground to the altitude of the plane, a the optical thickness to the altitude of the object, and θ the zenith angle of the slant path from the plane to the object. T is the transmission of the optics (aircraft window and lens) and $\o$ is the angle between the optical axis of the camera and the optical path from the lens to the image.

We refer the reader to Maccabee's analysis for an excellent discussion of the range of values of these parameters. He finds a value between 1.09 and 1.34 for the attenuation correction factor, a value of 0.7 for T, a shutter time of 1/125 seconds at f/8 and a value of 0.95 for $cos^4\o$. The average density over much of the image is estimated at 0.12, leading to the value of $H = 10^{-4} \ J/cm^2$.

Inserting these values into (Eq. 26-1) and (Eq. 26-2) gives estimates of the radiance of 1.7 to 2.0 W/sr cm^2 if the object was at distances of 6 or 20 kilometers, respectively. Assuming that the object was a Lambertian emitter with constant emittance over its surface, Maccabee finds a range 2.5×10^9 W (2,500 megawatts) to 3×10^{10} W (30,000 megawatts) for the power output within the spectral range of the film. As he rightly points out, however, "the total power emitted over all frequencies might be much greater."

Case No. 2: September 1965.
Fort-de-France, Martinique

On July 1, 1965, two French submarines, the *Junon* and the *Daphné*, escorted by the logistic support vessel *Rhône*, left the Toulon naval base in the Mediterranean and sailed toward Gibraltar. The ships traveled on, first to Horta in the Azores, then to Norfolk, Virginia, to conduct a series of joint operations with the U.S. Navy, which was engaged at the time in the recovery of a Gemini capsule near Bermuda. The French submarines escorted the aircraft carrier *Wasp*. Later the ships went through Hurricane Betsy, whose effects they avoided by diving to three hundred meters. On the way back to France they stopped for ten days at Pointe-à-Pitre, Guadeloupe, and for one day at Saintes before reaching the island of Martinique, where they anchored in late September 1965.

One evening during their layover in Fort-de-France, Martinique, in a dark sky and clear weather, a large luminous object arrived slowly and silently from the west, flew to the south, made three complete loops in the sky over the French vessels, and vanished like a rapidly extinguished lightbulb (see Vallee, 1990a).

The person who reported this case to us, Mr. Michel Figuet, was at the time first helmsman (*timonier*) of the French fleet of the Mediterranean. He observed the arrival of the object from his position on the deck of the submarine *Junon*. He had time to go up to the conning tower, where he took six pairs of binoculars and distributed them to his companions. There were three hundred witnesses, including four officers on the *Junon*, three officers on the *Daphné*, a dozen French sailors, and personnel of the weather observatory.

All witnesses aboard the *Junon* saw the object at 9:15 P.M. as a large ball of light or a disk on edge arriving from the west. It was the color of a fluorescent tube, about the same luminosity as the full moon. It moved slowly, horizontally, at a distance estimated at ten kilometers south of the ships, from west to east, leaving a whitish trace similar to the glow of a television screen.

When it was directly south of the ships, the object dropped toward the earth, made two complete loops, then hovered in the midst of a faint "halo" (Figure 26-3).

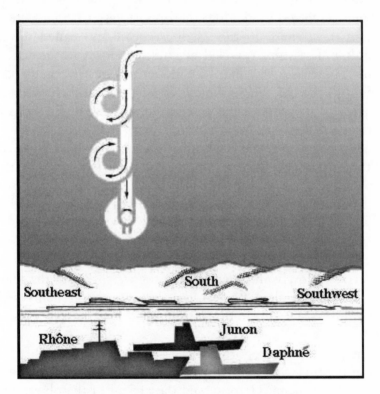

Figure 26-3. The harbor at Fort-de-France.

Mr. Figuet told the author that he observed the last part of this trajectory through binoculars; he was able to see two red spots under the disk. Shortly thereafter, the object vanished in the center of its glow "like a bulb turned off." The trail and the halo remained visible in the sky for a full minute. At 9:45 P.M., the halo reappeared at the same place, and the object seemed to emerge as if switched on. It rose, made two more loops, and flew away to the west, where it disappeared at 9:50 P.M. The next day Mr. Figuet compared notes with a communications engineer who had observed the same object from the navy fort. Together, they called the weather observatory at Fort-de-France. The man who answered the call had also observed the object. He stated that it was neither an aircraft nor a rocket.

In 1988 the author was able to interview Michel Figuet in Brussels. He confirmed the maneuvers and the appearance of the object and stated that he had met again with some of the crew members, whose recollections of the facts were equally precise.

A landscape illuminated by the full moon receives 0.318 lux, or 1.8×10^{-3} W/m². Since there is agreement among the observers that the object had approximately the same brightness as the full moon and was situated about 10 kilometers away, we can compute its total luminosity as:

$$P = I \times A \qquad \text{(Eq. 26-3)}$$

where I is the intensity in W/m² and A is the area over which light is spread. Here,

$$P = 1.8 \times 10^{-3} \times 4 \pi r^2 \qquad \text{(Eq. 26-4)}$$

where $r = 10{,}000$ meters, which gives $P = 2.3 \times 10^6$ W (2.3 Megawatt).

Case No. 3: December 30, 1966. Haynesville, Louisiana

The third case is drawn from official U.S. files. It took place at 8:15 P.M. on December 30, 1966, in the vicinity of Haynesville, Louisiana. The witnesses are a professor of physics, Dr. G., and his family. Inquiries with the weather bureau disclose that the weather was overcast, with fog and a light drizzle, ceiling about three hundred feet, parameters that are in agreement with the witnesses' statements. There was no thunderstorm.

In early 1967 the author came across this sighting while reviewing the files of the U.S. Air Force as an associate of Dr. J.
Allen Hynek at Northwestern University. Air Force personnel
had not followed up the report by Dr. G. and his family, so we
decided to pursue it on our own. Dr. G. told Dr. Hynek and
myself that he was driving north that night on U.S. Highway
79 between Haynesville and the Arkansas border when his
wife called his attention to a red-orange glow appearing
through and above the trees ahead to their left. They continued to observe it as they drove down the highway. It appeared as a luminous hemisphere, pulsating regularly, ranging
from dull red to bright orange, with a period of about two
seconds. There was no smoke or flame that would have been
characteristic of a fire.

When the car came to a point about one mile from the
source of the light, it suddenly brightened to a blinding white,
washing out the headlights and casting sharp shadows. This
burst of light not only forced Dr. G. to shield his eyes, but also
woke up his children who had been sleeping in the back seat.
After about four seconds it returned to its red-orange appearance.

Several sightings were described by other persons in the area.
One witness reported that about six days before, a similar
bright light had been seen near the same location.

When the University of Colorado received funding from the
U.S. Air Force for a scientific study of UFOs, the author called
Condon's attention to this case. A field investigation was conducted by several scientists from Boulder but failed to locate the
actual site. Condon concluded in his published report that the
case was "of interest," and it remained as one of the many
unidentified sightings in the University of Colorado files.

After the University of Colorado project was disbanded and
after the Air Force, following Condon's recommendations,
closed down Project Blue Book, study of the case was resumed
on a private basis. We came into contact with a qualified investigator, Mr. W., who had also pursued his own research with

Dr. G. Through them the author learned that Mr. W. and Dr. G. had pinpointed the actual site where the object had hovered. The area in question is a clearing about thirty feet in diameter, located to the west of some railroad tracks. The chief dispatcher stated that no rolling equipment was within fifty miles of the location that night. The nearest high-tension power lines are about nine miles away to the west.

All the trees at the periphery of the clearing exhibited a blackening or burning of the bark in a direction pointing to the center of the area, as if they had been exposed to an intense source of radiated energy. Clearly we would like to know whether the wood was burned by light energy, direct heat, or chemical combustion. From an estimate of the energy required to produce the depth of the burn, it may be possible to estimate the power of the source, assuming it was located in the center of the clearing fifteen feet away. However, this work has not been done.

Fortunately, there are other ways to arrive at a power estimate, as Dr. G. realized when he saw that the light from the object washed out his own headlights about ten feet ahead of the car. This enabled him to equate the intensity of the unknown object, which is given by its power output divided by the square of the distance, to the intensity of his headlights, which is given by their power output, known to be 150 watts, divided by the square of 10 feet. This leads to a lower limit for the power output of the UFO.

On using the inverse-square law for the intensity of a source as a function of distance, Dr. G. could calculate that it would take a lamp of power 4.86 megawatt to give the same intensity at a distance of 1,800 feet (the distance of the clearing from the observation point) as does a 150-watt automobile lamp at 10 feet. There are some uncertainties involved here. For instance, the headlamp is beamed, and an incandescent lamp has an efficiency of only about 2 percent. Hence, the luminous energy may be only about 10 to 100 kilowatts.

Case No. 4: November 5, 1976.
Grenoble, France

Another remarkable observation made near Grenoble, France, on November 5, 1976, by a senior French scientist is relevant here. As in the previous case, there were multiple witnesses, and the duration was long enough to allow details of the object and its trajectory to be seen and recalled. There were two other remarkable characteristics: First, it was possible to establish the distance of the object with precision; second, the exceptional qualifications of one of the witnesses provided some physical parameters that have rarely been available in UFO cases.

We are indebted to GEPAN, the French government's official UFO investigation task force, for communicating to me the details of the case, which the author had the opportunity to discuss with them at length prior to visiting the site in 1988. In accordance with their policies, the names of the witnesses have been changed. The official files, of course, contain full particulars and in-depth interviews with all concerned.

The first witness in the chronology of this observation is a Miss M., who was watching television at her home in the town of Rives, near Grenoble. The time was 8:08 P.M. She saw a bright light outside and called her father. Both went out on the balcony and observed an intense white source crossing the sky at high speed from the northwest to the southeast, disappearing behind the mountains in the direction of Montand. The father, when interrogated by the gendarmes, stated that the light appeared to be spinning.

While these two witnesses were observing the object in Rives, a French physicist we will call Dr. Serge was driving seven miles away near Voreppe on the road that goes from Rives to Grenoble. He had just returned from Paris on a plane that landed at Grenoble Airport, and he was driving to his home. Looking up, he saw a luminous disk moving in the sky. He stopped his car and got out to observe it carefully. The time was 8:10 P.M.

The disk, according to Dr. Serge, was brighter than the full moon. It was slightly flattened (with an aspect ratio of 0.9), and had an angular diameter of about 12 arc minutes (the full moon has an angular diameter of about 30 arc minutes). The object was white in the center and bluish white at the periphery. It was surrounded by an intense green halo about 2 or 3 arc minutes wide.

At the beginning of the observation, the disk was almost directly overhead. It flew at a constant velocity toward the east-southeast in less than 8 seconds, covering approximately 1.3 degrees of arc per second. At that point the disk stopped, without changing size, and hovered for 3 to 10 seconds. Then it started again in a different direction, 30 degrees away from the previous course, at much greater speed, covering about 8 degrees of arc per second and passing in front of Le Taillefer Mountain, 36 kilometers away. Dr. Serge lost sight of the disk when it passed behind Le Néron Mountain, 9 kilometers away.

The whole sighting had lasted about twenty to twenty-five seconds, and there was absolutely no sound at any time. The sky was clear, there was no wind at ground level, and the temperature was about 40 degrees Fahrenheit. Late in 1988 the author drove through the area where the sighting had been made. The photographs and the drawings included in the GEPAN report do not do justice to the majesty of the site. Mountains rise on both sides of the Isère River. In places the road runs at the foot of sheer granite walls. This topography provides a fair estimate of the object's distance at various points, since it was seen flying behind one mountain and in front of another.

It is noteworthy that the investigation by GEPAN disclosed that a similar object had been seen three hours earlier about eighteen miles east of Rives, leaving a trail, and that a bright disk was seen two hours later by the civilian traffic controller in the tower of the military airport at Aulnat. Shortly after 8:05 P.M. that same day, a witness located a few miles away near Vienne saw a slightly flattened sphere, whose light was similar to that of a very bright neon tube, with a fiery red-orange area underneath. It was about one-sixth of the diameter of the full moon and was flying very fast from the west-northwest to the east-southeast.

Given these detailed, competent observations, it is possible to bracket the energy and speed of the object with some reasonable numbers. From a careful reconstruction of the sighting it was estimated that the object was flying at an altitude of 1,500 to 2,500 feet, which would give it a diameter between 6 and 20 feet and a speed approximating 1 mile per second, or 3,600 miles per hour, during the second phase of its trajectory. Assuming that the disk gave off as much light as the full moon, as observed by Dr. Serge, its energy in the visible part of the spectrum was a modest 15 kilowatt. That is only a minimum value, based on the assumption that *the landscape directly underneath the object* was illuminated with an intensity comparable to that of the full moon. If illumination at the much greater distance where Dr. Serge was located was also that of the full moon we would be in conditions similar to those of Case No. 2, with a much higher power output value.

In the detailed interviews conducted by investigators of the French National Center for Space Studies (CNES), Dr. Serge expanded on his description of the object, noting that the halo reminded him of the color produced by the combustion of copper salts. It is also noteworthy that Dr. Serge, who serves as a director of a nuclear physics laboratory, did not report the sighting to anyone and did not mention it to his colleagues. It was only when the observation by Miss M. and her father was mentioned in newspapers that he volunteered his own experience. It should be noted further that, in addition to the reports from the gendarmes, the letters from the witnesses, and the investigations by GEPAN scientists, several of the observers were interviewed in person by a judge, a former president of the regional court of appeals.

Case No. 5: June 19, 1978.
Gujan-Mestras, France

This incident took place near Arcachon in France on June 19, 1978, and was also investigated in depth by GEPAN. While the

Grenoble case was remarkable for the convergence and high quality of the observations, the present case introduces another exceptional parameter: The UFO triggered the photocells that control the lights for the whole town. From the estimated distance and the threshold level of the cells, it is possible to derive an estimate of the power output of the object.

The town where the sighting took place is Gujan-Mestras. There were independent witnesses near Céon and La Réole. A local newspaper described how two frightened young men, an eighteen-year-old cook named Frank Pavia and a seventeen-year-old butcher's apprentice named Jean-Marc Guitard, knocked on the door of a baker, Mr. Varisse, who was preparing the next day's bread, at about 1:30 A.M.

The teenagers had stopped on the side of the road to repair the turn signal of their car when all the lights of the town were suddenly switched off. At the same time, a powerful rumble like an earthquake made them jump. Then they saw the object. It was, by their descriptions, oval, red, surrounded with white "flames," and it flew toward them at an altitude they estimated as 1,000 feet.

At this point Jean-Marc became unable to breathe, and he fainted. The object then changed direction and flew away. While telling their story to the baker (who reportedly laughed at them), both witnesses were reportedly terrified, had trouble speaking, and Jean-Marc had red, teary eyes.

At approximately the same time of night a thirty-five-year-old restaurant manager named Mr. Bachère, who was driving toward Bordeaux, saw "a large orange ball, very bright" that hovered over La Réole at about 1,000 feet before disappearing. It reappeared at the same spot one minute later. Mr. Bachère's wife confirmed his observation.

Given these reports, which were transmitted by law-enforcement officials to GEPAN in Toulouse, the task force decided to investigate immediately; three of their scientists were at the site the next day. They interviewed the witnesses at length, took them to the location, and had them point a theodolite to the places where the object had appeared and disappeared in an effort to establish triangulation. Finally, the witnesses were given a set of standard color samples from which they made a selection corresponding to the phenomenon they had seen.

This investigation brought to light the testimony of additional witnesses who had previously remained silent. For instance, Mr. B., a student who lived in Gujan, confirmed that he was outside when the town lights died at a time that he estimated as half an hour past midnight; concurrently, he had heard a strong, low rumble that scared him. Mr. B. saw orange flashes above the pine trees, below the cloud ceiling.

The measurements made in the field established that all witnesses had observed the same object, within the expected errors of human recall. There was rough agreement on time, duration, distance, trajectory, sound, and luminosity parameters. Understandably, there were also discrepancies regarding the apparent altitude and diameter of the object. One of the witnesses who gave the more consistent measures was used as the primary source for these estimates.

The manager of the town utility department was also interviewed. He showed the investigators the location of the photoelectric cells that control the streetlights. When these cells are exposed to a light that exceeds their threshold (10 mW/m^2), they assume that daylight has arrived and they turn off the system.

The results of the analysis bracket the distance between the cell and the UFO: between 135 meters and 480 meters, or roughly between 400 and 1,500 feet.

Although the diameter of the disk was estimated (5 meters), this is irrelevant to the calculation of the power output, which can be determined from the luminous flux at the photocell via Equation 26-5. Assuming a distance of 135 meters, one obtains

$$P \geq 0.01 \times 4\pi(135)^2 \qquad \text{(Eq. 26-5)}$$

hence $P \geq 2.3$ kW whereas for 480 m, $P \geq 29$ kW, assuming isotropic radiation from the object.

Case No. 6: August 24, 1990.
Greifswald, Germany

Numerous eyewitness reports, supported by videotapes and photographs, make this "one of the best-documented sightings in Europe," according to Dr. Illobrand Von Ludwiger, who has investigated this case. Independent witnesses observed formations of luminous spheres hovering in the sky northeast of Greifswald. Hundreds of tourists and local residents saw, photographed, and filmed the phenomena, characterized by rapid accelerations and abrupt changes of direction, inconsistent with known phenomena or manufactured objects. One private investigation group received six videotapes and eleven photographs from different individuals and interviewed in person more than a dozen witnesses.

The investigation concluded that the phenomena "consisted of two groups of luminous spheres that hovered nearly motionless for about 30 minutes between 8:30 P.M. and 9:00 P.M. over the Pomeranian sea. The brighter and closer group formed a circle of six luminous spheres. The second group formed the shape of a Y."

The German weather service reported that approximately five-eighths of the sky was covered with high, fleecy clouds in partly shaded masses, and gray, sheet-like clouds at 2,500 meters. There was a light east-northeast wind, and the temperature was about 16 degrees Centigrade, or 60 degrees Fahrenheit.

Given the number of precise observations, supported by photographs, it was possible to triangulate the position of the objects with some accuracy. From a distance of 14 kilometers the Y formation appeared to provide as much illumination as the full moon, according to one of the photographers, Mr. Ladwig. If the spectral distribution is equal to that of the moon, then the square distance law for the power output of the moon with 0.138 lux yields an estimated optical power output of $1.8 \times 10^{-3} \times 4\pi \times 14{,}000^2 = 4.4 \times 10^6$ W by following the same reasoning as in the Fort-de-France situation (Case No. 2).

DISCUSSION

Estimates from the six cases we have reviewed cover a considerable range. The estimates do not cluster around a particular value, and form no pattern. There may be several reasons for this. We may be in the position of a person trying to estimate the power of a truck by the intensity of its headlights; the actual energy figure may depart from our calculations by orders of magnitude.

Alternately, light emission may be only a side effect of a hypothetical propulsion mechanism, as carbon monoxide is a side effect in the exhaust of an automobile engine.

The impact of the observations on human witnesses can be dramatic, suggesting that other physiological and psychological parameters are present. The main witness in Case No. 3 (Dr. G.) was a physics professor who reported fear when confronted with the phenomenon. It forced him to shield his eyes and frightened his children, who woke up crying. One witness in Case No. 5, a seventeen-year-old male, developed breathing difficulties and fainted. Later his eyes appeared red and teary.

In discussing these figures, one must keep in mind that the literature contains equally reliable cases when the objects were dark or had a dull surface with no light emission whatsoever, although they performed the same evolutions as the objects studied here.

CONCLUSION

Many investigators have been discouraged by the difficulty of deriving reliable parameters from chance observations made under uncalibrated field conditions by surprised witnesses. The present study does show, however, that a small percentage of reported UFO cases meets sufficient criteria of reliability to yield quantitative data regarding distance and brightness. From these data we have shown that it was possible to arrive at a rough estimate of power output.

In the present state of our ignorance about the physical nature of the reported objects and given the lack of attention given to the subject by scientific and technical personnel who might be in a position to improve the quality of the data, we can only speculate on the mechanisms that give rise to these emissions. A complete examination of the data reveals cases when witnesses were temporarily blinded by the light from such objects, and other cases when physiological sequelae were reported, such as burns or skin injuries (Vallee, 1990a). Whether the reported phenomena turn out to be natural or artificial in nature, their widely reported impact on human witnesses should encourage us to pursue this research and extend the coverage of existing data-acquisition programs.

CHAPTER 27

Physical Traces

PHYSICAL ANALYSES IN TEN CASES OF UNEXPLAINED AERIAL OBJECTS WITH MATERIAL SAMPLES
(by Jacques F. Vallee)

INTRODUCTION

The combination of a reliable sighting of an unexplained aerial object with the recovery of a durable physical specimen is rare. While the media often allude to sensational finds, and at least one former military intelligence officer has stated that he once had custody of advanced technology coming from a "crash" (Corso, 1997), the material is not available for independent study and the details of its composition are scanty and contradictory.

At a more modest level, in the course of their investigations of the phenomenon around the world, civilian researchers acting privately have patiently assembled the embryo of a sample collection, starting from physical specimens reportedly gathered at the site of a close encounter or "maneuver"-type sighting.

The present paper summarizes the data, stressing methodology while refraining from proposing premature explanations for the origin of the samples. We strive to find those cases where (a) the literature gives sufficient ground to support the fact that an unusual aerial phenomenon occurred, (b) the circumstances of the actual recovery of the specimen are reported, (c) there is data to suggest that the specimen is in fact linked to the observed aerial object, and (d) physical analysis has been performed by a competent laboratory of known reliability. In several cases, the sample is available for continuing study by independent scientists. In the present paper we will try to establish the frequency of such cases and the type of analysis they suggest. In conclusion, we will examine hypotheses that may deserve further testing.

Statistical Frequency of Physical Sample Cases

In an earlier version of the catalog compiled by Larry Hatch (1999), we found over 17,375 unexplained reports of aerial phenomena reports. We could assign 15,181 of these cases according to the classification system used by this author (Vallee, 1990a), in order to bring out the distribution of incidents across various situations. Under this classification, inspired from Hynek's definition of "close encounters" (Hynek, 1972), each case is given a type and a category. Hynek used a single digit representing the "kind" or type of incident, ranging from "1" for a simple sighting and "2" for physical effects to "3" for report of a life form or living entity. We have extended this typology, using "4" in cases when witnesses experienced a transformation of their sense of reality (often corresponding to the popular characterization of the incident as an "abduction") and "5" in cases of lasting physiological impact, such as serious injury or death.

The categories to which the typology is applied range from "CE" for close encounters and "MA" for maneuvers (trajectory discontinuity) to "FB" for flyby (no observed discontinuity in flight) and "AN" for simple anomalies in which no UFO was reported. Unusual lights or unexplained entities fall into this last category.

Using this classification, we would speak of a particular case as a CE-3 incident, or an MA-2 incident, etc., leading to the simple matrix of Table 27-1, which provides a convenient way for establishing a baseline in comparing reports from various countries or from various epochs.

When the Hatch catalog is mapped into this classification, the resulting distribution is that of Table 27-2, showing 3,175 cases of physical effects, or 21 percent of the catalog, broken down as follows: 90 are associated with simple anomalies, 19 with a flyby, 1,782 with maneuvers, and 1,284 with close encounters. It should be noted that we are using the January 1997 version of

TABLE 27-1
Classification of Anomalies

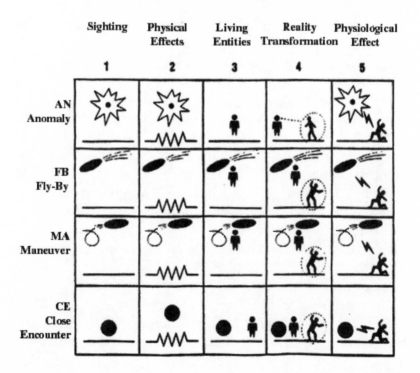

	Sighting	Physical Effects	Living Entities	Reality Transformation	Physiological Effect
	1	2	3	4	5
AN Anomaly					
FB Fly-By					
MA Maneuver					
CE Close Encounter					

TABLE 27-2
Incident Frequency in the Hatch Catalog

Type		1	2	3	4	5		
	Category	Sighting	Physical Effect	Lifeform	Reality Transformation	Physiological Effect	Subtotal	Fraction
AN	Anomaly	323	90	103	78	56	650	4.3%
FB	Fly-by	3,657	19	7	1	0	3,684	24.3%
MA	Maneuver	4,551	1,782	139	412	89	6,973	45.9%
CE	Close Encounter	1,158	1,284	593	530	309	3,874	25.5%
Subtotal		9,689	3,175	842	1,021	454	15,181	100%
Fraction		63.8%	20.9%	5.5%	6.7%	3.0%	100%	

the Hatch catalog, which is an evolving entity. Statistics performed on other versions may differ from those given here.

In Table 27-2, "physical effect" may refer to soil disturbances, broken tree limbs, crushed grass, burned areas, or to a variety of electromagnetic effects.

The Alleged Crash at Aurora, Texas. April 17, 1897

In order to provide some background to the analysis that follows, it is interesting to note that allegations of extraterrestrial "crashes" are nothing new and did not even begin in the present century.

In the course of a survey of early aerial phenomena in the United States, Donald Hanlon and the author found numerous reports of sightings in the period 1896–1897, which has become known in the literature as the "airship wave" (Hanlon and Vallee, 1967). One of the most remarkable cases had been reported on April 17, 1897, in the small town of Aurora, Texas.

The story, as told in a local newspaper, stated that an unidentified object "sailed over the public square and when it reached the north part of town collided with the tower of Judge Proctor's windmill and went to pieces with a terrific explosion, scattering debris over several acres."

Although Hanlon and this author regarded the story as an instance of early Americana and a probable hoax (in a context remarkably similar to that of Roswell, the press went on to state that the pilot of the ship, who "was not an inhabitant of this world," had died in the accident and that undecipherable papers were "found on his person"), our article reawakened interest in the case. It was investigated again in 1973 by William Case, a journalist with *The Dallas Times Herald*, and by personnel from the McDonnell Douglas aircraft company. While the 1897 story reported that the airship was "built of an unknown metal resembling somewhat a mixture of aluminum and silver," the fragment found by Case and his co-workers was determined to consist of aluminum (83 percent) and zinc (about 16 percent), with possible traces of manganese and copper. The combination could originate with numerous common aluminum alloys, according to the McDonnell Douglas scientists, but not prior to 1908 (Holliday, 1973).

While we cite this case for completeness, it is not included in the overall analysis.

CASE STUDIES

The cases that follow have been extracted from the small subset of physical effects cases where recovery of a material specimen was achieved under conditions that are of sufficient reliability to warrant serious follow-up. One case (the Council Bluffs incident of December 17, 1977) will be described in detail. Other incidents drawn from the literature and listed in chronological order will provide the relevant backdrop.

Case No. 1: Possibly 1933 or 1934, or Possibly 1957. Ubatuba, near São Paulo, Brazil— Classification: MA-2

This incident came to light in 1957 through the efforts of Dr. Olavo Fontès of Brazil and Jim and Coral Lorenzen, the founders of the Aerial Phenomena Research Organization, a now-defunct civilian research group in the United States. Witnesses on the beach at Ubatuba are said to have reported seeing a disk that plunged toward the ocean at high speed, rose again to about 100 feet, and exploded, showering the area with bright metallic fragments, some of which fell into shallow water. A few of the fragments were recovered and analyzed in Brazil by Dr. Luisa Barbosa at a laboratory that specialized in mineral-production studies. Dr. Barbosa identified the major component of the specimen as highly pure magnesium, more pure than commercially produced magnesium but possibly not as pure as multiply sublimed magnesium.

Subsequent work under the direction of Peter Sturrock has been conducted at Stanford University and at various laboratories in France, including Orsay University, confirming that the material was magnesium and magnesium oxide, but with substantial impurities (Sturrock, 1984), primarily aluminum, calcium, and iron. Analysis of this sample is still ongoing, with an effort to measure isotopic ratios that might help establish the origin of the material (Lorin and Havette, 1986).

The date of this event, often quoted in the literature as 1957, is actually imprecise. Dr. Pierre Kaufmann of São Paulo believes the original incident took place in 1933 or 1934, when a bolide indeed passed over Ubatuba and crashed at a nearby beach. The only aerial event to occur at or near Ubatuba in 1957 was the crash of a DC-3.

Case No. 2: June 21, 1947.
Maury Island, Washington—
Classification: MA-2

On the afternoon of June 21, 1947 (three days before the Kenneth Arnold case), four people who were on a boat close to the shore of Maury Island near Tacoma, Washington, reported an observation that has puzzled and divided researchers ever since. According to the published story, the witnesses were Mr. Harold Dahl (a salvage operator), his fifteen-year-old son, and two crewmen. They had a dog with them. They reported seeing a group of six large, flat doughnut-shaped objects flying at an estimated altitude of 2,000 feet. Their central holes were about 25 feet in diameter and they glistened with a gold-silvery color. One object suddenly started wobbling and dropped to an altitude of 500 feet above the boat. One of the disks came down (as if to "help" the one in difficulty, according to Dahl). A dull explosion was heard and numerous sheets of light, thin metal issued from the central opening in the troubled object. At the same time, the witnesses were showered with hot, dark fragments that resembled lava rock or slag compared to brass in color. The dog was reportedly hit by one of the fragments and died.

A man named Fred Crisman, to whom the incident was reported, allegedly went to the shore and found it littered with a glassy material and silver foil. Military authorities and the FBI, in a very confused series of investigations, attributed the case to a hoax: "Analysis of the fragments shows them to be from a Tacoma slag mill."* To this author's knowledge, however, the composition of the original samples, assuming that they were in fact studied by the FBI, was never released.

In a book he co-authored with Kenneth Arnold (whose own classic observation took place three days later, on June 24, 1947), popular writer Ray Palmer published an analysis of the original

*FBI teletype message, dated August 5, 1947, on file. The Maury Island case is mentioned in many books and magazines, notably by Ronald Story (1980), *Fate* magazine (1948), and Kenneth Arnold and Ray Palmer (1952).

fragments, whose primary constituents were calcium, iron, zinc, and titanium. Also found were aluminum, manganese, copper, magnesium and silicon, nickel, lead, strontium, and chromium. Traces of silver, tin, and cadmium were also reported.

Those investigators who regard the case as a hoax base their opinion on the fact that it was Crisman who initially sent the samples to Ray Palmer, linking them to alleged experiences involving the "Shaver Mystery," a science-fiction tale of underground beings. In their opinion, it is only after the Kenneth Arnold observation had been published that the story was changed to involve the alleged UFO incident. For the purpose of this discussion we will keep this weak case in the present list, but it is clear that no firm conclusion can be drawn from the reported facts. As Ray Palmer commented, "There we have it. The samples first sent by Crisman and Dahl were not slag, nor were they natural rock. What were they?"

Case No. 3: 1952. Washington, D.C.— Classification: MA-2

According to journalist Frank Edwards, a metallic fragment coming from an object that fell in 1952 was examined a few years later by a Canadian researcher, Mr. Wilbert Smith. The fragment had been sawed off from the recovered sample, representing about one-third of its volume. Over one inch in size, it was remarkably hard and reportedly consisted of "a matrix of magnesium orthosilicate" composed of "particles of 15 microns" (Edwards, 1966). Interviewed by two civilian researchers, C. W. Fitch of Cleveland, Ohio, and George Popovitch of Akron, Ohio, Smith stated that a navy pilot had been chasing a flying disk when he saw a bright "scintillating" fragment detach itself and fall to the ground. It was recovered an hour later and weighed in at 250 grams. Smith reportedly showed the sample to Admiral Knowles. Unfortunately there is no report of an independent analysis in the literature, and the sample is not available for further study.

Case No. 4: December 14, 1954.
Campinas, Brazil—Classification: MA-2

According to American journalist Frank Edwards (1966), numerous witnesses in Campinas observed three disk-shaped objects in flight over the city. Again, one of them started wobbling wildly and lost altitude. The other objects followed it down, and it stabilized at an altitude of about 300 feet. At that point the troubled disk emitted a thin stream of silvery liquid. The material was reported to splatter over a wide area, including roofs, streets, sidewalks, even clothes left outside to dry. An analysis by an unnamed Brazilian government laboratory is said to have identified tin as the main component of the collected samples. An independent analysis by a private chemist, Dr. Risvaldo Maffei, reported that 10 percent of the material was composed of substances other than tin, but gave no precise measurements.

Case No. 5: November 11, 1956.
Väddö Island, Sweden—Classification: CE-2

Another sample reportedly was recovered by two witnesses of an aerial phenomenon (one of whom has since died). Although the material appears to be common tungsten carbide, the original shape of the specimen was unusual and it has not been identified as an object serving a conventional use.

According to a summary of the case compiled by Von Ludwiger (1998), the two witnesses, Stig Ekberg and Harry Sjöberg, were building a house on the island of Väddö, about 90 kilometers north-northwest of Stockholm. At about 10 P.M., Ekberg was driving his Ford V8 pickup when they saw a bright flying object with the shape of a flattened sphere 8 meters wide and 3 meters high approaching from the right (from the east) against the clear night sky. They estimated that it flew about 1 kilometer in front of them at an altitude of 100 meters. Suddenly it made a sharp turn toward them, at which time the truck engine sputtered and died and the headlights went out. The object started "slowly gliding down." It seemed to rock back and forth until it came to a stop in the middle of the road, about 100 meters in front of them, 1 meter above the ground. "It was illuminating the surrounding landscape with such a tremendous amount of light that even a barn, half a kilometer away, was visible as if the sun was shining." The air smelled like ozone and smoldering insulation.

After about ten minutes the light of the object intensified, it lifted off the ground, moved to the left and up, made a sudden turn, and accelerated away in the direction from which it came. At that point Ekberg was able to restart the truck normally, and the headlights came back on. Observing that the grass at the landing site had been flattened, they investigated further and found a shiny "rock" that was hot to the touch. It was a three-sided piece of metal about the size of a matchbox, and had a heavy weight.

After several unsuccessful attempts to have the sample studied, it was taken to the SAAB airline manufacturing company, where Mr. Sven Schalin conducted a thorough analysis. Other tests were later run in laboratories in Sweden, Denmark, and Germany. The general conclusion was that the object was composed of tungsten carbide and cobalt, consistent with manufactured products. According to Von Ludwiger, "All industrial countries have companies which produce such hard metals, and the manufacturing technology is in principle the same. . . . The overall quality of the material was outstanding, but not unusual for the early 1950s."

Case No. 6: July 13, 1967.
Maumee, Ohio—Classification: CE-2*

At 11:26 P.M. EST, a collision reportedly took place near Maumee, involving a car driven by two men, and an unidenti-

---

*The author [Vallee] is indebted to Mark Rodeghier of the Center for UFO Studies for details of the Maumee, Ohio, incident.

fied light. Both witnesses were young navy veterans, one of them a radar specialist. In their report to police, they stated they had unexpectedly encountered an intense source of light in the middle of the pavement while traveling west on Stitt Road toward Whitehouse, Ohio. They could see no outline or structure in the object. The driver swerved to the left, skidding for about seventy feet and expecting a catastrophic collision. When they stopped, however, there was no trace of the object. The passenger confirmed the report, adding that the light appeared "bright as a welder's arc."

Following the event, the two men drove to Waterville, where they phoned police. They were instructed to proceed to the Maumee police station and await the arrival of the state highway patrol. They revisited the scene with two patrolmen. The car itself was examined, as well as the surrounding area, the road, and planted crops. No tangible evidence was reported, except for skid marks made by the vehicle and some damage to the car bumper and hood. Some time later the driver reported two metal samples he retrieved in the middle of the road and some "fibrous" metal found on the car. This fibrous sample turned out to contain 92 percent magnesium.

Neither witness experienced any unusual sensation during the incident, and their health was not affected.

Case No. 7: Early 1970s.
Kiana, Alaska—Classification: MA-2

In this case, an unknown person reported finding two pieces of material on a riverbank near Kiana and sent them to a national laboratory. Each specimen is silvery, lightweight, and looks as if it had been poured in a molten state from a source close to the ground. However, the laboratory made no effort to contact the witness and did not analyze the material.

Case No. 8: 1975 or 1976.
Bogotá, Columbia—Classification: MA-2

Two students at the University of Bogotá were about to take a cab at 4 A.M. when they heard a metallic sound overhead. They reported seeing a disk, about 12 feet in diameter, swinging in the air as if it had difficulty maintaining its altitude of 3,000 to 3,500 feet—obviously a very rough estimate since it is notoriously difficult to estimate the distance and size of luminous objects at night. Four other objects appeared, flying around the first one as if to provide assistance. Spouts of liquid were then ejected from the primary object. The witnesses took shelter under a tree and watched the liquid fall on the pavement, producing a vapor. The objects rose and disappeared into heavy rain clouds. After letting the material cool down for about 10 minutes, the witnesses were able to recover two metal chunks, about four inches by an inch and a quarter thick. The first analysis was performed in Central America by a mechanical engineer with a petroleum company. He concluded that the sample was an aluminum alloy with magnesium and tin. It was nonmagnetic and contained traces of unidentified materials. He also stated that the material was easy to cut and presented very fine granulation. In October 1985 the author was given a sample of this material by Mr. Ricardo Vilchez, a Latin American investigator, and brought it to the United States for analysis. Subsequent study led by Dr. Harold Puthoff and ourselves showed it to be formed mainly of aluminum (93.7 percent) with phosphorus (4.8 percent) and iron (0.9 percent) with traces of sulfur and an unexplained oxy-carbide layer.* The sample included no fluoride, contrary to most aluminum samples: fluoride is a common by-product of aluminum production. One side of the specimen showed evidence of violent activity and bubbling, while the other side was flat, with some embedded material, possibly from the road asphalt. Its appear-

---

*The analysis of the Bogotá sample conducted with Dr. Puthoff was first published in Vallee (1990a, pp. 44–45).

ance was typical of an overheat and was indeed consistent with the blowup of a machine, although the hoax hypothesis could not be totally excluded.

The sample was subjected to analysis with a scanning electron microscope (SEM), which produces an X-ray fluorescence spectrum, leading to the above composition findings. It was further analyzed with a secondary ion mass spectrometer (SIMS), which uses an ion beam in a vacuum, boring at various points into the material. This test found a surface layer of carbon, oxygen, and nitrogen, beyond which we encountered aluminum as well as magnesium (as reported by the initial analysis in Central America), with potassium, sulfur, sodium, and silicon. Phosphorus and iron also showed up in trace amounts.

Case No. 9: December 17, 1977.
Council Bluffs, Iowa—Classification: MA-2

In this incident (which is described at more length in the next section), two residents of Council Bluffs, Iowa, saw an object that crashed to the ground in the vicinity of a dike in Big Lake Park on the northern city limits. The time was 7:45 P.M. A bright flash was observed, followed by flames eight to ten feet high. When the witnesses reached the scene they found a large area of the dike covered with a mass of molten metal that glowed red-orange, igniting the grass.

As opposed to many of the previous cases, where few exact times and detailed witness accounts are available, this incident offers an abundance of information. Police and firefighters reached the scene within minutes of the event. One law officer described the molten mass "running, boiling down the edges of the levee" over an area of about four by six feet. The central portion remained warm to the touch for another two hours. There were eleven witnesses in all, eliminating the hoax hypothesis. Two of the witnesses had independently seen a hovering red object with lights blinking in sequence around the periphery. Inquiries made at Eppley Air Field and Offutt Air Force Base disclosed that no engine failure had taken place and there was no aircraft operation in the area.*

The recovered residue was analyzed at Iowa State University and at the Griffin Pipe Products company, leading to the determination that the metal was chiefly iron with small amounts of alloying metals such as nickel and chromium. This composition excludes a meteoritic origin.

Case No. 10: Circa 1978.
Jopala, near Puebla, Mexico—Classification: MA-2

While in Mexico in November 1978, the author was told by local investigators of the fall and recovery of a metallic residue following an observation of an unknown aerial phenomenon in the mountains near Puebla. The object was reportedly composed of iron with silicon (1.13 percent) and traces of manganese (0.84 percent), chromium (0.77 percent), and carbon (0.28 percent).†

ANALYSIS OF THE COUNCIL BLUFFS CASE

The weather in Council Bluffs the evening of Saturday, December 17, 1977, was overcast with a 2,500 foot ceiling, visibility 10 miles, temperature 32 degrees Fahrenheit. Wind was from the west-northwest at 16 mph, with gusts to 25 mph. The town is located on the southeastern shore of the Missouri River in Iowa, across from the city of Omaha (Figure 27-1). The object hit the ground in the vicinity of "Gilberts Pond" in Big Lake Park, across the Missouri from the Eppley airport. The exact street address is 1900 North Eighth Street. It fell at a point 16 feet from the paved road and 6 feet from the top of the

*Telephone conversation with investigators, September 1978.

†Personal [Vallee] investigation.

Figure 27-1. A city map of Council Bluffs, Iowa.

levee, burning an area 4 feet wide by 9 feet long. There was a secondary burn area 27 feet away on the side of the dike, measuring about 2 by 4 feet.

Some samples of the material were embedded in the ground in both areas, but no crater was discovered. There was an indentation 2 to 3 inches deep, and many metal spherules were found scattered about the area, particularly toward the northeast.

The initial witnesses were Kenny Drake and his wife, Carol, and Kenny's twelve-year-old nephew, Randy James. Two other witnesses, Mike Moore and his wife, Criss, reported seeing a hovering red object with lights as they crossed Sixteenth Street on their way downtown along Broadway. Criss reported "a big round thing hovering in the sky below the tree tops. It was hovering. It wasn't moving." She added that she saw red lights around the perimeter of the object, blinking in sequence. A middle-aged couple who saw the event spoke to the investigators by telephone, stating that they had seen "a bright red object rocket to the ground near Big Lake," but they refused to be identified. Four teenagers in a small foreign car spoke to the Drakes at the time of the incident but did not make a report.

Secondary witnesses who observed the metal were Jack E. Moore, assistant fire chief (who took the 911 call from Kenny Drake), police officer Dennis Murphy, and Robert E. Allen, who had served in the Air Force and wrote a weekly astronomy column for a local newspaper. Mr. Moore stated that the center of the metal mass was too hot to touch when he arrived on the scene about 8 P.M., only fifteen minutes after the initial incident, and that it remained so for about an hour (*Omaha World-Herald*, 1977).

Investigation proceeded as follows: Measurements taken at the impact point by Robert Allen indicate the object was traveling from the southwest to the northeast. Samples of the object were sent to the Ames Laboratory at Iowa State University, and others were taken to Griffin Pipe Products.

The material was determined to be carbon steel, "probably man-made," of a type common in manufacturing. The following four hypotheses were examined:

A. Hoax by Unknown Persons Pouring Molten Metal on the Ground

A check was made with every metal firm in the metropolitan area that has the remotest possibility of maintaining metal in a molten state. Griffin Pipe is the only company that has the capability for producing a similar product. Mr. Linton Stewart, works manager there, stated that they "drop the bottoms" from their cupolas on Friday afternoon and do no pouring until Monday. The melting point is close to 2,500°F, which would require transporting in a brick oven of 6 inch thickness with a large truck, to keep the material at the melting point. Conclusion: negative.

B. Hoax by Unknown Persons Using Thermite and Ordinary Metal

Professor Frank Kayser, of Iowa State University, observed that one might "collect the splatters from a casting or welding operation involving carbon steel," surround it with thermite powder and ignite it, heating the metal to the 1,000°C range. A cooling rate appropriate to wrought-iron microstructure could be achieved by spraying water on the mixture. However, the material was in a molten state when the witnesses arrived. The surface of the ground was frozen to a depth of at least 4 inches, and the air was at 32°F. Under such conditions, cooling by water spraying would have generated considerable amounts of ice. A check made with chemical and construction firms in the area disclosed no source of thermite. Negative conclusion.

C. Piece of Equipment from Aircraft

Because of the proximity to Eppley Air Field, it was thought the object could have fallen from an aircraft landing on the runway heading 320 degrees. However, a check with the airport indicated no abnormal aircraft activity at the time. All airlines operating into Eppley Field responded that they had no arrival using that runway, which would bring an aircraft within the vicinity of the impact site (Braniff had landed at 7:32 P.M.). Furthermore, the aircraft would be low and the metal would not be heated by the air to the melting point while falling. Negative conclusion.

D. Meteoritic Impact

There was no significant crater, the material remained in a molten state quite long, the composition is not compatible with meteoritic nature as noted above (very low nickel element in particular), and the spectrographic analysis did not disclose any metal components that should be an integral part of meteoritic materials. Negative.

The material sent to Ames Laboratory at Iowa State University was analyzed by Dr. Robert S. Hansen, director of the Ames Energy and Mineral Resources Research Institute. The material was found to consist of solid metal, slag, and white ash inclusions in the slag. These were examined by X-ray fluorescence, electron beam microprobe, and emission microscopic techniques under the supervision of Edward DeKalb of the analytical spectroscopy section.

Ames's findings were as follows: The metal is chiefly iron with very small amounts (less than 1 percent) of alloying metals such as nickel and chromium. The slag is a foam material containing metallic iron and aluminum with smaller amounts of magnesium, silicon, and titanium. The white ash was found to be calcium, with some magnesium.

In the course of research and follow-up for this paper, the author contacted Mr. Robert Allen, who confirmed that the case had remained unsolved after twenty years.* He kindly supplied us with copies of his correspondence with Air Force Space Systems, who had stated that in their opinion the material was not space debris from a man-made object, citing four reasons: (1) reentering spacecraft debris does not impact the Earth's surface in a molten state; (2) the 35- to 40-pound mass left no crater or indentation; (3) the reported visual sighting was at an altitude of only 500 to 600 feet, where reentering debris would not be glowing; and (4) the lack of structural indications is inconsistent with space debris.

---

*Author's [Vallee] telephone conversations and correspondence with R. Allen, September 1997.

DISCUSSION OF ELEMENT FREQUENCY

The samples described in the ten cases we have reviewed are summarized in Table 27-3. They belong, broadly speaking, in two major classes: samples resembling slag or industrial residue; and light silvery alloys, with one incident (Case No. 2, Maury Island) involving both types of materials. Unfortunately, as we have seen, the analysis of the original samples in this particular case was never released by authorities, and we can only refer to sources of dubious reliability. In incidents involving slag-like material, one primarily finds iron with traces of chromium, manganese, and silicon, notably in Jopala and in Council Bluffs.

In cases involving light silvery material, we find references to magnesium (Cases 1, 3, and 6) and aluminum (Cases 1 and 8), with iron mentioned in trace amounts. Some of the details of the composition remain puzzling: We cannot account for the very high degree of purity of the Ubatuba magnesium sample, claimed by the Brazilian analysts, or for the absence of fluoride in the Bogotá specimen.

We have encountered no case of unknown elements and no case with advanced technology materials exhibiting an unusual structure. However, the samples, as analyzed, appear to be consistent with the accounts given by witnesses, lending credibility to the reports in spite of their sometimes extraordinary details.

In summary, the analysis supports the thesis that an unidentified phenomenon has been repeatedly observed in various parts of the world over a long period, that it manifests through a physical, material support, and that it is amenable to scientific study. On the other hand, the patterns observed in the composition of the samples at our disposal do not point to any clear hypothesis for the nature of the phenomenon.

The fact that no exotic composition was found in these ten cases cannot be used to negate the theory that an advanced technology of unknown origin may have generated the samples. In the case of our own automobile industry, for example, environmentally compliant engines produce more mundane exhaust (such as pure water) than older models, where one could find complex combinations of gases.

LIQUID METAL TECHNOLOGY

The similarities among many of the above cases point to a common scenario for the generation of the recovered samples: Metal is observed to be ejected in molten form by an unidentified aerial object, commonly described as a disk, occasionally as a vehicle flying in an unstable condition. The material, in liquid form, falls over a fairly wide area, where it takes minutes to hours to cool down. When analyzed, it turns out to be made up of common terrestrial elements, often in a form resembling ordinary industrial by-products.

TABLE 27-3
Summary of Sample Composition

Case No.	Location	"Slag" Primary	"Slag" Secondary	"Light Silver Alloy" Primary	"Light Silver Alloy" Secondary
1	Ubatuba		none	Mg	Al, Ca, Fe
2	Maury Is.	Ca, Fe, Zn, Ti	Si, Cu, Ni, Pb, Cr, Al, Mg, Mn, Sr	Ag, Sn, Cd	
3	Washington		none	Mg, Si	
4	Campinas		none	Sn? (90%)	
5	Sweden	W (94.9%)	Co (4.1%) Zr (0.6%), Fe (0.3%)	none	
6	Maumee		none	Mg (92%)	
7	Kinana		none	yes	
8	Bogota		none	Al (94%)	P (5%), Fe (1%)
9	Council Bluffs	Fe	Ni, Cr, Mn, Si, Ti	none	
10	Jopala	Fe	Si (1%), Mn (0.8%), Cr (0.8%), C (0.3%)	none	

Given this scenario, it is appropriate to ask under what conditions one might want to use liquid metal in a flying vehicle. In the words of J. R. Bumby (1983) of the University of Durham, "The high conductivity of liquid metals makes them an attractive means of current collection for homopolar machines." Bumby goes on to cite a number of such machines, both superconducting and nonsuperconducting, that have been built (Watt, 1958; Doyle, 1974; and Chabrerie, 1972), and one that is commercially available (Lewis, 1971a, b). Similarly, liquid metal designs have been proposed for magnetohydrodynamic (MHD) generators, for the decomposition of toxic wastes, and for superconducting airborne platforms (Southall and Oberly, 1979). However, the composition of the liquids used in such machines is radically different from the list of elements found in Table 27-3. As noted by Bumby, "At room temperature the only pure liquid metal is mercury, although at slightly higher temperatures gallium (29.8°C) and sodium (97.8°C) become liquid." Actual machines are using sodium-potassium and gallium-indium mixtures as current conductors, thus minimizing wear and friction. The latter is liquid above 15.7°C. Yet none of these elements has been identified among the samples we have reviewed.

A different approach has been proposed by Dr. J. Roser in correspondence with the author. Noting the composition of the Bogotá specimen (Vallee, 1990a), he hypothesized a nuclear design for the object's power plant, utilizing direct energy conversion rather than a heat-driven mechanical prime mover. "A closed cycle MHD generator using a liquid metal working fluid with no vapor staging pumping could be configured in a torus or circular shape and would make very little noise due to the lack of moving parts," he wrote, adding that the nuclear process known as beta decay might allow the design to extract a surplus of power in the form of free electrons.

Assuming a working fluid of Aluminum 27 plus some percentage of Phosphorus 31 (solitary stable isotopes of their respective elements), Roser speculates that depleted fluid might need to be occasionally ejected: "This discarded material would contain Aluminum 27, Phosphorus 31, iron from original melt or housing erosion, plus isotopes of nuclei close to aluminum and phosphorus such as Magnesium, Sodium, Silicon, and Sulphur." Accordingly, he suggests isotopic analysis of the Bogotá sample to determine if it reveals anomalous isotopes such as Silicon 32 (half-life 280 years), which would indicate a nuclear-based power source.

CONCLUSION

Reports of unusual metallic residue following the observation of an unexplained aerial phenomenon are detailed enough for a comparative study to be undertaken. This research is hampered, however, by several problems of methodology where lack of money or analytical resources is only a secondary obstacle. The primary concerns have to do with inaccuracies in data gathering, lack of information about exact dates and times, lack of detailed, critical field investigation, and failure to provide an irrefutable chain of evidence in the collection, transportation, and examination of the samples.

In spite of these shortcomings (which could be addressed through the setting up of better standards and through collaborative agreements among investigators), this review has shown that significant progress has been made toward the analysis of a number of relevant incidents. In one case at least (Council Bluffs), the conditions of witness availability and reliability, on-site testimony by law-enforcement officers, chain of custody, and timely analysis were met. Other cases, such as Ubatuba and Bogotá, are sufficiently intriguing to encourage investigators to expand their work in the field.

Over the years, discussions of the UFO issue have remained narrowly polarized between advocates and adversaries of a single theory, namely the extraterrestrial hypothesis (ETH), defined as contact with an alien civilization originating in another solar system in our universe. This fixation on the ETH has narrowed and impoverished the debate, precluding examination of other possible theories of the phenomenon. To the extent that recovered samples did not show an exotic composition or complex structure supporting their preconceived hypothesis, both sides of the extraterrestrial argument lost interest in the cases. In the view of the present author, such lack of follow-up is unfortunate, because much could be learned from comparative analysis of such material even if it is mundane. Therefore our hope is that further field research may be stimulated by publication of the present survey.

CHAPTER 28

The Trans-en-Provence Case

INTRODUCTION

During the presentations at Pocantico, the panel took special interest in the case to be described in this chapter. Their interest may be ascribed to the following factors:

a. It was reported promptly to the local police authorities;
b. The first investigation was carried out promptly by the police;
c. The case was soon thereafter investigated by GEPAN; and
d. The case involved two types of physical evidence.

The event occurred near Trans-en-Provence, France, on January 8, 1981. The principal weakness of the case is that there was only a single witness. It was this consideration that led to the panel's recommendation that "studies should concentrate on cases which include as much independent physical evidence as possible *and strong witness testimony.*"

In this chapter, we reproduce two articles on this case that have been published in the *Journal of Scientific Exploration*: an article by Jean-Jacques Velasco (1990) and an article by Jacques

F. Vallee (1990b). The former is a translation (by Vallee) of material extracted from the official GEPAN report on this case (CNES, 1983). The latter is a report of Vallee's later and independent study of the case.

A third article on this case has been published in the *Journal of Scientific Exploration*, but this article is not reproduced here, since it is highly technical. This article is by Dr. Michel C. L. Bounias, Professor of Biochemistry at the University of Avignon in France. In his article, Bounias (1990) presents the results of his biochemical analysis of the alfalfa specimens taken a few days after the event, specimens taken 40 days after the event, and other specimens (from new growth) taken 730 days after the event. Bounias determined the biochemical composition of both the test plants and the control plants. He examined the variation of a number of biochemical compounds as a function of position with respect to the center of the ground trace. These measurements showed that there was a strong (statistically significant) correlation between the biochemical properties and the location of the specimens. There was also a strong (statistically significant) difference between specimens taken from the center of the trace close to the time of the event and comparable specimens taken from the same location 730 days later.

The upshot of these tests is that Bounias could conclude that the test plants taken from within the ring soon after the event had suffered some form of trauma that the control plants had not experienced. However, Bounias was unable to identify exactly what type of trauma would lead to the symptoms that he had identified.

REPORT ON THE ANALYSIS OF ANOMALOUS PHYSICAL TRACES
(by Jean-Jacques Velasco)

PART ONE: FIELD INVESTIGATION

1. *Chronology of the Trans-en-Provence Case*

On Friday January 9, 1981, police authorities in Draguignan, France, received a telephone call reporting a sighting of an aerial phenomenon that the author of the observation could not identify. In addition, the witness indicated the presence of physical traces on the ground at the site. These events were reported to have taken place on the previous day (Thursday, January 8) in the nearby town of Trans-en-Provence.

The Groupe d'Études des Phénomènes Aérospatiaux Non-identifiés, or Unidentified Aerospace Phenomena Study Group (GEPAN), organized within CNES, became aware of the case through the gendarmerie on the morning of Monday, January 12. It was learned that law-enforcement authorities had taken soil samples on the day of the report. Since it had rained heavily over the weekend, GEPAN investigators decided it would be fruitless to travel to the site immediately. Instead, they requested speedy delivery of the samples collected on the previous Friday.

GEPAN further learned about the nature of the traces through a Telex received during the afternoon of January 12. Several private groups also heard of the case through local press reports and went to the site. One of their investigators began his study on January 13.

2. Information Collected by Police Authorities

The Draguignan gendarmerie had first been alerted by the witness's neighbors. The site was visited by an officer on Friday, January 9, at about 11:30 A.M. The physical traces were observed, the witness was interviewed, photographs were taken, and soil samples were gathered according to standard police procedures. A few days later these samples were forwarded to GEPAN, and vegetal samples were sent to a laboratory of the National Institute for Agronomic Research (INRA).

A short time later, complementary samples were collected at the request of the analysis laboratories, as follows: (a) reference vegetal samples, gathered by the gendarmerie on January 23, and (b) a complete series of vegetal samples gathered by GEPAN itself on February 17.

The decision to intervene was made by GEPAN because this particular case presented two types of information that could be confronted and correlated, namely the single witness report and the physical traces observed at the site. GEPAN does not routinely investigate cases when a single source of information is present because in such instances the investigator is unable to make comparisons and inferences among data coming through different channels.

Under the methodology used by GEPAN, to each type of available information there corresponds a set of appropriate analysis techniques. Physical traces constitute a useful channel of information only to the extent that the analysis can be conducted before these physical effects have been dissipated. Among other requirements, this involves securing the site rapidly and obtaining rigorously controlled samples under normal weather conditions. These minimal prerequisites were found to be satisfied in the Trans-en-Provence case. GEPAN therefore proceeded with its full investigation.

3. Environment of the Site

The village of Trans-en-Provence is located three kilometers south of Draguignan. Mr. and Mrs. Renato Nicolai live on a property situated two kilometers east of Trans, on the side of a hill overlooking the valley of the Nartuby River (Figure 28-1). This valley is oriented east-west and contains numerous orchards and small agricultural plots. The sides of the valley are covered with woods and with Mediterranean vegetation. The sparse dwellings have their openings (windows, doors) facing the valley. Many terraces dug into the hillside make possible more intensive use of the soil for cultivation. Retaining walls, locally known as "restanques" and generally built out of native stone, have an average height of two meters.

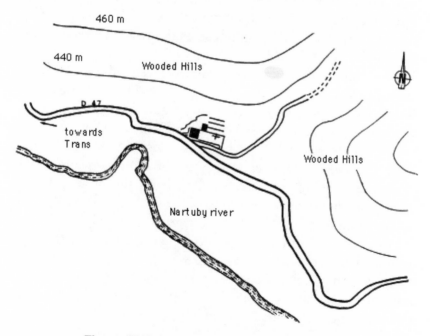

Figure 28-1. Location of the Nicolai property.

The plot of land owned by Mr. and Mrs. Nicolai is located some distance away from the D47 road, on the north side of the valley. A dirt road runs along the property. It ends 400 meters away at an isolated farmhouse. The property is structured in such a way as to make the best possible use of the contour of the hillside. The house is built over several levels of retaining walls, and it is partially dug into the hill. The driveway is covered with asphalt at the level of the basement, 30 meters away from the road running to the west. On the left side of the villa are some stairs leading to the living quarters. To the right a slope prevents access to the upper terrace, which is reached through the dirt road previously mentioned.

This terrace or platform is linked to the other levels through stairs located behind the house. However, it is almost never used, except to play "pétanque" (a game of skill using metal spheres, very popular in the south of France). To the northeast side of the hill are two higher levels (labeled Level 2 and Level 3 in Figure 28-2), each about one meter high. Two structures rest on these levels: a pump house at the edge of Level 3 and a stone cabin straddling both levels.

Above the larger platform are two levels, about 50 meters long and 2.5 meters wide, that are used as vegetable gardens. Woods of conifers and leaf-bearing trees some dozens of meters tall surround the property, except on the southwest side facing the Nartuby Valley. No obstacles of any significance, such as power lines, telephone lines, or TV relays, are visible from the Nicolai property. In fact, from the large platform where the phenomenon was seen, the visual field is totally open to the southwest over nearly 180 degrees. The only obstacle to the line of sight is the landscape on the other side of the valley about 2 kilometers away (Figure 28-1).

At the time of Mr. Nicolai's observation, the nearest weather station, 17 kilometers to the southwest of the site, registered the following measurements.

- Temperature: 6.8° Centigrade
- Humidity: 30 percent, no precipitation
- Wind: Southeast at 2 meters per second
- Clouds: 2/8, good visibility

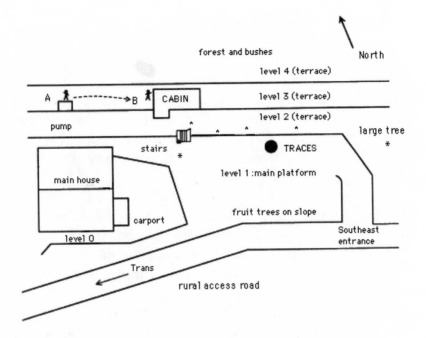

Figure 28-2. Map of the property (drawn by GEPAN).

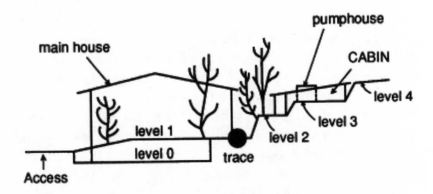

Figure 28-3. Details of the location.

4. Testimony of the Witness

I have lived in Trans-en-Provence at my current address for nearly fourteen years. My wife and I live alone. She is the cleaning lady at the social security office in Draguignan. I have not worked since November 1979. I was previously an employee of the S.C.N.I. company. This firm went out of business and I was laid off. I receive a disability pension because I suffered from a heart problem since 1973.

Yesterday, January 8, 1981, I was busy around the house as I am practically every day. I was behind the house, which is built over a "restanque" [raised level]. I was building a concrete shelter for a water pump. Behind my house on the same level is an expanse of flat ground. It is reached through a path along the base of the house.

It was about 5 P.M. The weather was turning colder. My attention was attracted by a slight noise, a sort of faint whistling. I turned around and I saw a device in the air at the height of a big pine tree on the edge of the property. This device, which was not spinning, was coming lower toward the ground. I was only hearing a slight whistling sound. I was not seeing any flames, either below or around this device.

While it was continuing to come down, I went closer by walking toward the stone cabin above my house. When I placed myself against the wall of the cabin I could see very well over the roof, since this cabin too is built over a raised level. I was on the higher level, about 1.2 meters from the roof [Figures 28-4 and 28-5]. From that position I clearly saw the device resting on the ground. Right away it lifted off, still emitting a slight whistling sound. Reaching a point above the trees, it left at high speed toward the forest of Trans, which is toward the northeast.

When the device lifted off, I saw four openings below, through which neither flame nor smoke was escaping. The device kicked up a little dust when it left the ground. At that instant I was about 30 meters away from the landing site. Later I

Figure 28-4. View of the site: retaining wall and forest.

Figure 28-5. View of the site: Mr. Nicolai's house
seen from the trace. Lines A and B point toward the
location of the witness when the object was first
observed and when it landed, respectively.

went to the spot and I noticed a circle about 2 meters in diameter. At certain places along the circumference of the circle were traces like abrasions.

When my wife came home in the evening, I told her what I

had seen. My wife thought I was joking. This morning in full daylight, I have shown her the trace of the circle. My wife called our neighbor Mr. X on the telephone. He came over with his wife. I showed them the trace, too. It is then that they advised us to call the gendarmerie.

The device had the shape of two saucers, one inverted on top of the other. It must have measured about 1.5 meters in height. It was the color of lead. This device had a ridge all the way around its circumference. Under the machine I saw two kinds of round pieces as it was lifting off; they could be reactors or feet. There were also two other circles, which looked like trap-doors. The two reactors, or feet, extended about 20 centimeters below the body of the machine. I have not felt any disturbance of the sense of vision or hearing.

[The witness was also interviewed separately by an investigator with a civilian research group, who summarized Mr. Nicolai's testimony as follows:]

Mr. Nicolai is busy with some masonry work on a terrace just above his villa. As the evening comes, he wants to finish the job before the night. Suddenly, at the end of the dirt platform he sees a round object, dark in color, "fall" from the sky just between the tops of two high trees. Since this fall was not accompanied by any noise, he is surprised and he looks carefully at the spot where the strange object has landed. He is about 80 meters away. The device is motionless against the retaining wall (half clay, half dry stones) that borders the platform toward the hillside, to a height of about 2 meters.

From his location the witness observes something like a large inverted bowl, dark gray in color, dull. Surprised, he walks toward this strange object and comes to a position at the edge of the level, about 45 meters away from the traces that will be observed after the departure of the object. Then he discovers a sort of ovoid vehicle, with the general shape of two half-spheres of unequal volume, clearly separated by a flat ledge, extending at least 15 centimeters and forming a ring around the metallic mass, which has a lead-aluminum appearance. The top part extends above the retaining wall, hence the machine has a height between 2 and 2.5 meters. The witness does not see any antenna, any porthole, any opening. He notices no extension, no external mechanical peculiarity. The whole thing seems smooth and compact to him. He estimates the horizontal diameter of this machine to be larger than its height. He has no time to continue his observation. The machine lifts off, making a slight amount of dust and with a soft whistling. Then it seems to tilt, exposing its underside, and it takes off at lightning speed, passing exactly between the two tall trees, at the exact spot from which it had seemed to "fall."

The witness has noticed that the landing trajectory is not identical to the takeoff trajectory. When the machine rises and tilts on its departing path, the witness notices four accessories under the device. He compares them to masonry pails in diameter and length. But he acknowledges that his description is imperfect and approximate, since the observation has been very brief because of the speed of the object and its most instantaneous disappearance. He has not heard any particular engine noise in the silence of the countryside. He has felt no heat, no vibration. He has felt no disturbance, either during the observation or afterward. He has only been very impressed by this unusual sight. He makes the drawing [shown in Figure 28-6] representing the device.

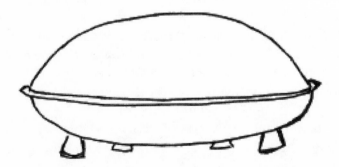

Figure 28-6. Drawing of the "device" by the witness for a private research group.

Worried and amazed, he goes inside his house and tells his wife about the sighting. Skeptical and distrustful, she recommends to him not to stay home, to avoid having another encounter. The next morning they go together to the place where Mr. Nicolai has noticed some clearly visible traces, which they are sure were not there the day before. Observing the material character of the sighting, they think it useful to call the local gendarmerie immediately for reassurance.

5. GEPAN's Reconstruction of the Phenomenon

Given the fact that this is a single-witness case (no additional witness was uncovered at a later date), the GEPAN investigation on February 17, 1981, centered on the gathering of additional samples, especially vegetal samples. The witness was interviewed as well as his wife, and a brief reconstruction of the sequence of events was conducted at the site.

Trajectory. The witness states he began to perceive the phenomenon in the sky above the trees at the back end of the large platform, more precisely between two tall conifers that tower above the wood. Mr. Nicolai states that the motion was fast and continuous, without sudden changes in speed, and that there was no stop until the time when contact was established with the ground (Figures 28-7 and 28-8). When asked to locate the impact area, Mr. Nicolai points to the spot, where the traces are still visible. The departure trajectory is described by the witness as similar to the path of arrival. However, some additional details will be given below (see "The Takeoff Phase").

Duration. According to our reconstruction, the arrival phase of the phenomenon was quite brief, of the order of a few seconds. Then the witness leaves his work and moves to the cabin wall. The phenomenon is at ground level on the terrace. The witness watches for a few seconds. Suddenly the phenomenon rises, flies over the wood, and goes away toward the east at a high rate of speed, rising in altitude according to its decrease in apparent diameter.

Figure 28-7. Landing trajectory.

Figure 28-8. Landing site: the platform and location of the trace.

From the data given by Mr. Nicolai, we estimate the overall duration of the sighting to be between 30 and 40 seconds. It is noteworthy that the witness was in good observing conditions throughout the event. His position on the higher level, behind the pump shelter or behind the cabin, provided a fairly open field of view of more than 90 degrees, with only three trees as obstacles.

Distance. If we consider the beginning of the approach phase until impact, the estimated distance may be about 20 meters. The distance between the pump house and the cabin is 17.5 meters. From that cabin to the impact point, the distance is 30 meters. It is likely that Mr. Nicolai was never more than 70 meters away from the phenomenon, and never less than 30 meters.

Shape. Mr. Nicolai does not say very much about the shape of the phenomenon as it descended. After it stopped and he was able to get nearer, he was better able to observe the object. This is consistent with the claim that the approach and the landing took place very fast. The witness gives a precise description of two phases: when the object was on the ground (Figure 28-9) and when it took off (Figure 28-10).

When the object was on the ground, the witness does not compare the phenomenon to a known object, but he refers to it as a device ("engine"). He stresses that on the side of this device was a thick ridge, flat in color, that circled the object. Under the device were two things compared to feet or pods.

When the object takes off, Mr. Nicolai is able to see it from underneath. Its shape is circular. In this visible area he observes four circles of smaller diameter, arranged symmetrically in a perpendicular position. They are clearly seen, and he compares them to masonry pails. (The witness was a professional contractor.)

Dimensions. Mr. Nicolai estimates the dimensions of the device with respect to available references before him. This is fairly simple to do since the object is located on a platform limited by a retaining wall of known height (2.5 meters). He states that the outside diameter is about 2.5 meters, the height is be-

Figure 28-9. Side view (object on the ground).

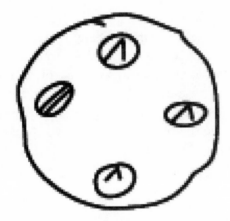

Figure 28-10. Bottom view (object taking off).

tween 1.7 and 1.8 meters, and the diameter of the small circles is that of a pail. It is noteworthy that the resulting diameter/height ratio (computed as 1.42) is very different from that shown on the witness's drawing of Figure 28-9 (computed as 5.66), and also from that drawn for the investigator of the private group (Figure 28-6), which is calculated to be 2.25.

Color. Mr. Nicolai states that the device is gray in color, comparable to zinc, darker and more flat in the thick lateral region. When he observes the bottom of the device, the four pods seem to him to be darker than the rest, but always of the same general color.

Sound. The witness states that it is the sound that drew his attention to the object in the first place, while he was busy on the pump shelter, about 70 meters away. He was then looking in the opposite direction and had to turn around to see it. He has great difficulty in defining the nature and the level of the sound. He compares it to a wind blowing fairly strongly. He does not say whether or not the sound stopped during the landing. The shock at the impact point was recalled like that of a stone falling on the ground. During the takeoff phase the sounds were of similar amplitude as they were during the approach.

The Takeoff Phase. It is during this phase that the witness observes the greatest quantity of details. This is understandable, since the witness is now at the closest point, about 30 meters. He has overcome his feelings of surprise and is able to react. According to him, the object was resting on the ground for several seconds before it suddenly rose vertically for several meters, tilted above the platform, continued to rise in this position, and disappeared into the sky.

6. GEPAN's Interview of the Witness

Mr. Nicolai is a man who has been ill for several years. He suffered an infarctus with subsequent relapse, which now prevents him from exercising his professional activity. He was very tired when we visited him. After the reconstruction of the events, he had to go inside and rest while we collected the samples. Afterwards, Mrs. Nicolai told us that he could see us again. She gave us some additional details about his observation, and she expected from us some explanations in return.

We had our conversation in the family kitchen, where Mr. Nicolai was waiting for us. He resumed his narrative, trying to find an explanation that would satisfy his curiosity. He reviewed the various kinds of flying craft (airplanes and especially helicopters) but he stated, "It isn't possible to land here; there are other sites in the valley that are more convenient, more flat."

Mr. Nicolai came back to the device, and especially to the marvelous technology it represented, repeating, "It made practically no sound, it flew vertically, it fell like a stone and it didn't break," and he concluded, "It's probably a military device; there are some nearby." He was alluding to the camp at Jouvan, not far from Trans.

We have stressed the fact that Mr. Nicolai did not observe the object passively; instead he went closer to this device that had landed on his property, while staying on guard behind the cabin wall. His first idea was that of a military craft. This was still his hypothesis when we came to see him, in spite of many visits by policemen, journalists, civilian investigators, and others. He felt sure he had been confronted with a type of military equipment he found remarkable for its flight characteristics and its landing precision. He eliminated right away the helicopter idea because of the proximity to the retaining wall: "The device was almost against the wall."

After the event, he resumed his work on the pump shelter. When his wife came home about an hour later, he tried to explain to her what he had seen that afternoon. Mrs. Nicolai did not believe her husband at all. Given his state of health, she even advised him to go and rest. The next morning he convinced her to come and see the traces, which were still visible. Mrs. Nicolai went with him and observed the traces. She then realized that something had indeed taken place and that her husband had not told her the story as a joke. She immediately decided to tell her neighbors, who had a certain social status (revenue service inspection), and who could advise her regarding the steps to be taken. These neighbors alerted the gendarmerie at Draguignan.

During our interview, Mr. Nicolai told us that he has heard the word UFO ("OVNI" in French) on television. The family TV set is in the kitchen, where he eats all his meals and where he spends several hours a day watching various programs. Otherwise, Mr. Nicolai tells us, he practically never reads, not even the newspapers. Thus, he does not know what the letters UFO stand for: We explain the meaning of the term to him.

The witness tells us that he has often heard this word since his observation. Private group members and journalists have spoken to him about "extraterrestrials" to find out if he had observed any. He answers frankly, without any hesitation and even with a little smile, that he has never seen any such thing. He then starts discussing life in the universe. He doesn't know precisely what this concept refers to; he confuses the notions of "universe" and of "galaxy." He speaks about the stars and believes that if there are stars there are other forms of life, and that such extraterrestrial life would manifest itself in a way identical to ours.

Regarding his religious beliefs and their evolution after his sighting, he answers that he believes in God and that this event changes nothing about his beliefs. His wife, who attends the interview, insists in getting into the discussion to answer in place of her husband. She speaks about her own religious views. She explains that for the last few years she has evolved toward less strong beliefs. She does not have a precise idea about the meaning of the terms "universe" or "space," and she shares her husband's notions about extraterrestrial life. At the end of our interview she insists in pointing out that we would never have met with her husband if it were not for the trace visible on the ground. She does not quite understand why people are so interested in what her husband has observed.

As a result of inquiries made to civilian and military agencies in the area regarding aerial traffic over Trans-en-Provence, we were told by ALAT that it seemed only a helicopter flight had taken place, at an altitude of 200 meters, at about 4:30 P.M. on January 8, 1981. Trans-en-Provence is located close to one of the largest camps for military maneuvers in France, at Jouvan. We alerted military authorities to find out if any unusual activity had taken place on that day. The only notable event around the time of the sighting was a short-distance firing of a tank gun using a blank shell. The gun fired toward the west, and the event took place more than 25 kilometers north of Trans-en-Provence.

7. *Synthesis of the Witness's Report*

There are very few differences, as the reader can observe, among the various versions of Mr. Nicolai's basic testimony. However, these versions are far from identical. The differences have to do with the choice of words. (In terms of linguistic analysis, these differences appear with the use of a neutral vocabulary, an evocative vocabulary, or a "significative" vocabulary.) Naturally, this choice of words may be due to the investigators themselves rather than to the witness.

Because of Mr. Nicolai's imperfect command of French, we tend to believe that the differences among the various versions are due to the investigators. For instance, in the version given by an investigator from a civilian group, the text is more literary and more dense: He "is surprised . . . strange object . . . impressed by this unusual sight . . . worried and amazed," and it often refers to preexisting imagery in the mind of the investigator: "He discovers a sort of ovoid object . . . the witness does not see any antenna, no porthole, no opening . . . lightning speed." This version fails to note that it is the slight sound (whistling) that attracted the witness's attention. The narration mentions a displacement of dust when the device leaves the ground, a detail that did not appear in the GEPAN interview. Finally, the drawing given by the witness to that private group is fairly different from that supplied to GEPAN: It is more in line with the "classic" UFO and it is drawn with a surer hand.

In summary, the differences we have noted do not lead to a negative assessment of the witness. His own subjectivity does not seem to have impacted his testimony either on the affective scale (expectations) or on the cognitive scale (existing hypotheses). However, the verbal expression difficulties that Mr. Nicolai experiences may have encouraged the investigators to inject their own subjective interpretations into the testimony. The analysis becomes too complex at this point to lead to a precise, detailed conclusion about this single-witness account. We can only state that it is generally consistent.

PART TWO: SOIL SAMPLE ANALYSIS

1. The Trace and Physical Samples

At the end of his observation, Mr. Nicolai went to the place where he thought the observed object had landed on the ground. At that precise location he discovered some unusual traces, clearly seen on the ground of the platform. These traces have now been examined, photographed, sampled, and analyzed in various laboratories.

The traces were located in the large platform at Level 1, near the dirt path at the southeast entrance to the property. They were visible on the hardened dirt near the retaining wall, 22 meters away from the tree to the left of which Mr. Nicolai saw the shape at the beginning of the sighting. As early as Friday, January 9, the Draguignan gendarmerie examined the traces and stated: "We observe the presence of two concentric circles, the first 2.20 meters in diameter, the second 2.40 meters in diameter. These two circles leave a crown 10 centimeters wide. On this crown two diametrically opposed sections are visible, about 80 centimeters long . . . which present black striations similar to abrasion traces."

A drawing was made (Figure 28-11) and four photographs were taken (Figures 28-12, 28-13, 28-14, and 28-15).

A few days later, the investigator sent by the private group gave a somewhat different version. Instead of two diametrically opposed sections, clearly more marked than the rest of the ring, he observes: "Rather a horseshoe which bears regular striations as if a metal had been dragged over the area . . . over this striated surface perfectly clean, all trace of vegetation has disappeared." (This last observation was incorrect.—J.-J.V.)

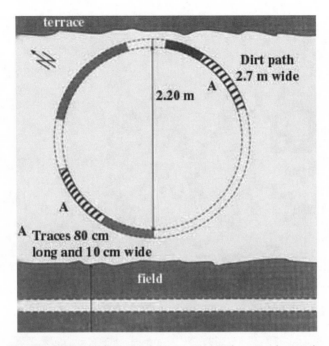

Figure 28-11. Drawing of the trace by the gendarmerie.

Figure 28-12. Location of the trace.

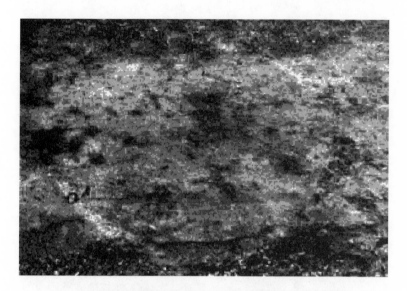

Figure 28-13. Location of the trace.

Figure 28-14. Close-up view of the trace.

Figure 28-15. Close-up view of the trace.

On February 17, 1981, or forty days after the sighting, the trace was still visible, probably because of the slight amount of precipitation since January 8 (a single storm shortly after that date), but also because this part of the property is not used often. One could still see an arc-shaped area, lighter than the rest of the terrain. The dirt was heavily compacted there, forming a crust about a centimeter thick. In some places the surface seemed to have been rubbed over a short distance.

Three sampling operations were conducted over this area.

- On January 9, four samples were taken by the gendarmerie, consisting of a dirt sample (P1), small quantities of surface soil (Q1) and depth soil below the crust (Q2), and an alfalfa sample.
- On January 23, the gendarmerie took new samples at the request of the biological analysis laboratory. These vegetal samples were taken far away from the trace (about twenty meters away).
- On February 17, GEPAN took a new series of eight vegetal samples. A new soil sample called P2 was collected outside of the trace area, three or four meters away.

Table 28-1 summarizes the characteristics of the four soil samples.

Table 28-1. Physical Samples

ID	Date	Location	Area	Description	Amount	Depth
P1	Jan 9	on the ring	tens of cm^2	surface spots	about 100	2 cm
P2	Feb 17	4 m away from ring	tens of cm^2	small shovelful of loose soil	about 200 g	surface
Q1	Jan 9	on the ring	few cm^2	surface soil	few grams	surface
Q2	Jan 9	on the ring	few cm^2	depth soil	few grams	2 cm

The analysis began at CNES with the visual examination of sample P1 using a binocular enlarging lens. A selection of areas presenting an interesting appearance were later examined under a microscope.

The samples were then forwarded to various laboratories equipped for physical and chemical analysis in an effort to determine the element composition of the P1 and P2 samples, and to identify possible variations between the two samples. It was thought that such systematic comparisons might lead to the discovery of mechanical, thermal, or radiation effects correlated with the phenomenon. (Samples Q1 and Q2 were not used at this stage.) The following sections present the results of these independent analyses.

2. Visual and Microscopic Analysis (CNES-Toulouse)

A series of photographs were taken using an optical microscope with low magnification. For these tests, sample P1 was divided into two parts, P1a and P1b.

Sample P1a showed heavily compacted dirt with a crust six to seven millimeters thick, predominantly composed of very dry limestone with only a few traces of desiccated vegetation in the form of moss. Curved striations are clearly seen on the surface, indicating that this dirt has been exposed to a rubbing effect that has resulted in the abrasion of some silicium grains (Figure 28-16). Further examination disclosed a spot where a small silex had been not only imprinted but ground to the level of the

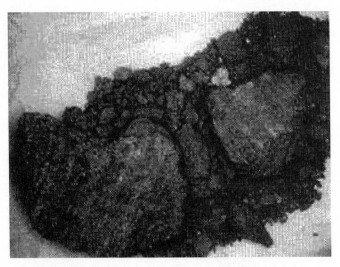

Figure 28-16. Sample P1a, magnification = 1.

surrounding dirt (Figure 28-17). The soil has been fractured on either side of this silex, possibly under a combination of mechanical and thermal action. To the right of this area in Figure 28-17, it appears that the soil is darker and contains small veg-

Figure 28-17. Sample P1a, magnification = 6.4.

Figure 28-18. Sample P1b, magnification = 1.

etal shoots that have germinated after the gathering of the sample. The abrasion effect is less visible in that area.

Sample P1b comes from the same part of the ring as P1a. It exhibits similar compression effects as well as striations. It also shows a darker area that could correspond to foreign material or even to a transformation of the surface material (Figure 28-18). This is clearly observable in Figure 28-19 and also in Figure 28-20, where some plants are germinating and pushing back the black material.

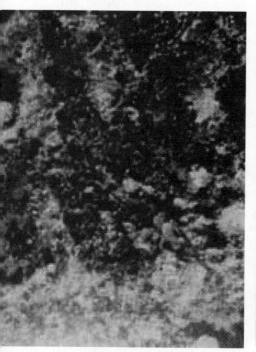 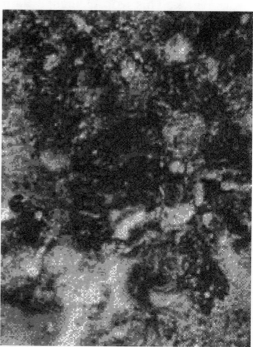

Figure 28-19. Sample P1b, magnification = 5.   **Figure 28-20.** Sample P1b, magnification = 13.

3. Physico-Chemical Analysis

The SNEAP laboratory in Boussens is often entrusted by GEPAN with preliminary analyses aimed at detecting and identifying organic or mineral items or elements in samples. In this particular case the laboratory conducted two types of analyses, the first one on the black area identified previously, the second one on the striations of sample P1b.

The analysis disclosed that the sample contained none of the organic compounds that are characteristic of combustion engines using hydrocarbons. An electronic microscopic analysis of the same P1b sample showed the presence of iron overlaid over limestone rocks in the form of striations about one micron thick. This iron element was not accompanied by chromium, manganese, or nickel, as is commonly found in steel. The technique employed here (using a CAMECA probe) did not allow the investigators to distinguish between free iron or iron oxide.

4. Electronic Diffraction Studies (Toulouse University)

Further analysis was conducted at Paul Sabatier University in Toulouse (Rangueil Faculty) by dissolving parts of the samples in water, desiccating them by ultrasound dispersion and processing them by electronic diffraction. When applied to P2, this analysis led to the identification of at least three compounds: $BaCa(CO_3)^2$, $(CaO_2,8H_2O)$, and, to a lesser extent, Fe_3O_4. The first two compounds may have been an artifact of the process itself.

When applied to P1b, a larger concentration of $(CaO_2,8H_2O)$ was found in crystalline form. It is noteworthy that at least one of the components of this sample is in a monocrystalline state, which is not found in the reference sample (namely P2).

5. Control Study (Metz): Mass Spectrometry by Ion Bombardment

In order to permit a more objective interpretation of the analytical results, GEPAN entrusted various laboratories with the same tasks. Thus the LAMMA analysis laboratory at Metz University was sent part of the soil, both from the reference sample and from the hardened ring. The scientists at Metz performed a mass spectrometry analysis by ion bombardment. When applied to the ring sample, they found the following:

- Negative ion analysis disclosed that the larger black particles (100 microns) exhibited the presence of C_2H_2O with a significant effective cross-section. They also found ions 63 and 79, which are typical of iron phosphate. The negative spectra thus obtained were analogous to those of some polymers or petrochemical residues.
- Positive ion analysis showed that the black particles differed from the surrounding dirt through the lack of aluminum. The elements sodium, magnesium, and titanium were present only in very small amounts. The dominant component was calcium. Other fragments already found in negative ion analysis confirmed the existence of a carbon-based polymer matrix.

From these tests it was concluded that the larger black particles appeared to be a combustion residue.

6. Control Study (Pau): Spark Mass Spectrometry

The Laboratoire d'Analyses Physiques (LDP), based in Pau, specializes in physico-chemical trace analysis applied to mineral and organic materials. The CNES staff has been familiar with this establishment since the days when it performed lunar-soil element analysis on behalf of CNES, working from rock samples provided by NASA. LDP uses a spark mass spectrometer and applied this instrument to fragments of the same soil samples that had been provided to the laboratories mentioned above.

The analysis showed that the sample contained common soil with a limestone-clay base. Little difference was found between the reference sample and the test sample, which contains a visible foreign deposit. The only detectable elements in this deposit are zinc and phosphate. The laboratory offers the hypothesis that this may be due to the rubbing of black paint based on "Carbon Black."

7. Synthesis of the Analysis Results

The various analyses reported above show that the area of ground where the phenomenon is reported to have been observed by Mr. Nicolai has indeed undergone certain alterations of a mechanical and thermal nature, as follows:

- Mechanical effects are exhibited in Figures 28-14 and 28-15, where one can see dark and light areas corresponding to curved striations with precise groove-like contours. A piece of silex has been cut and it even appears to have been superficially ground or polished. The dirt gathered at this particular spot is hardened, compacted, and it exhibits a crust that contrasts with the reference sample, which is loosely structured.
- Thermal effects produced by friction were noted by the SNEAP laboratory because the sandstone is found to be more compact under the black iron (or iron oxide) trace than at other locations. In addition, grains of $CaCO_3$ are not "swarming." Hence they cannot have been heated up to more than 600 degrees Centigrade, a process that would have dissociated, then recombined, this compound. Furthermore, the Rangueil laboratory failed to reproduce the observed microcrystallization by heating the sample to 1,000 degrees for two hours.

In summary, we find that a strong mechanical pressure, probably due to a shock, was exerted at the surface of the ground. Superficial modification of the structure (striations and erosion) took place. A heating effect that may have been caused by this shock, but that did not exceed 600 degrees, was subsequently observed. Foreign elements consisting of a small quantity of iron (or iron oxide) over a limestone grain, and a small but detectable amount of phosphate and zinc, were deposited at the site.

CONCLUSIONS

The report by Mr. Nicolai describes an observation made in daylight from a distance of about thirty meters, for a duration measured in multiples of tens of seconds, during which time the phenomenon was stationary. The investigation failed to discover any indication, either in the behavior or in the discourse of the witness, that would cast doubt on his report because of exaggeration, invention, or distortion. However, the absence of evidence is not evidence of absence, and this lack of grounds for doubt does not establish the truth of his testimony.

Complementary efforts were attempted through physical analysis of visible impressions in the environment. The particular conditions of the terrain did not allow precise measurement of mass, pressure, or thermal effects. However, we were able to show in quantitative fashion that a large-size event had indeed occurred, triggering mechanical deformations, heating, and perhaps even the depositing of trace materials. Possible interpretations (shock, friction) remain too vague for us to conclude that they absolutely verify the testimony of the witness.

Biochemical analyses encompassed the effects on photosynthesis, lipids, sugars, and amino acids in plants found at the site. Multiple differences were found between the reference vegetal samples collected far from the imprint and those that were located closer. In most cases these differences are graphically exhibited as logarithmic or bilogarithmic functions of distance, measured away from the center of the imprint. However, current knowledge about vegetal trauma is still too fragmentary for us to draw a single, precise conclusion from this remarkable set of results. We can only observe that they furnish yet another confirmation that a large-size effect did take place at this particular location. Whether or not it corresponds to the description given by the witness remains to be proven.

We find ourselves balancing between two expectations: first, the desire to "prove" that the witness's report is "true" (or, alternately, that it is "false"); second, the hope to reach a precise physical understanding of the events that have taken place, whatever they are. It is important to note that these two aspirations are not contradictory. In fact they meet precisely within the scientific mode of reasoning. It is only through understanding that one can demonstrate. Conversely, the "proofs" brought to light by physical analysis are to be gauged by the clarity and the precision of their interpretation.

At the present time these "proofs" remain vague. This state of affairs will last until more advanced research programs can address physical and chemical interactions both specifically and systematically. Thus, it is natural for the investigation we have presented to ask more questions than it solves. What is important here is that the right questions be posed. In this respect, we believe that the Trans-en-Provence case is one of the more enriching investigations undertaken by GEPAN.

RETURN TO TRANS-EN-PROVENCE
(by Jacques F. Vallee)

BACKGROUND

On Thursday, January 8, 1981, a remarkable phenomenon was observed on the outskirts of the French village of Trans-en-Provence by a single witness, Mr. Renato Nicolai, who reported the hard landing of a flying object and the ring-like traces it left on the ground. The gendarmerie, and later several French government scientists and laboratories, have extensively analyzed both the verbal report and the physical traces. In particular, Dr. Michel Bounias (1990) has reported on the effects the phenomenon produced on plants growing at the site.

During the time that has elapsed since the official study and Dr. Bounias's analysis, a number of individual investigators in France have also conducted their own studies of the Trans-en-Provence case, including inquiries among the neighbors of the witnesses. These investigations have revealed that one of the neighbors recalled observing a tractor used for drilling on the Nicolai property.* It was speculated that the wheels of a tractor maneuvering on the site could have produced the traces in question. Furthermore, it was pointed out that such drilling work involves the use of substances like cement in powder form as well as baryte, bantonite, and a lubricating product called "foramousse," which could have affected the plants. Such speculation, combined with our interest in a follow-up to the earlier analysis work, prompted us to reopen the case.

SITE VISIT

On November 19, 1988, the author and his wife (a psychologist by training) visited the site of the Trans-en-Provence phenomenon in the company of Dr. Bounias. Weather conditions were dry and clear as we arrived at the home of Mr. and Mrs. Nicolai, who collaborated fully with our requests and patiently answered our questions over the next two hours (Figure 28-21).

Mr. Nicolai told us that the well, which is clearly seen as one reaches the property from the west, had been built in 1966 at the same time as the main house. Water was found at a depth of forty-four feet. The well is located in the front yard, on the opposite side of the house from the site of the event. The witness also showed us the small shack he had been building at the time of the sighting. It was designed to house a new pump, immediately above the front yard. From that position, one does have a long view down to the flat area behind the house on the east side.

---

*Personal communication [Vallee] with M. Figuet, January 3, 1984.

Figure 28-21. The Trans-en-Provence site, photographed in 1988. (*Left to right*) Dr. Jacques F. Vallee, Dr. Michel Bounias, and the witness, Mr. Renato Nicolai.

We noted several other structures nearby: a small, one-story stone house near the pump shack, the ruins of a one-room stone cabin higher on the hill, and a round cavity lined with stones at the far eastern side of the property. It was used at one time as a garbage dump. Only the small house and the pump shelter show evidence of masonry work over the last ten years.

At the time of our visit, most of the site was overgrown with wild grass and weeds. There were some bare spots along the path, but any trace of the event had long been obliterated.

We questioned Mr. and Mrs. Nicolai at length about the sequence and the nature of the work to which the area had been subjected since they had assumed ownership. They told us that they had bought the property in 1966 and that the area where the event took place was initially planted with vines. Two years later (in the 1968–69 time frame), they moved some of the dirt from the hillside in order to level that piece of ground, consolidating the slope with a retaining wall that extends from the main house to the eastern boundary of the property. A dirt trail curves back from that area to the unpaved access road, which meets the two-lane highway below. The site is about twelve feet above the level of the access road.

When asked about the use of chemicals, construction materials, tractors, or other equipment at the site, Mr. Nicolai stated that he had definitely not dumped cement or any similar substances on the ground in that vicinity. It is important to note that a second well has been dug, to a depth of 110 feet, about 60 feet east of the back wall of the house and about 100 feet west of the site of the event itself. Equipment was indeed brought to the area for this work, Mr. Nicolai told us, but the drilling tools were brought from the main driveway and the tractor did not crawl over the site of the event. Most significant, this work took place in 1984, three years after the sighting. The most recent plant samples gathered by Dr. Bounias had been collected in 1983, one year before the drilling of this well. No pump has been installed, and the well has not been placed into operation, pending the possible sale of this parcel of the property.

A private conversation with Mrs. Nicolai disclosed her feelings at the time of the sighting: After her husband told her what he had seen, she was seriously worried about his health. Some time earlier he had suffered from cardiac problems and the doctor had prescribed frequent rest. Was he starting to hallucinate? She was so concerned she was unable to sleep that night. The next day she took her neighbors (Mr. and Mrs. Morin) into her confidence, not to engage in idle gossip but in search of advice; and it was out of a sense of civic duty that Mr. Morin, a tax inspector, insisted that the gendarmerie must be called.

Our impression of Mr. Nicolai was that he is a quiet man who highly values his privacy. The hypothesis that the witness had engineered a hoax in an attempt to gain publicity was not supported by observation of his behavior, either at the time of the event or in subsequent years. Indeed he has turned down several opportunities to appear on French television and to give media interviews, except for a single televised panel at which representatives of CNES were present. It is also difficult to believe that, if the initial report had been a joke, Mr. Nicolai would not have confessed it to his wife when he realized to what degree the event was upsetting her.

When we confronted Mr. and Mrs. Nicolai with the allegations that had been made about the presence of drilling equipment on their property, they quietly asserted that no drilling work had been done prior to 1984, and that the neighbors who had made such reports must simply have been mistaken about the date. None of the compounds (such as cement) cited as possible causes for the changes noted in the local plants were found in the soil analysis performed by CNES. However, there remained one avenue of verification, namely a comparison of the soil on the surface of the ring itself with the soil at the same spot but just below the surface. Mr. Velasco kindly supplied the author with samples (labeled Q1 and Q2) that had been gathered at the same time as the main samples but had not been used in the CNES analysis. We were able to perform a series of tests on these samples.

SAMPLE ANALYSIS

During 1988, samples of Q1 and Q2 were subjected to a number of analyses at a large, well-equipped California laboratory with the capability to process both biological specimens and physical substances. Unfortunately, there is no civilian organization similar to the Unidentified Aerial Phenomena Study Group within CNES (GEPAN) in the United States, and the analysis of physical evidence alleged to be related to UFO phenomena still carries considerable stigma in scientific circles. Accordingly, the analysis was performed as a personal favor to us and not as part of the normal work of the corporation in question, and we have agreed to keep its name confidential in any publication of the results. The samples are available, subject to the agreement of CNES, to any bona fide research organization that might show an interest in reproducing our analyses.

The technical staff who conducted the analysis were given the vials containing the Q1 and Q2 samples but were told nothing about their origin and nature, except for the fact that they were not hazardous in terms of radioactivity or toxicity and could be manipulated in normal fashion in the laboratory. Excerpts from the technical report are given below.

GROSS EXAMINATION AND OPTICAL MICROSCOPY

Sample Q1

This sample has the appearance of damp sand with tiny particles of varying size. It is predominantly beige in color with some brown, white, gray, or black particles. There are tiny dark brown fibers with branches that may be plant or animal in origin, the term "fiber" being used for lack of a better descriptor. There is evidence of a few insect parts (black round bodies with wings or black-brown bodies with a leg).There is an occasional black fiber without branches and very few white fibers. There are a few black particles that are soft, possibly insect bodies, and a very few tiny black particles that are hard (Figure 28-22).

Figure 28-22. The Q1 (surface) sample at magnification 2,000.

Figure 28-23. The Q2 (depth) sample
at magnification 2,000.

Sample Q2

This sample has the appearance of damp sand with tiny particles of varying size. It is predominantly beige in color with some
white, gray, or black particles. No fibers were seen in the whole
sample with the dissecting microscope (Figure 28-23).

These observations are consistent with the fact that Q1 was
taken from the surface, which is likely to include vegetal and insect material, while Q2 was taken below the surface in unex-
posed soil.

Random pinch-size aliquots were taken of both samples for
scanning electron microscopy (SEM); a second aliquot from
Q1, designated below as Q1b, was taken, concentrating on
black particles for SEM/X-ray analysis.

SCANNING ELECTRON MICROSCOPY

Aliquots of Q1 and Q2 were glued on aluminum specimen stubs with a layer of conductive colloidal graphite. The mounted specimens were then coated with a thin layer of carbon film in a high-vacuum evaporator. They were scanned under the SEM at an energy level of 20 keV.

Sample Q1a consists of homogeneous aggregates of particles that vary in size. In addition, there are tube-like structures intertwined in the clusters. These tubes appear to be hollow and differ greatly in size and length. There are some larger particles over 10 micrometers in size in the aggregate.

Sample Q1b comes from the area concentrating on the black particles viewed in optical microscopy. It appears to contain mostly aggregates of the same particles seen in Q1a, but without the tube-like structures.

Sample Q2 consists of homogeneous aggregates with particles of assorted size and shape, mostly ovoid or spherical. The particles range anywhere from 1.0 micrometer to 6.0 micrometers in size. In some fields there appear to be a few long tube-like structures protruding from the aggregates.

Again, these findings are consistent with the different depths of the material and the presence of biological material on the surface.

ENERGY DISPERSIVE X-RAY ANALYSIS

The samples identified as Q1 and Q2 were examined for elemental composition by energy dispersive X-ray analysis on the scanning electron microscope. More effort was directed toward the Q1 sample because of its greater interest to the scientists, due to its diversity. (Again, the scientists did not know the origin and nature of the samples and were guided only by their own deductions.)

The samples were analyzed using 20 keV electrons over several fields at both low and high magnification. Two other samples were examined to provide background information on common constituents of "dirt," which was the gross appearance of these samples.

Both samples contain aluminum, silicon, calcium, and iron. Sample Q1 also contains potassium in low concentration. The presence of sodium may have been masked by the high detector noise at low energy. One field from the examination of Q1 showed some evidence for the presence of copper.

When changing fields within these samples, the relative abundance of the elements changed somewhat, but all elements detected in the sample were present in each field examined, except possibly for copper.

Calcium or silicon was the predominant element in all fields examined. The calcium/iron ratio changed only by a factor of four or less. X-ray mapping was performed for calcium and again for iron in an attempt to see if there was a localized source of these elements, but none was identified. Spot analysis of the fibers was identical to the broad scan of the same area; however, bremsstrahlung is important at these small dimensions. One large rough-surfaced oval particle from Q1 was examined at high magnification and found to have a very low X-ray yield, indicative of organic material. The Q1b sample with more concentrated black particles did not differ from the Q1a sample.

To help understand the results from samples Q1 and Q2, a sample of "house dirt" from a vacuum cleaner bag and a sample of Mount Saint Helens ash collected in Montana were examined. The ash (very homogeneous) showed an identical X-ray spectrum, dominated by silicon, in each field examined. The "house dirt," however, was very heterogeneous. It contained aluminum, silicon, calcium, iron, potassium, sodium, copper, and sulfur. The interesting result was the dramatic difference in elemental composition between fields. Elements would appear and disappear as fields of view changed. These changes did not appear to correlate with the scanning electronic microscope images of the field.

No elements were detected in Q1 and Q2 that were not normal constituents of dust and dirt, and the ratio of elements does not appear to be unique.

CONCLUSION

The results of our analysis of the soil samples from Trans-en-Provence are consistent with the statements by the witness and his wife regarding the history of the soil. In particular, careful microscopic and physical analysis failed to detect any of the substances, such as cement or other construction and drilling materials, that have been proposed to "explain" the traces. Our results tend to support the earlier findings of the French laboratories consulted by CNES as well as the truthfulness of the witness's testimony.

CHAPTER 29

The Mansfield, Ohio, Case

A HELICOPTER-UFO ENCOUNTER OVER OHIO
(by Jennie Zeidman)

SUMMARY OF EVENTS REPORTED BY CREW

October 18, 1973: The four-man crew of an army reserve helicopter, based in Cleveland, Ohio, flew to Columbus for regularly scheduled physical exams. When finished, they left the medical facility at approximately 10:00 P.M., drove back to the airport (a distance of two miles), filed a flight plan, and took off at approximately 10:30 P.M.

The night was clear, calm, starry, and moonless, the temperature 43°F, and visibility 15 miles. Lieutenant Arrigo Jezzi was flying in the left-hand seat. The helicopter was cruising at 90 knots at an altitude of 2,500 feet mean sea level (msl) over mixed woods, farmland, and rolling hills averaging 1,100 to 1,200 feet elevation. (See Figure 29-1.)

Near Mansfield, Ohio, Sergeant John Healey, in the left rear seat, saw a single red light off to the left (west) heading south. It seemed brighter than a port wing-light of normal aircraft, but it was not relevant traffic, and he does not recall mentioning it.

At approximately 11:02 P.M., an estimated three to four minutes after Healey's observation, Sergeant Robert Yanacsek, in the right rear seat, noticed a single steady red light on the eastern horizon. It appeared to be pacing the helicopter.

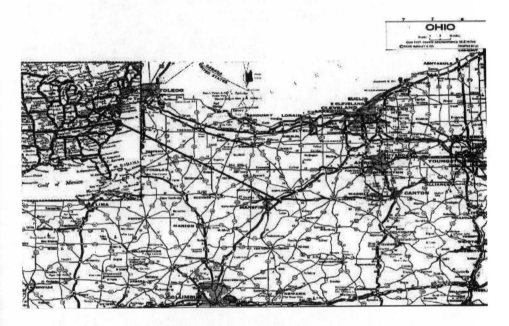

Figure 29-1. Location of sighting.

After watching it for perhaps a minute, he reported it to Captain Lawrence Coyne, the aircraft commander (see Figure 29-2), who instructed him to "keep an eye on it."

After approximately another thirty seconds, Yanacsek announced that the light appeared to be closing on their craft. Coyne and Yanacsek watched from their seats; Healey got up and stooped in the aisle to observe. Jezzi's view was obstructed.

The light continued its approach. Coyne grabbed the controls from Jezzi, began a powered descent of approximately 500 feet per minute, and almost simultaneously contacted

Figure 29-2. Captain Coyne and UH-1H helicopter.

Mansfield control tower, requesting information on possible jet traffic. After initial radio contact, the radios malfunctioned on both VHF and UHF.

The red light increased in intensity and appeared to be on a collision course at a speed estimated to be over 600 knots. Coyne increased the rate of descent to 2,000 fpm feet per minute. The last altitude he noted was 1,700 feet msl.

As a collision appeared imminent, the light decelerated and assumed a hovering relationship above and in front of the helicopter. Coyne, Healey, and Yanacsek reported that a cigar-shaped gray metallic object filled the entire front windshield. A red light was at the nose, a white light at the tail, and a distinctive green beam emanated from the lower part of the object.

The green beam swung up over the helicopter nose, through the main windshield, and into the upper tinted window panels, bathing the cockpit in green light. Jezzi reported only a white light from the upper windows. No noise or turbulence from the object was noted.

After a few seconds of hovering, the light accelerated and moved off to the west, showing only the white "tail" light. Coyne and Healey reported that the object made a decisive 45° course change to the right. Jezzi did not observe the course change. Yanacsek's view was partially obstructed.

While the object was still visible, Jezzi and Coyne noted that the altimeter read 3,500 feet with a rate of climb of 1,000 feet per minute. Coyne stated that the collective (see Figure 29-3) was still in the full-down position.

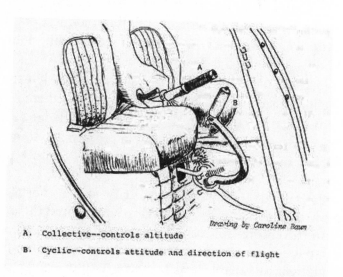

A. Collective--controls altitude
B. Cyclic--controls attitude and direction of flight

Figure 29-3. Side view of a helicopter's collective and cyclic controls.

Coyne gingerly raised the collective. The helicopter climbed nearly another 300 feet before positive control was regained. Then the crew felt a slight "bump."

Coyne descended to the previous cruise altitude of 2,500 feet; radio contact with Akron-Canton was easily achieved, and the flight continued to Cleveland without further incident.

The day following the incident, Captain Coyne went to P. J. Vollmer, Federal Aviation Authority chief of operations at Hopkins Field, to find how and where to report the occurrence. In a taped interview with Dr. J. Allen Hynek, Vollmer said:

I'll never, all the rest of my life, forget that man [Coyne] coming in here [at approximately 2 P.M.]. I have known Coyne for some time, not personally, not even socially, but I personally have an extremely high regard for his integrity and his capability. In a case of this kind, I don't know anybody that I would believe any more. I trust his judgment without a question of a doubt. I don't know what happened, but I do know—I could tell from the tremor of his voice, which wasn't much—that he was shook. He felt the feeling, inside of himself—this is what I gathered—that it had to come out of him. This knowledge and information. He needed advice on reporting it somewhere, but he didn't know where to go.

However, Vollmer could not suggest an official agency to which to report, so the matter rested until Coyne related the event to his cousin, a reporter for the *Cleveland Plain Dealer*. Even after the newspaper account, there was no official interest expressed in the matter, so Coyne filled out reports (see Figure 29-4) a month later in order that the incident be officially on record.

DISPOSITION FORM

For use of this form, see AR 340-15; the proponent agency is The Adjutant General's Office.

REFERENCE OR OFFICE SYMBOL	SUBJECT
	Near Midair Collision with UFO Report

TO	Commander	FROM	Flight Operations Off	DATE 23 Nov 73	CMT 1

TO Commander
83D USARCOM
ATTN: AHRCCG
Columbus Support Facility
Columbus, Ohio 43245

FROM Flight Operations Off
USAR Flight Facility
Cleveland Hopkins Airport
Cleveland, Ohio 44135

1. On 18 October 1973 at 2305 hours in the vicinity of Mansfield, Ohio, Army Helicopter 68-15444 assigned to Cleveland USARFFAC encountered a near midair collision with a unidentified flying object. Four crewmembers assigned to the Cleveland USARFFAC for flying proficiency were on AFTP status when this incident occurred. The flight crew assigned was CPT Lawrence J. Coyne, Pilot in Command, 1LT Arrigo Jezzi, Copilot, SSG Robert Yanacsek, Crew Chief, SSG John Healey, Flight Medic. All the above personnel are members of the 316th MED DET(HEL AMB), a tenant reserve unit of the Cleveland USARFFAC.

2. The reported incident happened as follows: Army Helicopter 68-15444 was returning from Columbus, Ohio to Cleveland, Ohio and at 2305 hours east, south east of Mansfield Airport in the vicinity of Mansfield, Ohio while flying at an altitude of 2500 feet and on a heading of 030 degrees, SSG Yanacsek observed a red light on the east horizon, 90 degrees to the flight path of the helicopter. Approximately 30 seconds later, SSG Yanacsek indicated the object was converging on the helicopter at the same altitude at a airspeed in excess of 600 knots and on a midair collision heading. Cpt Coyne observed the converging object, took over the controls of the aircraft and initiated a power descent from 2500 feet to 1700 feet to avoid impact with the object. A radio call was initiated to Mansfield Tower who acknowledged the helicopter and was asked by CPT Coyne if there were any high performance aircraft flying in the vicinity of Mansfield Airport however there was no response received from the tower. The crew expected impact from the object instead, the object was observed to hesistate momentarily over the helicopter and then slowly continued on a westerly course accelerating at a high rate of speed, clear west of Mansfield Airport then turn 45 degree heading to the Northwest. Cpt Coyne indicated the altimeter read a 1000 fpm climb and read 3500 feet with the collective in the full down position. The aircraft was returned to 2500 feet by CPT Coyne and flown back to Cleveland, Ohio. The Flight plan was closed and the FAA Flight Service Station notified of the incident. The FSS told CPT Coyne to report the incident to the FAA GADO office a Cleveland Hopkins Airport MR. Porter, 83d USARCOM was notified of the incident at 1530 hours on 19 Oct 73.

3. This report has been read and attested to by the crewmembers of the aircraft with signatures acknowledgeing this report.

REPLACES DD FORM 96, EXISTING SUPPLIES OF WHICH WILL BE ISSUED AND USED UNTIL 1 FEB 63 UNLESS SOONER EXHAUSTED. ☆U.S. GPO: 1972-473-063 P.2. 14

DA 2496

Figure 29-4 (a). Disposition Form: Near Midair Collision Report.

OPERATIONAL HAZARD REPORT

For use of this form, see AR 95-1; the proponent agency is Office of the Assistant Chief of Staff for Force Development.

(An operational hazard is any condition or act that affects or may affect the safe operation of Army aircraft, associated equipment, facilities, or cause injury to personnel.)

1. THIS HAZARD OCCURRED OR WAS OBSERVED WHILE:

a. ☒ IN-FLIGHT   c. ☐ OTHER(specify)

b. ☐ ON THE GROUND   d. ☐ LOCATED AT_____ DATE _18 OCT 73_ HOUR _2300_

2. THIS HAZARD IS CONCERNED WITH (select most appropriate category):

a. ☐ AIR TRAFFIC CONTROL   c. ☐ WEATHER   e. ☐ AIRCRAFT   g. ☒ OTHER (specify)
b. ☐ AIRFIELD   d. ☐ PUBLICATIONS   f. ☐ PERSONNEL   _UNIDENTIFIED_

3. IN THE AREA OF(select one or more to describe above category):

a. ☐ PROCEDURES/INSTRUCTIONS   d. ☐ FACILITIES   g. ☐ SERVICING(e.g., refueling)
b. ☐ POLICIES/REGULATIONS   e. ☐ MAINTENANCE INSPECTION   h. ☐ OTHER (specify)
c. ☐ OPERATION(S)   f. ☐ SERVICE(S) (e.g., wx)

4. IF THIS HAZARD OCCURRED WHILE IN FLIGHT, COMPLETE THE FOLLOWING:

a. A/C TYPE _UH-1H_   b. SERIAL NUMBER _68-16444_   c. MISSION _RETURNING FROM FLIGHT PHYSICALS_

d. DEPARTED FROM _COLUMBUS OHIO_   e. DESTINATION _CLEVELAND OHIO_

f. NEAREST NAVIGATION, FIX, FACILITY, OR AIRPORT _MANSFIELD AIRPORT_   ___ DISTANCE _WEST_ DIRECTION

g. YOUR AIRCRAFT WAS

☐ ON AIRWAYS   ☐ OUTBOUND FROM AIRPORT
☐ OFF AIRWAYS   ☐ INBOUND TO AIRPORT
☒ EN ROUTE   ☐ POSITIVE CONTROL AIRSPACE
☐ TERMINAL   ☐ OTHER (specify)
☐ IN CONTROL ZONE
☐ AIRPORT TRAFFIC PATTERN

h. YOUR AIRCRAFT OPERATING CONDITIONS

☒ VFR DD 175   ☐ IFR/VFR ON TOP
☐ VFR WITH IFR CLEARANCE   ☐ DVFR/ADIZ FLIGHT LIMITS
☐ IFR DD 175   ☐ LOCAL
☐ IFR WITH NO CLEARANCE

IF THIS HAZARD WAS A NEAR MIDAIR COLLISION WITH ANOTHER AIRCRAFT OR OBSTACLE, COMPLETE THE FOLLOWING:

FIRST SIGHTING OTHER AIRCRAFT | FLIGHT ATMOSPHERIC CONDITIONS

OTHER AIRCRAFT/OBSTACLE OBSERVED AT _3_ O'CLOCK

☐ ABOVE YOU   ☐ DIVERGING   ☐ YOUR RIGHT   ☐ OVERCAST   ☒ CLEAR   ☐ BROKEN CLOUDS
☐ BELOW YOU   ☐ CONVERGING   ☐ YOUR LEFT   ☐ SCATTERED   VISIBILITY MILES _15_
☒ SAME ALTITUDE   ☐ YOU OVERTOOK   ☐ OTHER OVERTOOK

WHAT FIRST DIRECTED ATTENTION TO THE OTHER AIRCRAFT/OBSTACLE ? _RED LIGHT PARALELLING OUR ACFT._

CLOUD PROXIMITY

☐ ABOVE   ☐ IN/OUT CLOUDS
☐ BELOW   ☐ IN CLOUDS   ☐ BETWEEN LAYERS

DISTANCE BETWEEN AIRCRAFT/OBSTACLE | DISTANCE TO CLOUDS

FIRST SIGHTING	CLOSEST PROXIMITY	HORIZONTAL	VERTICAL	HORIZONTAL	VERTICAL
5-10 mi.	500 FT.		500 FT.		

PHASE OF FLIGHT | FLIGHT CONDITIONS

YOU OTHER	PHASE	YOU OTHER	PHASE
☐ ☐	TAKEOFF	☐ ☐	TURNING
☐ ☐	CLIMB	☐ ☐	REFUELING
☒ ☒	LEVEL FLIGHT	☐ ☐	ACROBATICS
☐ ☐	DESCENDING	☐ ☐	OTHER(specify)
☐ ☐	LANDING		
☐ ☐	HOLDING PATTERN		

FLIGHT CONDITIONS

☐ BRIGHT DAY   ☐ DAWN   ☐ HAZE
☐ GLARING SUN   ☐ THUNDERSTORM   ☐ ICING
☒ NIGHT   ☐ PRECIPITATION   ☐ FOG
☐ DUSK   ☐ TURBULENCE

OTHER AIRCRAFT/OBSTACLE

TYPE A/C   OBSTACLE DESCRIPTION

UNIDENTIFIED

DESCRIPTION/EXPLANATION/COMMENTS (continue on reverse)

OBJECT APPROACHED AT SAME ALTITUDE FROM 5-10 mi. OUT, FROM THE EAST, FORCING ACFT. COMMANDER TO TAKE EVASIVE ACTION. OBJECT MADE NO ATTEMPT TO ALTER IT'S FLIGHT PATH

DI (Your Aviation Safety Officer)   YOUR SIGNATURE (optional)

DUTY _CREW CHIEF_   DATE _1 DEC 73_

DA FORM 2696, 1 AUG 68   PREVIOUS EDITION IS OBSOLETE.

109

Figure 29-4 (b). Operational Hazard Report.

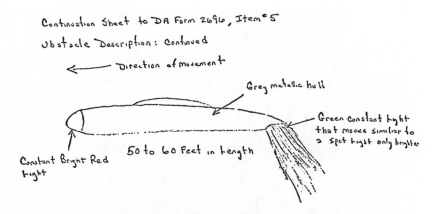

Figure 29-4 (c). Continuation of Report: Coyne's Drawing.

TESTIMONY: COYNE

After learning of the event from the press, Dr. Hynek interviewed Captain Coyne, the pilot in command, at the first opportunity, which was January 24, 1974. In the spring of 1976,
at Dr. Hynek's request, I talked with Coyne also.

Hynek Interview

Dr. Hynek's interview with Coyne took place at Cleveland
Hopkins Airport in a UH-1H helicopter, an identical model to
the one in which the event occurred.

COYNE: Basically, Jezzi was sitting here [see Figures 29-5 and
29-6] and I was sitting here, and John, he was sitting in this
seat, and Yanacsek, the crew chief, was seated here, looking out
this window. Jezzi had the controls. We were flying along, level
altitude, 2,500 feet. Yanacsek said, "There's a light on the
horizon," and I looked out and told him to keep an eye on it.
And I looked out this window here, to the right.

HYNEK: Coming in from the east, then. You were going
north.

Figure 29-5. Interior of helicopter with outward-facing rear seats.

COYNE: Yeah, and he said this thing was paralleling us, and I looked again and I said, "Well, check it out." And then he said that the thing was closing, and when I looked, the thing was coming at us. It was coming directly at the helicopter and it got larger and larger, and I'm looking out this window now. I told Jezzi, "I have the controls," and I took the controls, and the first thing I did was push it [the collective] down. We started to descend. Here's your vertical speed, right here, and we went down to 500 feet per minute, okay? And we're maintaining 90 knots, so then I took the cyclic and I pushed it forward. About 20 degrees lower than the horizon. Our airspeed went to 100 knots, our altimeter, which was reading 2,500, started down, 'cause it [vertical speed] was showing 2,000 fpm. It kept coming right at us, and I saw it was still coming, directly for the helicopter.

HYNEK: It was paralleling at first, though, you say. . . .

COYNE: It was paralleling us, right.

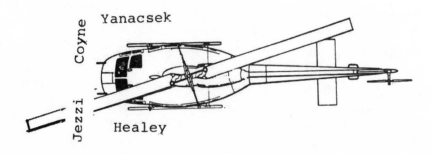

Figure 29-6. Positions of crew members within helicopter.

HYNEK: Was it gaining on you, would you say?

COYNE: No, it wasn't ahead of us or behind us; it was even with us.

HYNEK: But getting closer, though.

COYNE: Well, when it was paralleling, it didn't look like it was closing. Then it started coming at us, and as it came at us, I saw it was closing, and going faster and faster, and I said, "Holy Christ, that could be a jet," and [indistinct] said, "No, that's not a jet. It's moving too fast because of our altitude," and I looked and we were going through 2,000 feet now. [Note: Federal air-traffic regulations stipulate that below 10,000 feet msl aircraft speeds must not exceed 250 knots except to preserve the safety of the aircraft.]

HYNEK: Going through 2,000 feet, going down . . .

COYNE: We'd been at 2,500, and it started coming at us, and I pushed the collective down. And I saw it was coming at us, and I saw we weren't descending fast enough, so I pushed the cyclic forward to get our nose down, to get 2,000 feet per minute, and it still kept coming at us. We were going down in altitude, and it looked like it was still coming at us—it was descending in altitude also. It was coming to wipe us out, you know? We descended from 2,500, we're down 500 feet already, and then, let's see, I said the son of a gun is gonna hit us, y'know. And I braced—I figured this was it. What do you do when you have an automobile accident? You just stiffen up. And then they said "Look!" and I looked, and there it was, right here. . . .

HYNEK: At about your one-o'clock position, and 30 degrees up . . .

COYNE: Right about here, okay? And they were looking from your position, either out through here, or through here. . . .

HYNEK: By now it was close enough that they didn't have to look out the side windows.

COYNE: Right. Now, the light swung 90 degrees and came into the cockpit, here. Now, we fly at night and these instruments are all red lights, here. Everything turned green. Now, it could be, maybe because of this [indicates green-tinted panels of overhead windows].

HYNEK: But that's not very green.

COYNE: Here, I'll just give you an idea. [Holds up white card to sunlight coming through window.]

HYNEK: It looks yellow-green, but it looks mostly yellow, and also, that's sunlight. . . .

COYNE: They said "Look!" I looked and I saw it, right here, and then it moved this way, it went over this way, to the west.

HYNEK: Did it change its angle, or change its course, or . . .

COYNE: No, it stopped over us, and then it just slowly moved, while I thought we were descending, 'cause I remember it was 1,700 feet and I thought, Oh, this is it, and then I saw it right in front here, and I said, "That's no F-100!" Then it moved this way, and I looked at my altitude and we were at 3,500, climbing to 3,800, past 3,500, and the collective is still down. This [the cyclic, see Figures 29-3 and 29-18] is forward.

HYNEK: Now, who else saw the altimeter at that time?

COYNE: Rick [Jezzi] could see it, but I don't know whether John could or not. The first thing I looked at was this [the altimeter] and this [rate-of-climb indicator]. And I saw we were at 3,500, and I saw it was 1,000 fpm.

HYNEK: Vertical ascent.

COYNE: Vertical ascent. Climbing. We're still on a heading of 030. Our airspeed was 100 knots. And we're at 6,600 rpm. We were maintaining our rpm, but we were in position—the controls—for descent. You know, in autorotation, a controlled autorotation.

HYNEK: Hmmmm. This [collective] was still down.

COYNE: I had called Mansfield tower. Here's the radio. I had called Mansfield on UHF, 257.8. Now, this is the UHF frequency. If this doesn't work, you go to your VHF. Then here's your transponder, here. We had the transponder on. We called on this radio, and we called on this [other] radio, and we changed frequencies twice on it. Went from 257.8 to Cleveland radio, to Mansfield radio 255.4, and I think we called Mansfield tower on—what the hell is it—19.8 or something like that, on the VHF frequency. And when you key your mike, you hear a keying tone, you know? And we heard that, so when you press the key, the switch, you hear the transmitting sound, and there was nothing. They said, "Go ahead, Army One-five-triple-four."

HYNEK: They heard you.

COYNE: Yeah, they said they heard us and yet they say they can't find it on the tapes. They said they had three or four different tapes going, frequencies going.

HYNEK: You had radio communication to begin with?

COYNE: Yes, they acknowledged.

HYNEK: When did you first call Mansfield?

COYNE: Oh, it was still approaching us. When I saw the thing coming at us, and I said, "That thing looks like a fighter!" I said, "Do you have any high-performance aircraft in this area at 2,500 feet?" And there was no answer. I said, "Mansfield tower, this is Army One-five-triple-four." I said, "Do you have any high-performance aircraft flying in this area at a speed of 600 knots?" Nothing. I said, "Call them, Rick," and he called them. Nothing.

HYNEK: When you say "nothing," you mean no answer? You got no answer?

COYNE: Right. Now you change frequencies, change channels, you hear a channel tone. A buzzing sound and then a stop. That means the channel change. And it did change. And then—nothing.

HYNEK: By "nothing" you mean you weren't getting out or—

COYNE: There was the tone. But then there was nothing. And yet the radio worked, because we were talking to Mansfield just before, without a change, and we got Ashland and Medina— we made contact—the first people we made contact with [after] was Akron Approach, and we got a position report from them, and we just carried on, and I could see this object that was moved away. I saw the red as it was coming, and I saw a red and green here [as the object was in front] and this is where I drew the picture of the object.

The next portion of the tape concerns Dr. Hynek taking photos of Coyne pointing out the windshield and a discussion of the drawing made by Coyne (Figure 29-7).

HYNEK: Now Larry is showing me his drawing. The reason you put this first line here [the line around the nose] was why?

COYNE: Okay. The first line indicates where the red light stopped. To delineate where the red light stopped and the gray metallic structure began. You could also see the red reflection off the gray metallic structure. As you looked farther aft, in the center of the structure, you could see the gray, and in the trailing edge you could see the green light, and off the gray structure you could see the reflection of the green light.

HYNEK: Where was the white light that you saw?

COYNE: I didn't see the white light until it was moving west.

HYNEK: The green, then, was beaming down this way?

COYNE: Down on a 45 . . . and this light [the green] swung around from 180 degrees to . . . or swung 90 degrees to our position and came into the cockpit.

HYNEK: I see.

COYNE: It was just all gray. There were no lights or anything other than the red and the green.

HYNEK: The one thing I want to ask about the outlines: Were they fuzzy or sharp?

COYNE: Distinct. Distinct. Because the stars were blotted out, you know. It was dark, but you could see the ground. And with the stars you could actually see the outline of the structure.

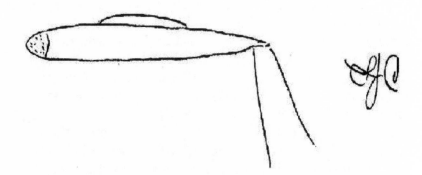

Figure 29-7. Coyne's drawing of the object.

That evening Hynek had dinner with Coyne, Healey, and Yanacsek. It was during their relaxed evening conversation that Coyne, describing the incident to Hynek, said, "It was like looking into another world."

Zeidman Interview

Two and a half years later, I reviewed the event with Coyne at Cleveland Hopkins Airport. Coyne was in the pilot's seat of a UH-1H; I was in the right rear seat immediately behind him.

> COYNE: I took a look and I could see the light and see it was moving toward the helicopter. At which time I got on the radio, with my heel mike here, and I pressed that. We were tuned into Mansfield and I said, "Mansfield, this is Army helicopter One-five-triple-four: Do you have any high-performance aircraft in your area?"
>
> I let go of the mike, and he came back and said, "This is Mansfield Approach, go ahead Army One-five-triple-four." I stepped on it again. "This is One-five-triple-four. Do you have any high-performance aircraft in your area?" I let go of the mike. Nothing [Coyne means there was no response.] Yanacsek said, "The aircraft is closing."

I saw it. I tell Jezzi, "I have the controls," and I grabbed the controls from Jezzi. I saw it was coming and I pushed down on the collective and we began to settle. Generally we descend at 500 fpm. A general procedure. But I can't give you the time. I just went down a little. I'm watching the object and checking my instruments. I'm watching and reacting. It's moving at us, and it looks like it's going to ram us right by the door. I take the collective and push it all the way down.

Looking now, our airspeed is 90 knots. I push the cyclic forward and increase our speed to 100 knots to help get the aircraft moving, and the helicopter begins to descend. Okay. The object is coming closer and I'm checking my instruments 'cause I see the ground is coming up and . . . 1,700 feet . . . it looks like the thing is going to impact with us. And Healey says, "Look!" And I look at the altimeter and it says 1,700 feet and I look up and the thing is right there, in front of us. The object was all across the window. I could see it very clearly. It covered the entire window, not just a spot. The red light was here. And where the red light stopped you could see the red reflecting on the structure. Very definite. The red constant glow. And behind it the green light comes out—a pyramid-shaped light—and swings 90 degrees and just comes this way, and comes into this window and it seems like it takes up the whole aircraft. Everything turns green. And I said, "That's no F-100!" And Yanacsek is looking over my shoulder and Healey is looking over and Jezzi is staring. Then the light . . . the aircraft . . . the vehicle . . . begins to move this way, and I asked Jezzi, "Do you have it?" and he says, "I see a white light." And Healey is looking at it through here [front] and part of it up there [above]. And then we could see it moving towards Mansfield. The faster it accelerated the brighter the white light got. It did a 45-degree turn when it cleared between Mansfield and the Mansfield airport, headed toward Lake Erie and the Sandusky area, and in the Sandusky area it did a 45 attitude climb, out into space. The light became very bright until it disappeared.

ZEIDMAN: How did it disappear, and how did you know it

was going away, if it was getting brighter? Going away and getting brighter is against the laws of physics.

COYNE: It just suddenly snapped out, and you could tell it was receding because of the flight path, the trajectory. There was no doubt it was going away. At that time we contacted Akron-Canton. We could not get hold of Mansfield at all. We called Akron-Canton Radio, and they answered. The radios were functioning fine then, and Akron-Canton says, "You are over the—you are so many miles north of Ashland."

ZEIDMAN: You got a transponder fix?

COYNE: Yeah, right. And we said, "Fine." All we said was what was our position. And I said, "Healey and Yanacsek, keep an eye out for that thing in case it comes back to take another pass at us." In my opinion, that thing tried to ram us. To kill us. That's what my fear was.

And I moved us back to Cleveland at 110 knots, almost max airspeed. But before that point, while we could still see it, I says, "My God, we're at 3,500 feet," and I says, "What's happening?" The collective was bottomed. It wouldn't go down any farther, and while I was looking at the instruments, the altimeter was going up to 3,800. I pulled the collective up and then pushed it down and the helicopter seemed to settle. I never touched this [collective] until I noticed the helicopter was at 3,500 feet and climbing.

ZEIDMAN: But you didn't see it [the altimeter]?

COYNE: Yes, I did. I noticed there was a climb, but I didn't think there would be that rate of a climb.

ZEIDMAN: Well, didn't you wonder "Why are we climbing—the collective is down!"

COYNE: I figured turbulence.

ZEIDMAN: Did you feel the climb? Did you feel any turbulence?

COYNE: No. That's what's weird. There was no turbulence, no noise. We didn't hear anything, we didn't feel anything; all we could do was see. And the fact that this thing was up to here—3,500 feet—and this needle [rate of climb] was up to here—1,000 fpm, and it was climbing. From the bottom position I had to pull it up, push it down, and then the helicopter seemed to bump, like it hit turbulence then. But the thing was way to the west. It was already in the Mansfield area when we began to settle. When I saw the 1,000 fpm climb and read the altimeter, the collective was still in the down position. The throttle was still in the same position as when I descended. The needles were still joined together, still running at a regular rpm. It was a powered descent, not an autorotation.

I asked Coyne specifically about the location of the event. Coyne said that he was unable to pinpoint the exact site, although, he said, "I've flown that route a hundred times. We were just passing Mansfield. We could see Mansfield, and the Mansfield airport, and then Ashland, straight ahead. Jezzi was flying, and we were following the lights of I-71 and cross-checking with Cleveland VOR. We had the Mansfield NDB [nondirectional beacon] cranked in—we always keep to the right [east] of the NDB so as to keep away from the Mansfield control area. I knew where we were, but the exact spot over the ground I can't tell you." [See locations in Figure 29-8.]

While I was talking with Coyne on another occasion at Port Columbus, again seated in a UH-1H, we reviewed the sequence of events. He mentioned, almost as an afterthought, the helicopter compass malfunction.

COYNE: And we began to settle, and the magnetic compass was—

ZEIDMAN: Yes, go ahead.

COYNE: . . . was spinning.

ZEIDMAN: This has never come out before, that the compass was spinning.

COYNE: It was completely shot. The mechanics took it out of the box and shipped it. I thought this information was in the . . .

ZEIDMAN: No. No way. This has never come out before.

COYNE: It began spinning when the vehicle, the thing, was in front of us, while it was still coming to us.

ZEIDMAN: And you were looking at all these things [the instruments] at the same time?

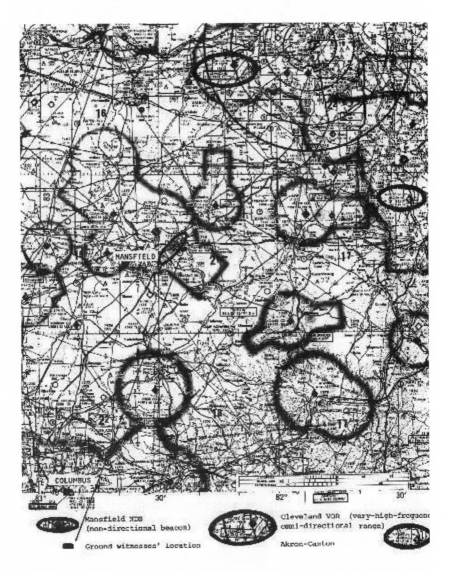

Figure 29-8. Aeronautical chart showing location of beacon, towers, and ground witnesses.

COYNE: Yep. This didn't spin [the RMI, radio magnetic in-dicator]. This did [the magnetic compass]. This remained con-stant—our radio magnetic indicator. But this just began to spin. Like crazy. It was spinning the next day after we landed. The mechanics came out. The thing was just shot. The compass was useless. We can show you the aircraft records. The compass was removed because it was completely unserviceable.

ZEIDMAN: All right. So, how did you get reoriented, and get your heading, and so on?

COYNE: Well, we never varied. I don't think we even deviated. There was no pedal. The problem was not the heading; it was descent and airspeed.

ZEIDMAN: On one of the tapes, Healey said the compass remained the same.

COYNE: This compass—the RMI. There was no malfunction in any of these instruments, here. We had the Cleveland VOR on; the altimeter, the RPM, the torque—all the instruments were functioning. The only thing—this [the magnetic compass] began to spin. Now, this thing will spin, a compass will drift 20 degrees when you turn on the landing light. But this thing just kept on turning, in one direction. Kept going around: 90, 180, 270, zero, 90—continuously. It didn't drift back.

ZEIDMAN: How fast was the compass spinning?

COYNE: About like that [motioning], maybe four or five— say four times a minute.

ZEIDMAN: And the compass was actually removed?

COYNE: It was replaced. The tech inspectors went over the aircraft with the Magnaflux. They checked with the light for skin stress on the aircraft and there were no stress factors on the aircraft.[*] Nothing damaged. The only thing that was bad was the compass.

---

[*]In the Zyglo method of the Magnaflux Corporation, a fluorescent penetrant is sprayed on the metal to be tested and the surface is then examined under a source of ultraviolet radiation.

Testimony: Healey

The verbatim transcript below represents the first recorded description of the event: a tape made on October 19, 1973. Sergeant John Healey related his experience to a colleague in the Cleveland Police Department less than eighteen hours after it happened. He presented a calm and straightforward account interspersed with moments of restrained desperation and hysterical, almost sobbing laughter:

"The light seemed to be getting brighter and brighter. And it appeared that it was on a collision course. And we were at about 3,000 feet, and the pilot took the controls from the copilot and he put the helicopter into a power dive and we lost 500 feet immediately if not sooner. And this object cleared our aircraft by about 500 feet. It had a steady red light on the nose; it was cigar-shaped and had a green light shining down from the aft end. It was like a gunmetal gray and it made no noise, nor were there any vibrations or air turbulences. It went from the eastern horizon to our point in a matter of about two minutes, and then from there it continued in a direction of about 270 degrees till it got near the horizon. Then it broke off and did about a . . . to 340 degrees and was lost on the horizon, just like that. When it was all over we were all pretty scared because at the speed this thing was moving . . . now it's a funny thing, it came from the horizon very quickly but when it went over our aircraft, its speed was very slow until it passed over our aircraft and then it picked up speed again. This is the odd thing about it. Because the helicopter has green . . . we call it the greenhouse. It's a green roof, green windows, over the top of the pilot and copilot so they can see directly up; it's tinted against the sun. I was standing right in the aisle between the pilot and copilot and we were looking right there through the greenhouse watching this thing, and it damn near came to a stop right over us. And then it started up again. So we all got a very good look at it. There were no windows that I could see.

"It just hesitated for a moment—dropped its airspeed very

low—and then just picked right up again and took off. And there's nothing we've got that's that slow and fast in the air, that can slow down and start up again that fast. There were no engines, and no air turbulence. This thing didn't have any wings. I don't know how the hell he got around, but he did. And if we hadn't dived, we probably would have been involved in a collision, because this thing only cleared us by about 500 feet. If we had stayed on 3,000 feet it probably would have hit us. The speed that this thing moved from the horizon was fantastic; it really put on the k's.

"When we first observed this little red light it looked like a navigation light, way out in the distance, but as it got closer this light got very big and very bright. It was almost like the landing lights of a 727, that's how bright this light was. Like, our navigation lights are very small bulbs on the sides of our aircraft, but this had a great big spotlight on the front of it, and that's why you could just tell from the size of it . . . This light kept getting bigger and bigger and bigger, so we didn't know what it was until it was right over us, and we could see its outline. All we could see coming at us was this one big red light. It had no blinking lights at all, or the anticollision beacon, just the red light in the front, the green light underneath, and the white light in the back. It looked like the real bright landing lights we had just seen at Port Columbus. It was a steady light. And it scared the living hell right out of me.

"Well, everybody looks at me and they laugh as I talk to people about it. They say 'Ha ha ha,' and I laugh about it too now. [Laughs hysterically for four to five seconds, then stops soberly.] Well, all four of us were on board this aircraft last night. None of us ever expected to see something like this, and we've never encountered anyone who had seen anything like it, so it was a brand new experience altogether. I'll tell you the truth: Any time I've ever heard anything about UFOs, I've just glanced at it; I never really got absorbed with it because I never believed in it, but now I think I'd start reading the articles, because maybe somebody'll describe what I saw.

"And we had just taken our flight physicals that evening so

we were all cold sober and in perfect health—we'd all passed
our physicals—so it wasn't a case of we'd been out drinking or
something. You just don't go near an aircraft when you've been
drinking. And we left the hospital at 10:00, and we pulled pitch
at 10:30, and it took us fifteen minutes to get to the airfield and
we filed our flight plan, and it took about fifteen minutes to
warm up the aircraft, and at 10:30 we were leaving, so there
was no time to stop at a bar and even get halfway wasted,
'cause we can account for every minute of our time."

Healey's testimony remains consistent. Talking with his
cousin Laura Gallagher a year later, he said:
"We were almost struck by an aircraft. This thing tracked us
for a long time, out on the eastern horizon, and then it started
on an intercepting path, so it was probably trying to dope us
out, you know. Then I figure he just came in for a closer look.
He was curious like we were curious, but he had the ability to
outrun us. . . .
"But after he took off, I watched that light for a couple of
minutes, just watched it take off in a westerly direction. Then
when it got near the horizon, it did a right turn of about 45°
and just followed the contour of the earth, and over the horizon
it went. I sat and watched it. I had nothing else to do. And it
made a 45° turn and went over the edge of the world."
In December 1976, talking with CUFOS consultant Dr. Tom
Evans, Professor of Psychology at John Carroll University in
Cleveland, Healey said:
"It had no windows, and it was a cigar-shaped affair. It
looked as though it was a solid object. It definitely had sub-
stance. If I had to guess what material it was, I'd say metal.
Some of the light reflected on the object. From my point, between the seats, it appeared to take up the entire—both—front
windows. Surprisingly, I looked at it as a disinterested party. I
had no fear that we would be involved [in a collision]. It was
just something interesting to watch. I was hoping it would turn
around so I could get a better look."

Evans asked Healey what left him with the greatest emotional impression. Healey replied:

"The shaft of green light coming out of the underside of the aircraft. You could actually see a cone of light, a definitive cone, a light that stuck out at right angles. A spotlight has a condensed cone from the source—the filament—to the target; it doesn't grow that big. But this opened up in a triangular shape. It opened up. It wasn't just a straight beam of light coming down. It was going straight down from the aircraft, but it wasn't a condensed beam. I saw the green beam as the [object] was in front of me, out the front windshield. I didn't see it as it was going away [to the west]. Then I saw the taillight—a white light. I saw the red light coming toward us, and when the aircraft was perpendicular to us through the windshield. What happened was I had crouched down between the two seats and that way I could look right through the windshield. I couldn't see the bright spot, the filament of the light; I could just see the cone.

"I really don't remember the inside of the aircraft [the helicopter] turning green. I don't remember the green cockpit or the descent or the climb. I know Larry said the light swiveled, but I don't remember that."

Dr. Evans then talked about the perceptual phenomenon of "closure," in which the human mind is capable of taking three or more distinct points and "filling in" or "closing" them into a shape or pattern that is identifiable with respect to past experience. Healey replied that indeed he had tried to "form the cigar shape into a recognizable aircraft, something that I could identify, an F-100 or something," but that he was unable to do so. He concluded: "We had enough time where we could watch this thing come at us, [but] when you see this thing, it staggers you because you don't know what the hell you're looking at. It was just a solid metal thing, with no rivets or seams or anything like that. I'll never forget that damn thing."

Testimony: Yanacsek

Sergeant Robert Yanacsek had had a previous UFO experience in Vietnam. While crew chief of a Chinook helicopter, he watched three white lights flying in tight formation, passing beneath his helicopter as it was flying 3,000 feet above the ground at night. The lights maintained their precise relationship throughout the twenty- to thirty-second observation and did not appear to be attached to anything. During the Mansfield incident, Yanacsek was seated directly behind Coyne and had an unobstructed continuous view of the object from the time he first noticed it on the eastern horizon, through the encounter point when the object was maintaining a fixed relationship to the helicopter.

Describing his experience, Yanacsek said:

"It was a clear night, a beautiful clear night, and a steady red light appeared on my right—a steady red light, not flashing—and naturally I thought it was an aircraft. It was so far away that I looked at it for some time before I mentioned it; it wasn't that important, it was so far away, and we were coming up on Mansfield, and we'd be having [radio] contact with the ground so I didn't want to bother Larry. We were too high, in my estimation, for it to be a radio tower, but it was either that or an aircraft. I figured it was an aircraft, since it wasn't flashing.

"I must have watched it for a minute, oh, a minute and a half, before I said anything. A long time. [Great emphasis in Yanacsek's voice.] There was no question in my mind that it was manmade, whether it was a tower or a plane. It wasn't a star or anything. It was a red light, and it was kind of hard to miss it.

"As the object was closing, and I hate to call it a crash dive, but that's basically what it was—a last-ditch effort [of the helicopter] to get out of the way in the last twenty seconds or so when it was driving straight toward us. It was obvious that it was coming at us. There was no question there. We were positive it was going to intercept us, especially since the object or whatever it was had turned in our direction to begin with. It didn't try to stay apart; it was turning toward us at the same altitude and was obviously going to come at us and intercept us. It was red the total time. There was no flashing; it was just bright red, a bright red. I saw a white light only when it was directly overhead, or—correction, correction—I think as it approached me there was a white light. Yes, I think there was because it lit up the tail a little bit and gave definite proof, if you want to say, that it was something solid, something solid and metallic. It lit up the area around the light. It was because it was coming at us at an oblique angle that it [the white light] couldn't be seen immediately.

"It easily filled up the entire windshield. If I had been sitting in the front seat I probably wouldn't have been able to see anything but the aircraft, or whatever it was. The object may have hovered over us for ten to twelve seconds. It seemed like a long time; it seemed like it was there for so damn long. It was just stopped, for maybe ten to twelve seconds, and I mean stopped. It wasn't cruising, it was stopped. It didn't waver, it didn't put on the brakes, it didn't gyrate—it was just like in a cartoon. It was coming at us, and then, in the next "frame," it was there, just like that. No noise, no flaps. It reminded me very much of a submarine. Silent and gliding, and just there. I really didn't think we would really collide, because the object was obviously completely in control of the situation.

"The edges were sharp, because it was an exceedingly clear night out, and the solid part of it blotted out the stars right behind it, and if it had been a dark, cloudy night I probably couldn't have told too well, but it blotted out the stars in an oval shape."

Yanacsek mentioned also that there was the suggestion of a line of separate, possibly round "windows" between the main oval shape and the slight "dome section" of the object. The light from the "windows" was insignificant compared to that of the other three brighter lights on the object.

"The green was in the cockpit, but I think it came from the 'greenhouse.' It was green inside the cockpit. The green light also came in through the windshield, which is not tinted. What happened there . . . it wasn't just a one-shot light; it seemed to swivel. Now again, whether we flew through it, or it swiveled, at any rate the light traveled across our nose into the cockpit and then up into the green area, and it washed out the entire cockpit. It might have been a maneuverable spotlight, or it might be we were passing under it; it did shine in the front. It came up over the nose into the cockpit windshield, and then it came up into the 'greenhouse.' It was wide and intense, like an aircraft light.

"After it got out John Healey's side . . . I think we had litters and equipment and stuff, and I couldn't really see it over the copilot's head until it got out Healey's window. At that time it was almost as small as when it started. Very small. And white. It was way over near Mansfield. The time it took to get over there was between thirty seconds and a minute."

TESTIMONY: JEZZI

Lieutenant Jezzi was not available for an interview until February 12, 1977, when Dr. Hynek and I met with him. We asked Jezzi to simply "begin talking," and he quite readily launched into his description of the event.

JEZZI: That was my first flight with the unit. I hadn't flown for three months before that. We were through with our physicals and we took off without refueling. The weather was beautiful, and our visibility was unlimited. I was flying at the time, and we were cruising at 2,000 or 2,500 feet, I don't remember exactly, and we were flying east of Mansfield, and there had been some conversation previously about UFOs because at the time there were a lot of stories coming out . . . the governor of Ohio had seen them. We were flying about ten miles east of Mansfield . . . there's that F-100 Air Guard squadron stationed there, so you always look out for the jets. I think we had called the [Mansfield] tower and cleared ourselves through the zone.

At that time there was a mention of a red light on the horizon, the eastern horizon, to our right, and the conversation was that it looked like a radio tower, but it wasn't flashing, and then a few seconds later [Yanacsek] said, "No, it's not a radio tower, it appears to be moving." The next comment I heard was "It's coming toward us" and very shortly thereafter . . . I was sitting on the left side of the cockpit . . . I couldn't see what was going on, it's very hard to look toward the right, so Captain Coyne took the controls from me, put the collective down, reduced pitch, and we descended, and we dropped, oh maybe 1,000 feet to about 1,500 msl. We were trying to contact Mansfield but we couldn't get them. And then all hell broke loose in the cockpit. Everybody was yelling and screaming about what the hell it was and that it almost hit us. That kind of conversation kept up for several minutes.* Now, I never saw the object until it was almost vertically on top of us. I never saw a body to it at all. I would say it was about 100 feet above us and maybe 500 feet to our front. Fairly close. The only thing I recall seeing was a white light, a very bright, intense white light on the aft portion of the object, on the back side moving away from us. I followed that light all the way to the horizon.

ZEIDMAN: Did it fade out, or did it snap out, or what?

JEZZI: I just saw it go away and disappear. I assume it went over the curvature. What bothers me is that it was a very intense white light, comparable to some of the approach or landing lights on a smaller aircraft. Not at all like an aft-position light, which is an extremely small one, not very bright. It was much too bright, extremely bright, to be an aft-position light.

ZEIDMAN: All the time you saw the light, did it vary in color or intensity?

JEZZI: No, it stayed very bright.

ZEIDMAN: Even as it receded?

---

*During the April 2, 1978, meeting, Yanacsek indignantly stated that there was not a lot of yelling and screaming. He resented Jezzi's remarks. "We were under emotional control," he said.

JEZZI: Yes. As I said, it was different than an aft-position light. It was like a little ball of white light.

HYNEK: How big, would you say? What kind of object held at arm's length?

JEZZI: A nickel.

HYNEK: Was it bigger than a point source?

JEZZI: Oh, yes.

HYNEK: If the full moon had been visible at the time, would it have been bigger or smaller?

JEZZI: Smaller.

ZEIDMAN: How would you compare it to an aspirin held at arm's length?

JEZZI: About as big as two aspirins at arm's length.

HYNEK: Well, the full moon would just be covered by one aspirin.

JEZZI: Oh, I've seen moons bigger than that!

There were a few moments of digression while Dr. Hynek explained the apparent angular-diameter relationship between sun, moon, and an aspirin tablet.

ZEIDMAN: Well, were the edges fuzzy or distinct? Did it leave a beam?

HYNEK: A trail? Did it at any time leave a trail, a luminous trail?

JEZZI: No. As I say, it was a very intense white light. It did not leave a beam of light, like a spotlight, you get a beam. It didn't give that effect at all. It was just a single, isolated light, extremely bright.

ZEIDMAN: What was its trajectory? A straight flight path, or . . .

JEZZI: Linear. Its course was linear. Now, it was mentioned that there was a greenish light that colored the aircraft, that turned the Huey green for a moment as it went by. I didn't see that or sense it, and I think that since the cockpit has a greenhouse—a green Plexiglas roof—that was the effect we saw. There was conversation while it was happening that it was stopping over the helicopter, that it hovered, but I didn't see that. I hadn't caught sight of it yet.

HYNEK: How long was it in view? How long did it . . .

JEZZI: Minutes. The whole episode was over in minutes.

HYNEK: The length of time you saw it . . .

JEZZI: It's hard to say. From when I first caught sight of it and followed it to the horizon, it's hard to say whether it was a minute or 30 seconds. The whole episode took place in minutes. Maybe two? Maybe more. For my part, I saw it, I'd say, for from 30 seconds to a minute.

ZEIDMAN: Well, you've never established how fast it was going.

JEZZI: I don't know the approach speed because I didn't see it, but as it receded it was going faster than the 250 knot limit for aircraft under 10,000—faster than 250 knots but not as fast as 600 knots, the speed that the others reported as the approach speed. I will say that it was moving faster than normal traffic at that low altitude. Closer to the 250 than the 600. In a way, I'm kind of the oddball in this situation because I couldn't see over to the right, and I really didn't see the first part, what the others saw.

ZEIDMAN: Were you aware of the dive, and the climb?

JEZZI: I was aware of the dive. Your stomach went. Because Coyne really grabbed it from me. You could tell he was concerned. He was much more aware of the proximity of the object than I was. I hadn't seen it. I wasn't aware of the climb at all—and 1,000 fpm—it could have been less. It was not that much of a climb, that steep, that much acceleration. But the climbing is something that occurs somewhat easily in a helicopter if you're not paying attention. If you're flying the aircraft and thinking of something else. We were talking rapidly about what was happening. You get excited and you just go like this [demonstrates by raising left arm] and you're climbing. And going from 1,500 to 3,000 feet in two or three minutes is not going to be extraordinary. There are thermals that are so bad that you put your collective down and you're still climbing. I've had it happen to me.

ZEIDMAN: Do you think Larry was responsible for the climb?

JEZZI: I don't know. Larry said, "Son of a gun, it pulled us up!"

ZEIDMAN: You weren't following through [on the controls]. . . .

JEZZI: No, I didn't have the controls. I don't know what he did. I saw the altitude. I recall it was over 3,000, it could have been 3,500 feet, and we were still talking, still trying to get Mansfield on the radio. I'm pretty sure it [the object] had disappeared by then because it faded out, and I immediately looked back over [at the instruments] and that's when I caught the altitude. The object must have been gone by then because while I could still see it, I was looking at it.

HYNEK: Now sort of lean back and take a deep breath and try to recall—take as much time as you want—and recall the conversation just after it happened.

JEZZI: After it disappeared? Well, I recall Coyne's comment about the different light colorations. And the word "cigar-like shape" came out at that time. And they talked that it appeared to hover over us. Of course, there was a lot of "What the hell was it?" and "We almost got killed," and then they talked about the climb. Was the climb the result of the vacuum the other aircraft left? I don't know. It's hard to really explain. I really did not see what the others did see. The thing that really grabs me, it was so spontaneous. The remarks in the cockpit, the dialogue was so spontaneous. There was something there, and it was different. That these people, who had been flying a long time, couldn't identify it. The light didn't vary in color or intensity all the time I saw it, even as it went away from us. It was very bright. It was different from an air navigation light. As I said, it was just like a little ball. . . .

ZEIDMAN: Going back to the radio malfunction, to what do you attribute the radio malfunction? Was that an unusual event?

JEZZI: In that unit, no. It happened from time to time. Because our maintenance, our avionics, were not that good. Things like—you'd have poor transmission and then all of a sudden it came in, or it was garbled. So I don't know if it was part of the incident or not. We had VHF. Some of the birds didn't have the two radios, and I recall it was always hard to transmit and receive on UHF because everybody prefers VHF civilian-wise, but we tried to receive on the VOR and transmit on UHF, et cetera, Fox Mike, the whole thing, and we couldn't get contact until very close to Cleveland.

ZEIDMAN: Do you know anything about the magnetic compass malfunctioning?

JEZZI: Oh, yes. Triple-four's magnetic compass was never the same afterwards. Whether it was like that before I don't know.

ZEIDMAN: Larry says the compass was changed, replaced.

JEZZI: Yeah, they did that, I recall. I know they did that after the incident. That mag compass never worked.

ZEIDMAN: He said the RMI was fine.

JEZZI: Yeah. But that's true about the mag compass. But I think the new one was goofy, too. It was funny because I did fly that aircraft months later, and it would do a 360 without any reason at all. . . .

ZEIDMAN: Wait a minute. You flew Triple-four months later and the new compass didn't work?

JEZZI: The new compass was still bad. You could check the records. . . .

ZEIDMAN: I've asked Larry for the records. He says he can't find them.

JEZZI: Huh. Strange. The records are supposed to stay.

ZEIDMAN: Right, stay with the aircraft for the life of the aircraft.* While all this was going on, was there any particular time when you were especially worried about what was going on?

JEZZI: No. Well, I was worried about this approaching object or whatever it was, because I couldn't see it.

ZEIDMAN: They thought you were going to have a collision.

---

*Jezzi and I were both wrong. I have since been informed by the head of avionics at the helicopter maintenance facility that records of minor instrument changes are only kept for sixty days.

JEZZI: I didn't experience that because I never saw how close it was until after it had crossed over. So I have no idea how close we came.

HYNEK: Do you think it has a natural explanation?

JEZZI: Well, I was trying to figure out if it was an aircraft or a jet with a navigational light problem, and if it were flying, let's say, from southeast to northwest, which is really what happened—and the angle—and if he's flying that way, and we're going to see the left wing light first, red, okay?

ZEIDMAN: But if he were having a problem, and all *your* lights were working, he wouldn't come straight at you, he'd try to *avoid* you.

JEZZI: Sure, and there is no reason to think he didn't see us. According to what the others said, he was acting like he deliberately—er, that he *did* see us. But the thing is the aft light. And the discrepancy I see here is that it was very, very bright for an aft light.

And we didn't see a strobe or a rotating beacon, either. Which is an FAA regulation. You've got to have it to fly at night. But the lighting [configuration] shoots my whole theory down. If it was a high-performance aircraft, it must have had a nut for a pilot. The lights were all wrong, and only 500 feet above the hills? At night? I'd hate to do that with a Lear at that speed.

ZEIDMAN: Was there any noise or any turbulence?

JEZZI: No, none. But you said about being worried. We flew back to Cleveland and almost ran out of gas. Had nine gallons of fuel left in our Huey.* We had flown 12 minutes into the 20-minute fuel-warning light. That's what really scared me the most, the fuel problem. I had my shoulder harness locked, and I was praying. I knew it was going to be close. We got clearance from Cleveland, and we came right on in.

I came back to the airport on Saturday to fly for an extra

---

*When asked later about this point, Coyne said that he had been unaware of the "nine gallon" figure, although he realized he was using more fuel than usual, hightailing it back to Cleveland. Jezzi did not give his source for the fuel measurement.

training period, and at that time Coyne was talking to a reporter from a Cleveland paper. He had a picture of the cigar-shaped object with the slight cockpit and the thick light on the bottom and a kind of red nose. Bob Yanacsek came in later that day with the same picture, and it was interesting—the coincidence that two people drew the same thing. Yanacsek had just come in so I don't think, I don't know, if they had compared them before.

THE GROUND WITNESSES

Recognizing the potential value of locating ground witnesses to the event, the Civil Commission on Aerial Phenomena (CCAP), a small group of technically oriented central Ohio people interested in UFOs, had published in the *Mansfield News Journal* of August 19, 1976, a story reviewing the Coyne case and calling for witnesses to come forth. That same evening, Warren Nicholson, CCAP director, received a long-distance call from Charles C.,* a youth who claimed that he, his mother, and his siblings had witnessed the event. Within a few days, Nicholson and his associate William E. Jones conducted an extensive interview with the family.

On a second extensive interview, Nicholson was accompanied by CCAP investigators John Lenihan (a police helicopter pilot) and Tim Wegner. My follow-up interview consisted of a nearly two-hour session with the family at the site. Nicholson remains the principal investigator of the ground witnesses, and the preponderance of the following quoted material is excerpted from his tapes. To preserve continuity and clarify the sequence of events, I have integrated verbatim quotes from both my tapes and the Nicholson transcripts into a chronological narrative.

---

* His mother requested that the family's name not be published.

At approximately 10:40 P.M. on October 18, 1973, Mrs. C. left the Mansfield home of her mother-in-law to return to her own home in rural Ashland County. (Locations relevant to the ground-witness testimony may be found on the map, Figure 29-9.) Accompanying her were her three children: Charles, then aged thirteen; Camille, eleven; and Curt, ten. Also in the car was Karen B., thirteen, a stepsister of Mrs. C.'s husband. They were all aware of the current flurry of UFO activity in the central Ohio area and the subject had been mentioned earlier in the evening.

As they drove south on Laver Road at a speed of approximately 35 mph, a bright red light caught the attention of Mrs. C., Camille, Charlie, and Karen. Curt's view was obstructed (see Figure 29-10 for seating arrangement). The light was at two o'clock high when first seen. It seemed, Mrs. C. said, to be at medium altitude, and was flying south, paralleling Laver

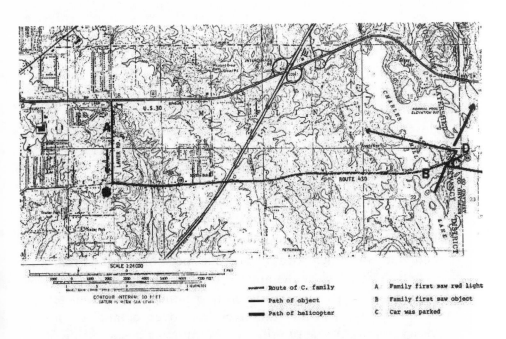

Figure 29-9. Map: U.S. Geological Survey, Pavonia, Ohio, quadrangle.

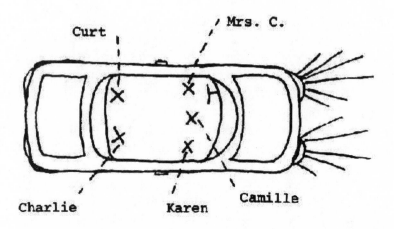

Figure 29-10. Positions of ground witnesses within the car.

Road. The family's attention was attracted to it only because it was a single steady light, decidedly brighter than a star or a plane. The speed of the light was "about that of a jet," and as it proceeded ahead of them it remained just the one steady red light—no other colors, no strobe, no rotating beacon. The red light pursued its southerly course and had already disappeared from view over the trees at the intersection where Laver Road ends at Route 430 by the time the car had reached that point.

The family's next increment of travel was eastward, from the intersection of Laver Road and Route 430, to the Route 430 bridge over the Charles Mill Reservoir, a distance of 3.6 miles, which they covered in approximately five minutes, steadily descending toward the lake at an average speed of about 45 mph.

The last 500 feet of the approach to the bridge is desolate, flat, and swampy. The road berm is trimmed back about ten feet and then brush and tall trees take over, a tangled, uninviting terrain. A line of utility poles follows the south side of the road.

As they entered that portion of the road they saw ahead in their one o'clock position (almost due east) a red and a green light, moving together, coming down rapidly toward them. They first thought it was a light plane, flying low over the lake, but changed their minds almost immediately; the red was too bright, especially compared to the green.

"It looked like a big red light. It wasn't flashing," Mrs. C. told Nicholson. "The red light appeared to be more toward the front. The lights stayed on; they never flashed."

Mrs. C. began to slow the car.

There was general agreement among the children that the red light was the brighter of the two and that it appeared to be the leading, forward light. They could see no shape to the object, and no noise was discernible at that time.

As the car slowed down, the lights appeared to move more slowly and farther to the right, to the car's two to three o'clock position. "It looked like at one time that it stood still," Mrs. C. reported.

The space between the lights increased as their distance from the car appeared to decrease. Camille reported that just before the lights moved out of her view to the right, she could make out a shape. Her drawing (Figure 29-11) shows a domed shape with a yellow light, the only yellow light mentioned by any of the witnesses. There was strong agreement that at this point the object seemed almost stationary.

Now with the car halted at the roadside but with the motor and lights still on, Mrs. C., Camille, and Charlie became aware of a second group of lights, some of them flashing, approaching from behind them (the southwest). At this point they became aware of noise for the first time. Mrs. C. thought the two sets of lights were helicopters about to crash.

CHARLES: There was a whole bunch of noise.

JONES: What kind of noise was it?

CHARLES: A bunch of racket. It was sort of rattling, like tin or a knocking sound [raps on table].

JONES: Where did the noise come from?

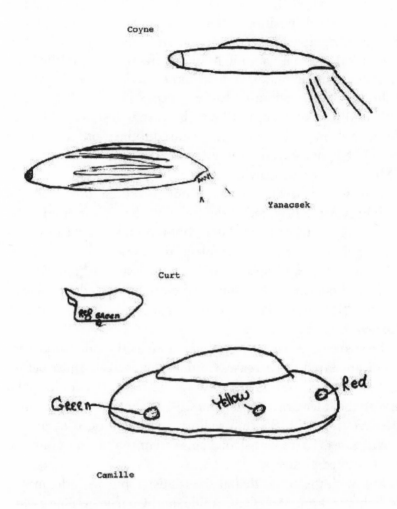

Figure 29-11. Witnesses' drawings of object.

CHARLES: Up in the sky. It was like beating the air.[*]

According to Mrs. C., Charles and Camille, twisting around in the car, could see through the side windows that the steady-lighted object and the object with flashing lights were con-

[*]An excellent description of the very distinctive sound of a Huey helicopter.

verging. The witnesses believe it was at about this point that they first realized that a helicopter was involved.

MRS. C.: The one object went over the top of the other one. And then it stopped.

NICHOLSON: Did any of the lights appear to be a streak? By a streak I mean if you take a sparkler and move it very fast through the air and you see a sort of streak through the air, or did it appear to be more of a pinpoint type of light?

MRS. C.: There was no streaking to them at all.

NICHOLSON: Are you sure? Did it move so fast that a streak . . .

MRS. C.: No. Neither one did.

JONES: What color was this object?

MRS. C.: What do you mean?

JONES: What color did you see from it?

MRS. C.: Just the red and the green.

JONES: Do you mean from the helicopter?

MRS. C.: No, from the object above the helicopter.

JONES: Were the red and the green the same size?

MRS. C.: No, the green light seemed smaller. It was not of the same brightness.

JONES: The green was smaller?

MRS. C.: Yes. There are different versions. I know the kids have seen something. . . . They say they see something a little different than I do, but I'm just telling you what I saw. We parked down here by the bridge. The helicopter seemed to be coming basically from the south or southwest and the object was also basically south of me.

After probably less than thirty seconds of watching the objects, and over the mother's protestations, Karen and Charlie piled out of the car and stood by the right rear fender. Karen did not want to leave the car, but was forced to by Charles in his zeal to get out of the two-door vehicle. The illustration (Figure 29-12) drawn by co-investigator Allan Hendry is based upon the witnesses' description and a photo of the site taken by Nicholson.

Figure 29-12. The ground witnesses' observation
(drawing by Allan Hendry).

CHARLES: When we got out of the car it was right there, sitting there [standing outside of the car at the site, pointing toward the southwest].

ZEIDMAN: How long did it remain stationary?

CHARLES: Two minutes. No. Not even that long. And it was longways, like this [indicates that horizontal axis of object was toward observers].

ZEIDMAN: Hold something at arm's length. How big would it be? Would a dime cover it? [Hands Karen a dime.]

KAREN: [Holds dime at arm's length.] Oh, bigger.

ZEIDMAN: Well, there's the sun. While it's behind the cloud, take a quick squint at it. Was the thing bigger than the sun?

CHARLES: Bigger than that. It was a big ol' thing.

KAREN: Yeah.

ZEIDMAN: Describe it to me.

CHARLES: It was something like a blimp. Shaped like a blimp.

ZEIDMAN: What color was it? Tell me if it was painted—like the whole thing was painted, or was the whole thing glowing? Were the edges fuzzy or sharp?

CHARLES: You couldn't see them. I mean you could see them, but it was dark, and you couldn't tell how it was built.

Charles had described the shape to Nicholson as "long and kind of round. It would be kind of pear-shaped with the big part of the pear facing toward you. The light seemed to be coming from the bottom." Karen had mentioned that the light "seemed to come from the side or the back," and that at one point after the object and helicopter converged they appeared to move together westward "for a little ways" (estimated less than 100 feet) parallel to the road. She was the only one who reported this motion.

Throughout the three interviews, Charles and Karen repeatedly mentioned a flare-up of the green light.

CHARLES: When we got out, everything was green. I saw that thing and the helicopter.

KAREN: Everything turned green.

CHARLES: It lit up everything green. It couldn't have been no higher than . . . it was a great big thing. I don't know exactly how high it was. . . . It was a great big thing. There was a whole bunch of noise. We were driving out 430, going home, and all of a sudden we heard this noise and I looked up and out the back window. . . .

NICHOLSON: Was the light a flash or was it long-lasting?

CHARLES: We saw the green light for ten seconds. Not very high. Maybe 500 feet. It was a light, dull green. I know it sounds crazy, but it was a light, dull green. Everything just turned green. I think the green came from above the helicopter. It kind of looked like rays coming down.

KAREN: We wanted to go home and lock the doors. We were scared.

NICHOLSON: [In the second interview] When it lit up green, did it light up the whole countryside or just the immediate area?

CHARLES: It was so bright that you couldn't see too far. It just seemed that right around us . . . it was . . . everything was green. The trees, the car, everything.

NICHOLSON: Do you remember what color the helicopter was?

CHARLES: Green.

NICHOLSON: Why was it green?

CHARLES: Because of the light from the thing up above! I think I could see windows in the helicopter.

WEGNER: Did the thing above the helicopter remind you of anything you have ever seen before or on TV, or in a movie, or anything like that?

CHARLES: Uh-uh [negative]—except maybe a school bus.

WEGNER: Was the helicopter bigger or smaller or the same size as the object?

CHARLES: The helicopter was smaller.

NICHOLSON: Do you remember seeing anyone fishing [in the nearby lake]?

CHARLES: No, I don't remember seeing anyone fishing. You couldn't see too far, anyhow. Everything was just so green from it, you could only see a short way 'cause it was just so bright.

NICHOLSON: Where was the helicopter in relation to the thing?

CHARLES: Just barely ahead and below—the helicopter was ahead and below. And then the helicopter seemed to pass over us and we looked around and couldn't see the thing then. It was gone. It was just gone. When the light went out you couldn't see the object.

WEGNER: You couldn't see it anymore? Did it fly off?

CHARLES: I don't know. It was just gone. And then we saw this helicopter fly across the road.

WEGNER: What direction was the helicopter going?

CHARLES: Northeast. The helicopter went northeast. Then we got back in the car and went on. The thing could have been right overhead. I don't know. We got back into the car and then we saw it [the helicopter] fly out over the lake.

ZEIDMAN: [In the third interview] Were you already back in the car when it crossed the road? Did you actually see it cross the road?

KAREN: When we got back in the car it started.

ZEIDMAN: How far back of you did it cross the road?

CURT: Just beyond those trees [estimated 100 to 150 feet].

ZEIDMAN: Did it cast any reflection on the road?

KAREN: Uh-huh [affirmative].

CAMILLE: A green light.

CHARLES: Everything was green.

CURT: We looked back and it was crossing the road. It kept coming at us and getting bigger and then it crossed the road. Then the car started moving and it seemed like it followed us.

CHARLES: We looked back and it was gone!

CURT: Uh-uh [negative]. It didn't! When we started going we looked around and we could see it over there [out left side of car]. It was going just like that [indicating that it appeared to be pacing the car].

CHARLES: Following the car—it was just gone.

CURT: [Negative sound] We turned around and *saw* it, heading out that way, toward Mansfield. We were going faster, all right. It just flew off and got smaller and smaller toward the northwest.

MRS. C.: We were scared.

CURT: When it went back toward Mansfield it went behind the trees; that's the way it disappeared. I saw it go back. I didn't see it turn around. It just stopped and went back.

ZEIDMAN: It reversed itself?

CURT: It just went backward.

CAMILLE: [In the third interview] That light was so bright, when Charlie was standing outside. But nobody else could see it.

ZEIDMAN: What do you mean, Camille?

CAMILLE: When we were looking up there, and Charlie was

standing outside, that light seemed to be so bright, but nobody else around here could see it. [No one else reported it.—J.Z.]

CHARLES: You should have been able to see that light from *anywhere.*

CURT: *Miles!*

CAMILLE: It was high up when we first saw it, and then it came down lower. When it was beside us it was about the same as the trees.

Charles and Karen said they were out of the car for about a minute and that the green flare-up lasted about ten seconds. Mrs. C. estimated the total time the car was actually stopped as "not over a couple of minutes." She remembers the green light, but not an intense flare. Her comment that the red light was brighter than the green refers to the appearance of the object as it approached from the east. When the two objects were at a relatively high angular elevation behind the car, her view was obstructed. She was becoming quite apprehensive by that time, was worried about the two children outside the car, and she thought she was looking forward, eastward across the bridge, in the hope (vain) that other road traffic would appear. Although both helicopter and object were seen separately after they diverged, the actual break-off of the two objects was reported by no one. The testimony, however, suggests that the divergence occurred close in time to when the two objects crossed the road. When last seen by Curt and Charlie, the group of lights they identified as the helicopter was proceeding alone northeast over the lake—at a higher altitude than when previously seen south of the road. Curt's attention and angle of view were directed primarily toward the departing object; Charlie, in the midsection of the car, could see best toward the northeast.

COMMENTARY ON THE GROUND WITNESSES' TESTIMONY

Throughout the three interviews with the ground witnesses, there was a constant lively exchange among them. The observers were not trying to please the investigators or each other, especially concerning the motions of helicopter and object during the period when the two objects were crossing the road. This is not surprising since the witnesses' attentions were variously focused upon reentering the car (Charles and Karen) and looking out the right window (Camille), the rear window (Curt), and the front windshield (Mrs. C.). The ground-witness tapes have been repeatedly reviewed and there exists not the slightest hint of collusion between the mother and the four children. At no time in the three interviews did the mother "coach" the children into a response; she listened to their reports and presented her own, regardless of variation. No one in the family used the terms "UFO" or "flying saucer" in describing the event; usually they referred to "the object" or "the thing."

At no time throughout the more than five hours of the three interviews was there any indication that the thought of remuneration or publicity had ever entered their minds. The family was in domestic upheaval and Mrs. C. was adamant that she did not want to "make waves." Had it not been for the newspaper story and Charles's assertiveness in phoning Nicholson (a toll call), they never would have reported the incident at all; indeed, before the newspaper story mentioning Nicholson, they had no idea where to report it.

The use of "leading questions" in the three interviews could have provided ample opportunity for the witnesses to agree with the previously suggested responses: that the object moved fast enough to cause a "streak"; that the object was "cigar-shaped," as illustrated and described in the newspaper article; that the object was glowing; or that it reminded the witnesses of something in a movie or on TV. However, all of these "suggestions" were rejected.

Nicholson and Jones met with Mrs. C.'s mother-in-law at the

time of the first interview. She corroborated that the witnesses had told her of the incident within a few days of its occurrence. I met with her also, and to me she said, "They've been telling the same story all along. Everything lit up—that's what she [Karen] told me."

THE SOUND-AND-LIGHT WITNESSES

Fifteen years after the event and nine years after the initial publication of this report, two additional witnesses, albeit indirect ones, were interviewed. During the interim, there had been several leads suggesting other witnesses, but follow-ups and evaluations had been unproductive. Then in 1988, the serendipitous occurred. John Timmerman (a CUFOS vice president) and Jennie Zeidman, manning a traveling CUFOS photo exhibit, were approached at the Mansfield mall by a mother and son, Jeanne and John Elias.

On the evening of October 18, 1973, Mrs. Jeanne Elias had gone to bed and was propped up watching the eleven o'clock news. She remembers the date precisely because it was her younger son's birthday and there had been a family party that day. Her husband had retired earlier and was already asleep. Suddenly she heard loud helicopter noise. "We are right in the path of the landing for Mansfield airport," she said, "and the planes fly over our house, and I was very nervous about those planes, because once in a while they fly over very low, and our house is on an elevation." The helicopter seemed so close that—fearing it was about to crash into the house—"I stuck my head under the pillow so if it crashed I could maybe save part of me."

Just then John, then fourteen, called to her from his room. When she went in to see him, he asked if she had seen "the green light." She said no, that she had had her head under the pillow. John said, "The whole room lit up green." He had not gotten out of bed to determine its source. When presented with the extensive set of color-cards carried by Zeidman in her investigator kit, John identified exactly the same shade as that identified by the other ground witnesses.

The Elias house (twice visited by Zeidman) is 1.75 miles southwest of the ground-witness location. It is undetermined what the helicopter's airspeed was at the precise moment it passed over the Elias house. However, it must have been (according to two separate testimonies by Coyne) between 90 and 100 knots. At 90 knots, the helicopter would have reached the Charles Mill Reservoir site in approximately 60 seconds. If the speed was 100 knots, the 1.75 miles would have been covered in about 55 seconds. The "green spotlight" phase of this encounter must have endured for a minimum of 55 seconds.

Table 29-1. Comparison of Observer Testimony

Observer/ Interviewer	Observer Looking Through	Object Shape/ Appearance	Approach color	Departure Color	Departure Duration	Movement of Object at Closest Point	Movement of Green Light	Shape of Green Light
Coyne to Hynek and to Zeidman	Front wind-shield	Cigar; distinct sharp edges	Red	White	Still in view when 3500' alt. noticed	Stopped momentarily	Swung 90° into cockpit	Pyramid
Healey to Zeidman/ Evans	Both front end upper windows	Oval/ cigar, solid	Red	White	A couple of minutes	Nearly stopped	No movement seen	Triangular cone
Jezzi to Zeidman/ Hynek	Upper window	Ball of intense light	View obstructed	White	30 secs. to a min.	Very slow	No green seen	Not seen
Yanacsek to Zeidman	Upper window and Front window	Light Solid, submarine	Red	White	Between 30 secs. and a minute	Stopped for 10-12 seconds	Swung into aircraft	Wide and intense
Ground witnesses to Nicholson and Zeidman	Car windows, open air	Pear, blimp, solid	Red	Not stated	View obscured by tree	Stationary at least 30 seconds	Not stated	Like rays coming down

POINTS OF SIMILARITY AND DISSIMILARITY

It is apparent from the previous testimony that there is substantial agreement among air and ground witnesses concerning the major aspects of the event. Table 29-1 compares the various facets of observer testimony.

Points of Similarity

1. The date was October 18, 1973, the time a few minutes past 11:00 P.M.
2. The location was east of Mansfield, Ohio, east of I-71, and east of the Mansfield NDB (see Figure 29-8).
3. The helicopter approached from the southwest.
4. The object approached from east-southeast.
5. The steady red light was on the front of the object.
6. There was a short-lived bright green flare or beam of unusual nature.
7. Except for a few seconds of green flare-up, the red light was the predominant one.
8. The object was not entirely symmetrical.
9. The object assumed a position over the helicopter.
10. The helicopter did not deviate; its last direction was northeast.
11. The object's last reported direction of travel was northwest.
12. The flight path of the object as described by the ground witnesses corresponds to its flight path based upon the crew testimony.

The portion of the object's flight path described by the ground observers as "crossing the road" and "following the car eastward" at first appears to be a discrepancy with respect to the crew testimony. However, it is easily shown to be a point of corroboration, and it is listed as Point 12 above. To the crew within the moving helicopter, the motion of the object was perceived as (1) approaching from the east, (2) decelerating/hovering, and (3) resuming a westward course. The crew did not distinguish the actual forward motion of the object; it was perceived by them as the hovering phase of the event. Figure 29-9 and Figure 29-13 below show these components of the object's flight path; they are also easily demonstrated by taking one's two hands and describing the linear motion of the helicopter (left hand) and the "zigzag" motion of the object (right hand). Curt's report that the object "seemed like it followed us" (paced the car eastward for a short distance) can now be shown to be a product of the object's flight path northeast relative to the east-northeast path of the car. (I am indebted to Mr. Philip J. Klass, who first brought this to my attention by pronouncing it a discrepancy.)

A separate point of coincidence, apart from the actual UFO/helicopter encounter at the Route 430 bridge, is the steady red light observed as the C. family was driving south on Laver Road. That incident preceded the Route 430 encounter

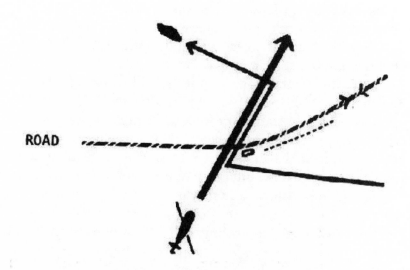

ROAD

Figure 29-13. Object's zigzag flight path.

by five minutes or more. Healey had observed a single red light flying south, off to his left, "three to four" minutes before Yanacsek's first mention of the red light on the southeast horizon.

Dissimilarities

Jezzi's account is somewhat different from those of the other eight witnesses. Because his view was obstructed by Coyne's body, Jezzi came in "in the middle" of the event, at the point when the object was just passing the helicopter's meridian. From that point on, all four crewmen reported only a bright white light heading off to the northwest. At the time the others were exclaiming that the object was stopping, it had not yet entered Jezzi's view.

Considering only the last portion of the event, the difference between Jezzi's account and the others' involves the object's course (Jezzi described it as linear, Coyne and Healey reported a 45° turn near the western horizon), and the point in time of the disappearance. (Jezzi said it disappeared just before he looked at the altimeter and became aware of the climb, whereas Coyne stated that the object was still easily in view after he noted the 3,500 feet altimeter reading.)

Another discrepancy involves the ground witnesses who testified that both helicopter and object, after their convergence, appeared to remain stationary for a discernible period of time, perhaps even several seconds, before they started to cross Route 430. The aircrew was unaware of this. Their attentions were solidly focused upon the unknown object/light as it appeared in front of and above them, and they assumed their machine was progressing forward at a speed of approximately 100 knots. I would not discount the possibility that "the objects remained stationary" increment was a misperception by the ground witnesses of the flight paths of helicopter and object at the point where the helicopter was in transition from dive to climb, and it and the object were moving essentially on line of sight toward the observers.

Karen B., on the ground, described both the aircraft and the object moving westward "a little ways," later estimated as less than 100 feet. She was the only one to report that motion.

THE UNKNOWN OBJECT

The characteristics of the unknown object that preclude its identification in terms of known phenomena are its appearance, its motion, the length of time it was visible, and the peculiar nature of a green light on its aft portion. The crew's first assumption was that it was a plane, though other commentators have advanced the hypothesis of a meteor to explain the event.

Appearance

The unknown object appeared only as a red light during the first portion of the event. At the closest approach to the helicopter, its appearance was that of a solid, cigar- or oval-shaped, gray, metallic structure, slightly domed, with sharply defined edges. The silhouette of the object blotted out the background stars. Charlie C., on the ground, described it as "like a blimp," "kind of pear-shaped," "a big ol' thing." Coyne, Healey, and Yanacsek all reported three precisely positioned lights: red emanating from the nose, a green "beam" with maneuverable spotlight capabilities emanating from the under/aft portion of the structure, and a bright white light, which came from the "tail" of the object. The ground witnesses reported the red nose and green beam lights. Jezzi, who did not witness the object's approach, concurred with his crewmates that during the departure phase, only the bright white light was visible.

The Distance/Size of the Object

With an unfamiliar object of unknown dimensions, it is impossible to arrive at any accurate estimate of size or distance, unless a familiar object of known dimension can be seen in direct relationship to the unknown.

What is curious in this case is the agreement in the estimate of each crew member on the size and distance of the object. Both Coyne and Healey stated it was about 60 feet in length (about the size of their helicopter), 100 feet above, and 500 feet away. Jezzi described it as a light 100 feet above and 500 feet in front of the helicopter (see Figure 29-14).

According to Coyne, the object at its closest point (in front of and slightly above the helicopter) "filled an entire front windshield panel" (see Figure 29-15). For Healey, crouching between the seats, it seemed to fill both windshield panels. Yanacsek said that it easily filled one windshield panel, and he thought that had he been sitting in the front seat, it would have filled both windows.

Determination of the distance and size of the object was attempted by graphical methods using the distance from the observers' eyes to points on the precisely measurable windshield panel. Measurements from Yanacsek's position (twisting and cringing to the left) and from Healey's (crouching behind the front seats) were considered, but found too variable for this purpose. Coyne's position in the front seat was more reliably measured, and those figures produced an angle of view (for Coyne) of approximately 75 degrees (see Figure 29-16).

The relationships between length of an object and distance (in feet) from an observer for objects that subtend an angle of 75 degrees are as follows:

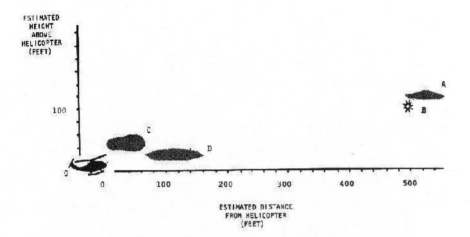

A Coyne and Healey described object as 100' above and 500' in front of helicopter and 60' in length.

B Jezzi described intense white ball of light as 100' above and 500' in front.

C Ground witnesses saw helicopter and object in relationship to one another.

D Apparent object size measured against window frame suggests length of 100' and distance of 65.'

Figure 29-14. Four perspectives of object-helicopter relationship.

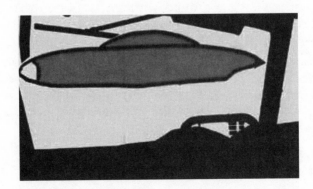

Figure 29-15. Coyne's drawing of object superimposed on a photo of the windshield.

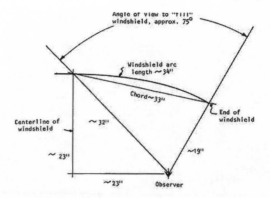

Figure 29-16. Geometrical relationship of length
that "filled windshield" to distance.

Overall length of object	Distance from observer to object
20	13
60	39
100	65
300	195
767	500

Thus it is suggested that the "500 feet away and 60 feet long" estimates provided by Coyne, Healey, and Jezzi are not compatible with the more objective figures obtained through trigonometric computation and the direct visual report of the ground witnesses. The ground witnesses reported that the object and the helicopter were close together, one essentially over the other, and although they reported that the UFO was "larger than the helicopter," none of them reported that it was "much larger," as would be indicated on the table for a 500-foot distance. An approximate distance of 65 feet and a linear size of approximately 100 feet best fits the distance and proportions described by the ground witnesses.

Motion

The reported motion of the object can best be shown by listing the various increments of its flight path:

Table 29-2. Reported Motion of Object

Motion	Observer(s)	Est. Speed
Light appeared stationary on horizon (did not change relationship with helicopter)	Yanacsek Coyne	
Light appeared to turn toward helicopter	Yanacsek	
Light appeared to be rapidly approaching	Yanacsek Coyne Healey Ground witnesses	600 kts
Object appeared to decelerate or actually stop as it passed closest to helicopter (course and speed decreased to match that of helicopter)	Yanacsek Coyne Healey Ground witnesses	0 kts
Object moved from S to N side of road at an oblique angle to approach path	Ground witnesses	slow
Object flew off to NW	Crew Jezzi	> 250 kts
Object made 45-degree turn before disappearance	Coyne Healey	

Thus both aircrew and ground witness testimony indicate that during continuous observation the object exhibited flight trajectories that included precise hard-angle turns and an apparent range of speed from zero to 600 knots. Both characteristics disqualify it for identification in terms of a natural phenomenon.

Duration of the Observation

How long was the object under observation? Table 29-2 presents the various increments of the encounter based upon analysis of witness testimony, and Table 29-3 translates those increments into movement through space.

Consistently, Coyne has stated that the object was still visible after he noticed the climb, and even until the helicopter was again descending to cruising altitude. At variance is Jezzi's recollection that the object disappeared immediately before he noticed the altimeter. Jezzi had the better view to the west and he did not have the controls to contend with; however, more than three years had elapsed after the event before he was queried as to the specific details of the incident. The two men in the rear of the helicopter cannot contribute to this point: their attention was fixed upon the departing object; they were not concerned with the technicalities of the helicopter's flight or instruments; and they were unaware of the climb until Coyne brought it to their attention.

Thus it is the discrepancy between Coyne and Jezzi that provides the 60-second spread to the final segments of the event, and is responsible for the "15-second leveling off and regaining control" and the "10-second departure" increments in the Median column of Table 29-3.

The climb duration of 108 seconds is based upon the 1,700 feet-to-3,500 feet altimeter readings and the 1,000 feet per minute vertical ascent reading. It does not include the undetermined extra time necessary for acceleration into the climb from the level flight attitude.

Although in Table 29-3 and Figure 29-17 the climb duration is presented as an assumption, it actually reflects only a supposition. If the climb were a "normal" one (using the only "hard" figures we have—an 1,800-foot climb at 1,000 fpm), it must have taken longer than 108 seconds. Of course, if the climb were not normal—i.e., if the object had somehow affected the helicopter's flight—then theoretically the climb could have consumed any length of time.

Returning to the various crew testimonies, if Jezzi is correct, then the object disappeared after an elapsed time of approximately 275 seconds. If Coyne is correct, it could have remained in view for 330 seconds or even longer. The "compromise"

Table 29-3. Elapsed Time Analysis

Description	Estimated Time (seconds)		
	Short	Long	Median
Object Approach "It was so far away that I looked at it for some time before I mentioned it. I must have watched it for a minute, oh, a minute and a half, before I said anything" (Yanacsek).	30	90	60
"Yanacsek said, 'There's a red light on the horizon at about 3 o'clock—are there any radio towers over that way?' I told him to keep an eye on it" (Coyne).	10	15	13
"After approximately another 30 seconds, Yanacsek indicated that the light was converging on the helicopter" (Coyne on Report Form 2496).	15	30	30
Coyne looks over, evaluates, decides to take evasive action (Coyne).	5	5	5
Aircraft Descent 2500'- 1700'= 800' in two increments: 1st = 500 fpm, 2nd= 2000 fpm, as consistently reported by Coyne. Altitude change in each segment unknown.	24 18 (a)	48 12 (b)	36 15 (c)
Closest Point "It damn near came to a stop right over us." (Healey).	3	10	8
"It wasn't cruising, it was stopped for maybe 10-12 seconds, and I mean stopped" (Yanacsek).			
"It stopped over us, and then it just slowly moved" (Coyne).			
"The object came over the helicopter, and then it just stopped, for about 10 seconds" (ground witnesses).			
Aircraft Ascent From 1700' to 3500'= 1800' at 1000 fpm (Coyne).	108	108	108
Leveling, Regaining Control 3500' to "near 3800'" "From the bottom position, I had to pull it up [the collective], push it down, and then the helicopter seemed to bump like it hit turbulence" (Coyne).		20	15
Object Departure "But the thing was way to the west. It was already in the Mansfield area when we began to settle. The first people we made contact with was Akron Approach, and I could see this object that was moved away" (Coyne).		60	10
"I watched it depart for a couple of minutes" (Healey).			
Total	213	398	300

(a) 200' @ 500 fpm = 24s. (b) 400' @ 500 fpm = 48s. (c) 300' @ 500 fpm = 36s.
   600' @ 2000 fpm = 18s.   400' @ 2000 fpm = 12s.   500' @ 2000 fpm = 15s.

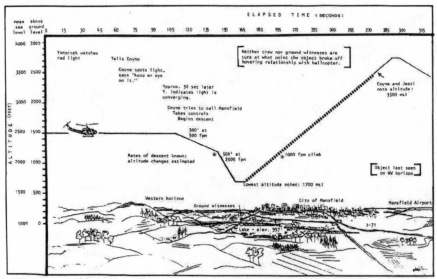

Figure 29-17. Length of observation from witnesses' accounts.

figure of "300 seconds ±30" takes into consideration Jezzi's statements that the object was traveling faster than 250 knots and slower than 600 knots, that he thought it was "closer to 250 than 600," and that he followed it all the way to the horizon. If we choose 350 knots as the object's departure speed, and 15 miles as the horizon distance, then a time of 134 seconds for the departure would be indicated. Healey, also on the left side of the helicopter, reported "a couple of minutes" as the departure time. Yanacsek said "30 seconds to a minute." The men sitting on the left side of the helicopter should probably be given higher observer ratings than Coyne, who was busy with the controls, or Yanacsek, whose view was interrupted by Jezzi's body and pieces of equipment.

The Beam of Green Light

The joint testimony indicates that just as the object reached the helicopter's "meridian," a green light on the aft underportion of the object became visible to Yanacsek, Coyne, and Healey. It was visible to the ground witnesses as the object approached. The green light became a beam while the object was in front of the helicopter. The beam appeared to travel upward across the helicopter nose and windshield, and when it reached the upper, tinted windows, the maximum effect was achieved and "everything turned green." Before that point, there was no glare effect and the object's shape was easily defined.

The most impressive aspect of the entire experience, Coyne said (as had Healey), was the peculiar quality of the green light that emanated from or near the indentation of the aft end of the otherwise symmetrical shape of the unknown craft:

COYNE: The aft engine light [*sic*] did not leave a trail, just a white, bright reflection that dissolved into the night. When the light of the green light penetrated into the night, it cut right through the night, the darkness, and it was definitely shaped like a pyramid. The further in length it went, the wider it got, whereas the white light dissolved into the darkness. You could see the white as the thing passed over us, but it became more apparent as it was moving away. The object moved very slowly away from us, and then it began to accelerate. As it began to accelerate, that white light became even brighter. Very bright.

ZEIDMAN: But still the same color?

COYNE: Oh, yes. Stayed white. Just brighter in intensity. And then when it turned, it became brighter and went over the horizon and just [snaps finger] went out. But the green light was definitely different. It cut through the night. Now, the night lights [the helicopter instrument lights], which are red—everything turned green in here. The light didn't come through here, where it's green [indicating overhead window panels]. It came through here [front windshield]. This green [upper panels] wouldn't make the red disappear.

Healey had also emphasized "a definitive cone, a light that stuck out at right angles . . . [which] opened up in a triangular shape . . . it wasn't a condensed beam." The young ground witnesses also had repeatedly mentioned the green light as the outstanding feature of their experience. Directly comparable to the statements of Coyne and Healey is Charlie's description: "It was like rays coming down."

PRELIMINARY EXPLANATORY HYPOTHESES

There are two obvious prosaic possible explanations for the reported phenomenon: The object was a meteor or the object was an aircraft. The following two sections consider these two possibilities in detail.

Possibility of High-Performance Aircraft

As the Huey flew northward from Columbus into the Mansfield area, Yanacsek and Healey, sitting in the rear seats facing outward, were charged with the normal procedure of observing and reporting any relevant traffic. The four men were well aware that they would be flying through a zone of possible low-altitude jet aircraft from the Mansfield Air National Guard base; they were also aware of the current flurry of UFO activity in the area, but were on a routine flight, which three of them had made many times before. Were they exceptionally alert or taking any particular precautions? I think not. Healey told me, in a tone of some apology, that he had been drowsy. Coyne described himself as "relaxing, smoking."

When Yanacsek first reported a red light, like an obstruction light on the southeast horizon, Coyne merely told him to "check it out," and the initial report created no interest. When Yanacsek subsequently reported that the light appeared to be moving toward them, Coyne became concerned, began actively observing the light, and called the Mansfield tower with his request for local traffic conditions.

As the light approached, all of the crew assumed it to be a high-performance aircraft—probably an F-100 from Mansfield.

As they dived evasively and the object decelerated, Coyne remembers yelling, "That's no F-100!"

Could the object have been a high-performance aircraft? Aspects of that possibility are presented in Table 29-4.

In addition, when Captain Coyne checked with the FAA, he could find no record of any other aircraft in the area, and the last known F-100 of the Mansfield Air National Guard landed at 10:47 P.M.

The object thus appears not to have been any kind of conventional aircraft.

The Meteor Hypothesis

A meteor, by commonly accepted definition, is the luminosity produced by the friction of air resistance as a meteoroid (a material particle) hurtles through the atmosphere, exciting and ionizing atoms along its path.

Appearance. A meteor trail is by its very nature diffuse and luminous. It does not appear opaque, blotting out the background of stars, or possess a precisely delineated structure, as was reported by the witnesses in the helicopter and on the ground. The red, white, and green lights were reported in precise positions on the object's structure. There were no reports of a diffuse, overall luminescence, trail effect, or lingering afterimage. Even Jezzi, who reported only an intense white light, reported no trail or general luminosity other than that from the concentrated light source itself.

Motion. The components of the object's motions are discussed in detail in this report. Obviously, the flight path of the object, with its rapid approach, deceleration, hovering, and departure at moderate speed as reported by both crew and ground witnesses, does not qualify as meteor behavior. A meteor, if very slow, if in orbit many tens of kilometers above the helicopter, and if (most important) it could "keep itself alive," would appear to climb halfway across the sky during the first increment alone; it would not maintain the same position on the horizon. (Witness the path of an artificial satellite as it crosses the celestial sphere.) Any object moving across the observer's line of

Table 29-4.
The Possibility of High-Performance Aircraft

Reported	However
1. Object approached at speed estimated at 600 kts, decelerated rapidly, hovered over helicopter as it moved forward, then passed off to the NW.	a. A fixed-wing aircraft would not have the capacity of decelerating from high velocity to hover or near-hover in only a few seconds. b. A helicopter would have the capacity of hovering, but would not be capable of the high forward speeds reported.
2. Object was at its slowest speed as it passed directly in front of and closest to the helicopter.	a. A fixed-wing aircraft moving across the line of sight at generally constant velocity would appear to move more rapidly when passing directly in front of an observer.
3. No noise or turbulence was noticed during the close approach of the object.	a. A conventional aircraft, if within 500 ft., would have produced noise heard inside the helicopter. b. The night was calm and the flight totally smooth. Any turbulence would have been noted as an anomaly.
4. Object was described by Coyne, Healey, Yanacsek, and ground witnesses as a smooth, cigar-shape, with slight dome on top, and lights. Jezzi reported no object, only a light.	a. At such close quarters, some of the features of a conventional aircraft should have been identifiable—wings, engine pods, windows, empennage, numbers.

Table 29-4 (continued)

Reported	However
5. Color configuration showed the red light leading.	a. No conventionally lighted aircraft carries a bright red light on its nose.
	b. In order for any fixed-wing aircraft to present the reported color configuration, the aircraft would have to have been flying:

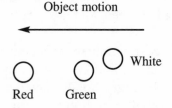

Object motion

Red   Green

Light positions

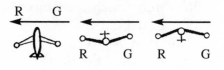

Top view   Tail view   Upside down, head-on

Reported	However
6. Unknown object had bright white light on aft portion.	a. Conventional aircraft may have white tail lights, but not of the exceptional brilliance or intensity described by crew members.
	b. Neither piston nor jet aircraft present bright white engine exhaust.
7. All lights on the object were constant.	a. FAA requires either a strobe or a rotating beacon on top or bottom of fuselage.
	b. The night was calm and the
8. The object was reported at speeds as high as 600 kts at an altitude as low as 1800 ft msl.	a. FAR Part 91 requires that below 10,000 ft mal no aircraft shall fly faster than 250 kts.

sight at a constant speed will appear to move most rapidly as it crosses directly in front of, and is closest to, the observer.

If the object were an exceptionally bright fireball (suggesting that it was at considerable altitude and distance from the observers), the question is raised why it was not reported, that clear balmy evening, by numerous observers as it passed so leisurely over the several-hundred-mile path of Pennsylvania, Ohio, Indiana, or Michigan, or even out over Lake Erie, where in the starry darkness dozens of ore freighter seamen must have been at the watch. To our knowledge, no bright meteors were reported at all that night over the many thousands of square miles from which the object—had it been at high altitude—would have been visible.

Duration. Meteors are short-lived phenomena. Once a meteor has entered the Earth's atmosphere, its fiery flight can endure for only a very few seconds. Average shower meteors are visible for less than two seconds; fireballs and bolides rarely last more than ten seconds. The Orionid meteor shower (associated with the orbit of Halley's comet), which occurs every year between October 18 and 23, is a relatively minor meteor shower characterized by swift streaks, persistent trains, and velocities of about 40 miles per second.

Meteors "ignite" and become visible at altitudes from 100 kilometers down to about 80 kilometers (60 to 50 miles). For an observer essentially at sea level, objects between 80 and 100 kilometers (60 and 80 miles) could theoretically be visible over flight paths from 720 to 1,150 kilometers (446 to 713 miles) in radius. For meteors at the altitude of 80 kilometers (50 miles), an Orionid at 66 kilometers per second (41 miles per second) could theoretically cross the sky in less than 22 seconds; a sporadic meteor traveling at the average meteor velocity of 40 kilometers per second (25 miles per second) could traverse the entire sky in less than 36 seconds, and an extremely slow fireball with a velocity of 12 kilometers per second (7.4 miles per second) could theoretically cross the entire visible sky in about 110 seconds.

But theory and reality are not always compatible. All of the above figures are based upon the premises that a meteor head could maintain its altitude of entry, could stay in a circular orbit without decay, and could continue to burn without disintegration, for more than 2,300 kilometers (1,400 miles). Empirical evidence corroborated by radar measurements indicate that these phenomena do not occur. Meteors are not observed to travel 180° from horizon to horizon. Faint (shower) meteors have a usual path length of only about 60 kilometers (87 miles); bright meteors may have a path length of up to 300 kilometers (186 miles), but in fact to be visible they must be within 150 to 200 kilometers (90 to 125 miles) of the observer. Angular velocities average about 20° per second.

I consulted extensively on this problem with Dr. William M. Protheroe, professor of astronomy at Ohio State University, who supplied the formulae and checked their application to the flight times of meteors. Dr. Hynek also considered this problem. Their conclusion is that the generally accepted time for longest meteor head visibility, under the most favorable conditions, would be of the order of 30 to 40 seconds.

Thus the appearance of the object, the nature of its motion, and the length of time it remained visible all provide grave difficulties for a meteor hypothesis as an explanation for the reported events.

During the nineteen years since the publication of this report, there has been (to my knowledge) only one published objector to the "Coyne case" as exemplifying a genuine unidentified (i.e., unexplainable) flying object. Within a few days of its occurrence, Philip Klass, an aviation journalist, propounded that the object was merely "a bolide of the Orionid meteor shower." Klass maintains that position to this day. Repeatedly asked to submit a second-by-second time-line analysis based on his own research, Klass has steadfastly declined to do so. Klass and Coyne have never met. Klass has never visited the site of the encounter. His only contact with the nine visual and two sound-and-light witnesses has consisted of two phone calls to Coyne and a talk-show chat and supper with Healey. When I asked Klass why he had never talked to the witnesses, he wrote that he "didn't have to talk to the witnesses: Woodward and Bernstein never talked to Nixon" (J. Z., July 1998).

ANOMALIES WITHIN THE AIRCRAFT

While the men of the helicopter crew were watching the object in astonishment and fear, they were also experiencing certain anomalies within the aircraft. First the radios abruptly malfunctioned on all frequencies, then they noticed that the magnetic compass disk was rotating, and finally, as the object moved to the west of their aircraft, they discovered they were in a 1,000 feet per minute climb with the collective full down.

The Radio Malfunction

As the object/light approached the helicopter, first Coyne and then Jezzi attempted to make radio contact with the Mansfield control tower to check possible aircraft in the area.

ZEIDMAN: Now, on this business of the radio, the apparent radio malfunction . . .

COYNE: That's the problem. Now, Jezzi was calling while I was handling the aircraft. Jezzi called on this radio, the VHF. There was no answer. He depressed the mike. You'd hear the keying sound, and you'd hear him talking on the air through your own earphones, but then there was nothing coming back.

ZEIDMAN: The keying sound indicates that you are transmitting?

COYNE: Right. Then he changed frequencies, and called on the alternate. He called Tower on VHF, then he called on UHF. The frequencies are published in the IFR [Instrument Flight Rules]. He had the IFR supplement in his hand, and we heard the channel tone every time he changed frequencies, the channel tone and the keying sound. The radios were functioning, but we had no transmission. They weren't receiving us.

ZEIDMAN: Okay. Now, the channeling tone.

COYNE: When you change like this [click, click], you hear a channeling tone, every time you change channels.

ZEIDMAN: And it lasts a second or so?

COYNE: Right, a couple seconds or less.

ZEIDMAN: And it indicates that you have changed frequencies?

COYNE: And when you hit the mike you hear the keying sound.

ZEIDMAN: Now, there are two ways to activate the mike. . . .

COYNE: Right. Here [a heel pedal] and here [the mike button on the cyclic stick]. And yet we had perfect transmission with Canton-Akron after, and with Columbus prior, and with Cleveland when we landed. And Mansfield was just eight miles away [See map, Figure 29-8.]

ZEIDMAN: The shortest distance of all.

COYNE: Right. We could see over there.

Certainly, Mansfield was well within radio range, and previous contact with the tower had been no problem. According to Coyne, no exactly comparable malfunction of this specific aircraft's radios had occurred, either before or after the October 18 incident.

Coyne reported that the day following the event, he phoned the Mansfield tower and asked that they replay the previous night's tapes. As Coyne told Dr. Hynek, "They said they heard us and yet they say they can't find it on the tapes." There is no record of even the initial transmission between the helicopter and the tower.

In many UFO encounters, pilots have reported a temporary failure of aircraft radios, instruments, or sometimes total electrical systems. Dr. Richard Haines, psychologist-physicist, has commented, "Ionized air is known to block radio transmission, as evidenced by numerous studies. A well-known example occurs during a spacecraft re-entry during ablation of the heat shield when all communication is lost."

Could this have caused the radio silence?

The Compass Rotation

At the most intense moment of the encounter, after the helicopter had dived to avoid a collision and after the beam of green light had penetrated the cockpit, the magnetic compass began rotating slowly, while the RMI (radio magnetic indicator) remained apparently unaffected.

The magnetic compass, most basic of navigation instruments, is a simple device consisting of one central unit on which two bar magnets are fastened on a two-point suspension system, which is permitted to rotate freely in response to local variations in magnetic field (see Figure 29-18). As the plane changes direction, the compass heading is read directly from a disk, which rotates around a pivot. The magnetic compass is acutely sensitive to changes in the plane's attitude (turning, banking) and is subject to error (but not to the extent of continuous rotation), unless the aircraft is in straight and level, constant-speed flight. The instrument also reacts to ferrous metals or electrical currents in the vicinity (as evidenced by Coyne's mention that the compass would deviate by 20° when the aircraft's landing lights were turned on), and for this reason it is placed as far away as possible from such potential disturbances in the cockpit (see Figure 29-18). Every aircraft has its

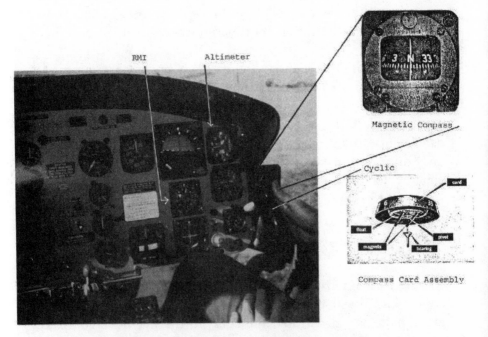

Figure 29-18. View of the instrumental panel (with compass obstructed by cyclic) (Photo by Hynek).

own residual magnetic fields that are balanced out at the time of installation of a magnetic compass.

The RMI (in this case, an AN/ASN-43 built by the Sperry Gyroscope Co.) is a multipurpose instrument used with three different navigation systems: a DG (directional gyrocompass), the ADF (automatic direction finder), and the VOR (very-high-frequency omnidirection range). The RMI "clock-face" is itself only an indicator, and is capable of presenting simultaneous readings from all three systems. The remote sensor for the DG portion of the system is located in the tail boom of the UH-1 helicopter and consists of an induction compass transmitter and a magnetic flux compensator. The gyro itself is located in the aft radio compartment. Only through the DG mode could the instrument be affected by changes in the magnetic field. Coyne reported that all three modes were operational at the time of the encounter.

The head of the avionics laboratory at the helicopter maintenance facility has commented:

> If the directional gyro (DG) system were subjected to a disturbance or variation in magnetic field, it would not respond with any drastic needle swinging on the instrument face, but by displaying either a "+" or "–" symbol located in a small synchronization knob located at one corner of the instrument. Under the circumstances [the excitement of the encounter], such an error indication could easily be missed by the pilots.

Guidance and control specialist Dr. Robert Wood has speculated:

> If an aircraft were subjected to a strong transient magnetic field, it could change the aircraft's own residual magnetic signature, resulting in deviation of the magnetic compass. In the encounter with the UFO, since the compass made about four complete rotations per minute, the local magnetic field (at the

compass itself) apparently modulated at that rate. However, a pulsating magnetic field emanating from the unknown object that could cause a compass rotation at the time of the encounter would not explain the continued rotation into the next day, unless the friction in the compass bearings was extremely low.

In response to questions raised by Jezzi's testimony, Coyne stated that the magnetic compass had never malfunctioned previously, and that although the replacement compass did not function properly, this was finally attributed to faulty installation. When it was reinstalled, there was no further trouble with the instrument.

The Unexpected Ascent

The highest elevations in the southeast Mansfield area are 1,300 feet above sea level. Coyne reported that as the red light approached and a collision appeared imminent, the last altitude he noted was 1,700 feet, with a 2,000 fpm dive in progress. However, we know from the location of the ground witnesses that the site is lower than the surrounding hills—the lake elevation is 997 feet—and the trees near the shore are approximately 30 to 50 feet high. The 1,700-foot altitude thus reflected an actual above-the-trees level of perhaps 650 to 670 feet.

"The reason I didn't crash into the ground," Coyne told me, "was because I could see the ground. I had night vision. We were down to 500 feet, maybe. But I've flown a helicopter low-level many times—200 feet, even 50 feet. The big thing of course is wires, obstructions."

We do not know at what precise altitude the helicopter ceased diving and began to climb. There are two reasons to suspect that the dive-to-climb change was not an abrupt one: none of the crew felt the g-forces of a sudden directional change (yet they were all acutely aware of the dive), and the ground witnesses reported that the two craft were maintaining the same altitude while the two children got out of the car.

Coyne says that the collective was in the full-down position when he noticed the climb, the cyclic in a "nose-down 20°" position (out of a 40° nose-down capability), and his power setting had never been changed at all from the cruising setting of 6,600 rpm.

"It was 3,500 feet when I noticed it [the climb]," Coyne said, "and this [the collective] was still bottomed. No lift. I didn't have that much time to think. Something not normal was happening. It continued to the point where we topped out at 3,800 feet."

Coyne remembers that his left arm was stiff (elbow straight) on the collective. When I pointed out (during the April 2, 1978, review meeting at Port Columbus) that if he had been reared back looking upward through the "greenhouse," he could have maintained a stiff arm and still have been pulling up on the collective, Yanacsek immediately broke in and said that he remembered definitely that Coyne, seated directly in front of him, had been hunched over in a protective, flinching posture, not reared back. Coyne agreed, remembering how he instinctively stiffened and flinched in anticipation of a collision, and how his attention had been focused primarily on the front, not upward through the "greenhouse."

Coyne's description of the abnormal control response and the concurrence of all four crewmen that they were unaware of both climb and g-forces remain among the most puzzling aspects of this event. The implication of the Coyne crew testimony is that the helicopter's climb was not a normal one.

ANOTHER EVENT THE SAME EVENING

Walter and Mary Kowalchik live southwest of Mansfield in a hilly, wooded, suburban area. On October 18, 1973, they were talking on the local network of their ham radio group at about 9 P.M. with Richard Swain, a technical sergeant in the Air Force, who was in Galion, Ohio (see Figure 29-19).

Kowalchik reported: "Swain said, 'There's something

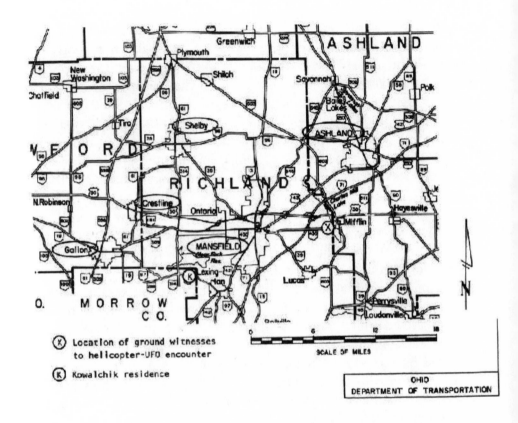

Ⓧ Location of ground witnesses
to helicopter-UFO encounter

Ⓚ Kowalchik residence

SCALE OF MILES

OHIO
DEPARTMENT OF TRANSPORTATION

Figure 29-19. The area around Mansfield.

strange. First of all, it's a strange light. No airplane has a light
like that. It's an orange glow, rather than a flashing red or
green. And secondly,' he said, 'it isn't behaving like an aircraft.
Now wait a minute, there's something strange here!' And he
was all excited. He was in Galion and he said it was heading towards Shelby.

"Now, it so happens that Mr. Eldon Heck was also on the
air, and he sent his wife out in the yard to scan the skies while
he was on the air. Sure enough, she came back to report that she
was sighting something strange over the Shelby area. It was
heading towards Mansfield. So we have a report from Galion,

we have a report from Shelby, and then we have a report from Gordon Sponseller, who was also in the Air National Guard, and he said, 'There is a strange object. I can't identify it because all I can see is a light. I cannot see an object, but I can see a strange light, maneuvering in a strange way. It moves very rapidly in one direction and then there is a sudden stop.' Sponseller said that no object with any mass at all could possibly stop that suddenly. 'Something is strange,' he said. 'Either someone is shining a light against some clouds, or it's a type of maneuvering that is very fast.'

"And by that time I [Kowalchik] came out here and told Mary, because at that time we had a very clear view of the sky in that direction. At that time there were no leaves on that dogwood tree. We had a very clear view of the skyline, and Mary said, 'Well now, I do see an orange glow over there,' but she also sighted an aircraft in the sky, and she knew it was an aircraft because of the flashing lights on the craft, and it was moving at a very steady rate across the sky like an airplane would, whereas the other object was moving very rapidly from spot to spot on the skyline. So Mary called me out and as I got there she said, 'Look at that! Oh my God, they're gonna crash!' Because they were on a collision course—at least it appeared from here, and they did come close together and veered off— the orange object veered off, and the plane kept going on, and that's about the extent of our sighting."

Mrs. Kowalchik then gave her version of the incident:

"I watched it with the binoculars and I kept track of it. We've seen other lights, unidentified lights, in other parts of the sky, but this one seemed to be staying and staying in one place for the longest time, and finally I came to the conclusion that it couldn't possibly be a plane. When I did see the plane come, the two of them seemed to come right together. I really let out a scream be- cause it looked from here—of course that was a ways away—but the way I could see them with the binoculars it looked like they were coming right into each other. The two of them seemed to be coming right toward each other. It seemed that way because the object had seemed to sit in the sky for a long time before."

I asked Mrs. Kowalchik what the object did after the apparent close approach.

"It was visible for a little while, then it seemed to suddenly disappear. I could see the plane going off."

"Was the aircraft a fixed-wing plane or a helicopter?"

"I really don't know. It seemed that the plane kept on its course."

Mr. Kowalchik interrupted. "As near as I can recall, the plane continued on the course, but the glow or the light veered upward suddenly. The plane was at a fairly low altitude. It was just above the skyline. It appeared to be just beyond Mansfield, to the northeast."

Mrs. Kowalchik continued: "It was an orange glow, a very bright orange glow. It was definitely not a red. Also, it was a lot brighter than any airplane light. We can watch the planes, lots of times we watch, and even when they're close and the lights look larger—but this wasn't anything like that.

She went on to say, "It stayed in one area for a long time. I could tell from the relationship to the skyline and to the dogwood tree. You know, I watch hummingbirds a lot. And they're so mobile, and I couldn't help but think how interesting that was, that the object was also so mobile. A helicopter couldn't do that."

I asked, "Did you see any meteors, any shooting stars?"

Mrs. Kowalchik replied, "Oh, I've seen meteors sometimes, but not that night. It wasn't anything like a shooting star, it really wasn't."

Mr. Kowalchik said, "I won't even attempt to offer any type of explanation for this, but there was an object. It was not any aircraft. Obviously not an aircraft because no aircraft could possibly move in this fashion where it would hover, be stationary, then move very quickly. And particularly near the near-collision—it seemed to rise straight up in the air. I can't remember how it disappeared, just faded away."

"I know the plane went on its way," Mrs. Kowalchik added, "because I felt such a great sense of relief, because obviously nothing had happened."

Referring to his ham log, Mr. Kowalchik established that the sighting occurred on October 18, 1973. The net started at 7:30 P.M. and they were off the air at 9:30. The incident happened during the later part of the time interval, about 9:00 P.M.

Obviously, this was not the helicopter encounter that occurred at 11:05 P.M. Obviously, too, without other witnesses on the ground or a report from the pilot, there is no way of knowing if the plane and the object did nearly collide. In the dark, even through binoculars, the line of sight could have been very deceiving. Since the plane did not deviate, it is entirely possible that the pilot was totally unaware of the object, or could see the object and knew that it did not constitute a threat.

CONCLUSION

The object encountered by the Coyne helicopter crew remains unidentified despite many hours of face-to-face interviews with the observers and many months of supplementary investigation, consultation, and analysis. All of the witnesses were cooperative over extended periods of time. Because the aircrew and ground witnesses (who have never communicated with each other) reported substantially the same description and chronology, the probability is very high that they were participants in the same event. Certainly there is no indication of collusion or hoax among them, and, independent of one another, the testimony of each set of witnesses represents a valid UFO experience.

The possibilities that the object was either a meteor or a high-performance aircraft have been considered at length and have been shown to be untenable. The degree to which the object affected the helicopter's instruments or flight path is unresolved, although similar magnetic compass and radio malfunctions, as well as unexplained climbs and apparent near-collisions, have been recorded in other incidents of interaction between UFOs and aircraft.

One interpretation of the reported observations is that the

phenomenon was an object with physical reality at the time of the sighting. Another possible interpretation could be that of a projected image similar to that of a hologram.

I [Jennie Zeidman] am not proposing any theory as to the mechanisms or the origins of UFO phenomena, or to the specific identity of this particular unknown object. This report offers only a presentation of the facts and my unswerving conviction that we are being confronted with new empirical data that deserve the serious attention of both behavioral and physical scientists.

REFERENCES IN THE TEXT

Allen, C. W. (1963). *Astrophysical Quantities*. London: The Athlone Press.

Altschuler, M. D. (1968). *Scientific Study of Unidentified Flying Objects*. E. Gilmore, ed. New York: Bantam Books, p. 733.

Arnold, K., and Palmer, Ray (1952). *The Coming of the Saucers*. pp. 106–108.

Bounias, M. C. L. (1990). "Biochemical Traumatology as a Potent Tool for Identifying Actual Stresses Elicited by an Unidentified Source: Evidence for Plant Metabolic Disorders in Correlation with a UFO Landing." *Journal of Scientific Exploration*, 4, pp. 1–18.

Bumby, J. R. (1983). *Superconducting Rotating Electrical Machines*. Oxford: Clarendon Press.

Cappa, P., and Winter, A. (1979). "E Nel Livornese," *Notiziario UFO*, 11, No. 2, p. 15.

Chabrerie, J. P., Fournet, G., and Mailfert, A. (1972). "Flooded Rotor, Direct Current Acyclic Motor, with Superconducting Field Winding." *Proceedings of the Applied Superconductivity Conference*, Annapolis.

Childerhose, R. J. (1958). Affidavit written in May 1958, and private communication to Dr. B. Maccabee.

Chiu, H. Y. (1969). "The Condon Report, Scientific Study of Unidentified Flying Objects" (book review). *Icarus*, 11, pp. 447–450.

Clark, J. (1998). *The UFO Encyclopedia*. 2nd edition. Detroit, MI: Omnigraphics.

Clemence, G. M., et al. (1969). "Review of the University of Colorado Report on Unidentified Flying Objects, by a Panel of the National Academy of Sciences," *Icarus*, 11, pp. 440–443.

CNES (1983). *Enquête 81/01: Analyse d'une Trace. Note Technique numero 16*. (CT/GEPAN-000 13). Toulouse: Groupe d'Étude des Phénomènes Aérospatiaux Nonidentifiés, March 1, 1983.

Colorado Project (1967). Air Force briefing, January 12, 1967. Philadelphia: American Philosophical Library, Colorado Project Archives.

Condon, E. U. (project director), and Gillmor, D. S. (ed.). (1969). *Scientific Study of Unidentified Flying Objects*. New York: Bantam.

Corso, P. J. (1997). *The Day after Roswell*. New York: Pocket Books.

Cosmovici, C., Bowyer, S. and Wertheimer, D. (eds.) (1997). IAU Colloquium 161, Proceedings of the Fifth International Conference on Bioastronomy, July 1–5, 1996, Capri. Capri: Editrice Compositori.

Doyle, A. C. (1994). *The Sign of Four*. Oxford University Press.

Doyle, J. T. (1974). "Shaped Field Superconductive D.C. Ship Drive Systems." *Advances in Cryogenic Engineering*, 19, p. 162.

Eastman Kodak Co. (1973). *Understanding Graininess and Granularity* (Publication F-20). New York: Eastman Kodak Co.

Eastman Kodak Co. (1980). *Kodacolor II Film Specifications* (Publication DS-11). New York: Eastman Kodak Co.

Edwards, F. (1966). *Flying Saucers—Serious Business*. New York: Lyle Stuart.

Fate Magazine (1948). Number 1, p. 31.

Feynman, R. P. (1998). *The Meaning of It All: Thoughts of a Citizen Scientist*. Reading, MA: Perseus Books, p. 75.

GEPAN (1976). GEPAN Case No. 76305443, Grenoble observation.

Greenler, R. (1980). *Rainbows, Halos, and Glories*. Cambridge: Cambridge University Press.

Haines, R. F. (1978). "UFO Drawings by Witnesses and Non Witnesses: Is There Something in Common?" *UFO Phenomena*, 2, pp. 123–151.

Haines, R. F. (1979a). "A Review of Selected Sightings from Aircraft—1973 to 1978." *Proceedings 1979 MUFON UFO Symposium*. San Francisco, CA, July, 1979, pp. 114–140.

Haines, R. F. (1979b). "What Do UFO Drawings by Alleged Eyewitnesses and Non-Eyewitnesses Have in Common?" In R. F. Haines (ed.), *UFO Phenomena and the Behavioral Scientist* (Chapter 12). Metuchen, NJ: The Scarecrow Press.

Haines, R. F. (1983). "A Review of Selected Aerial Phenomenon Sightings from Aircraft from 1942 to 1952." *Proceedings 1983 MUFON UFO Symposium*. Pasadena, CA, July 1983, pp. 14–44.

Haines, R. F. (1987). "Analysis of a UFO Photograph." *Journal of Scientific Exploration*, 1, pp. 129–147.

Haines, R. F. (1992). Fifty-six Aircraft Pilot Sightings Involving Electromagnetic Effects. *Proceedings 1992 MUFON UFO Symposium*, Albuquerque, NM, July 1992, p. 102.

Hall, M. P. M., and Barklay, L. W. (eds.) (1989). *Radiowave Propagation*. London: Peter Peregrinus, Ltd.

Hanlon, D., and Vallee, J. F., (1967). "Airships over Texas." *Flying Saucer Review*, 13, 1, p. 20. In the same issue, see also the letter on page 27.

Hatch, L. (1999). *U* Database. See his web site at *www.jps.net/larryhat*.

Hippler, R. R. (1967). Letter to Robert J. Low dated January 16, 1967. Philadelphia: American Philosophical Library, Colorado Project Archives.

Holliday, J. E. (1973). McDonnell Douglas report on the Aurora case, based on the on-site investigation by Ronald A. and N. Joseph Gurney on 12 May 1973.

Hynek, J. A. (1969). "The Condon Report and UFOs." *Bulletin of the Atomic Scientists*, 25, pp. 39–42.

Hynek, J. A. (1972). *The UFO Experience*. Chicago: Henry Regnery.

Jacobs, D. M. (1975). *The UFO Controversy in America*. Bloomington: Indiana University Press.

Klass, P. (1968). *UFOs Identified*. New York: Random House.

Kuettner, J. P. et al. (1970). "UFO: An Appraisal of the Problem, A Statement by the UFO Subcommittee of the AIAA." *Astronautics and Aeronautics*, 8, No. 11, pp. 49–51.

Lewis, D. L. (1971a). "Practical Homopolar Machines. Use of Liquid Metal Slip Rings." *Journal of Science and Technology*, 38, 2, p. 46.

Lewis, D. L. (1971b). "Homopolar d.c. Machines for Industry," *Electronics Review*, July 23, 1971.

Lorin, J. C., and Havette, A. (1986). *Isotopic and Elemental Characterization of a Magnesium Sample of Unknown Origin Collected in Brazil in 1957*. Unpublished paper, personal communication.

Low, R. J. (1967). Letter to Lieutenant Colonel Robert J. Hippler dated January 27, 1967. Philadelphia, PA: American Philosophical Library, Colorado Project Archives.

Maccabee, B. (1999). "Optical Power Output of an Unidentified High Altitude Light Source." *Journal of Scientific Exploration*, 13, pp. 199–211.

McDonald, J. E. (1969). "The Condon Report: Scientific Study of Unidentified Flying Objects" (book review). *Icarus*, 11, pp. 443–447.

McDonald, J. E. (1971). "UFO Encounter I, Sample Case Selected by the UFO Subcommittee of the AIAA, Lakenheath, England: Radar-Visual Case, Aug. 13–14, 1956." *Astronautics and Aeronautics*, 9 No. 7, pp. 66–70.

McKay, D. S., et al. (1996). "Search for a Past Life on Mars: Possible Relic Biogenic Activity in Martian Meteorite ALH 84001." *Science*, 237, p. 924.

Menzel, D. H. (1953). *Flying Saucers*. Cambridge, MA: Harvard University Press.

Menzel, D. H., and Boyd, L. G. (1963). *The World of Flying Saucers: A Scientific Examination of a Major Myth of the Space Age*. Garden City, NY: Doubleday and Company.

Menzel, D. H., and Taves, E. H. (1977). *The UFO Enigma: The Definitive Explanation of the UFO Phenomenon*. Garden City, NY: Doubleday and Company.

National Military Establishment. (1949). Memorandum to the Press No. M 26–49. Washington, D.C.: National Military Establishment, Office of Public Information, April 27, 1949.

Nature (1969). "A Sledgehammer for Nuts." 221, pp. 899–900.

Neblette, C. B. (1965). *Photographic Lenses*. New York: Morgan and Morgan Publishing.

Omaha World-Herald (1977). "Mystery Flaming Object Definitely not Meteorite." December 20, 1977.

Pasko, V. P., Inan, U. S., and Bell, T. F. (1996). "Sprites as Luminous Columns of Ionization Produced by Quasi-Electrostatic Thundercloud Fields." *Geophysics Research Letters*, 23, p. 649.

Perry, T. S., and Geppert, L. (1997). "Do Portable Electronics Endanger Flight? Part I." *Air Line Pilot*, August 1997, p. 20.

Petit, J. P. (1986, September). "Shockwave Cancellation in Gas by Lorentz Force Action." *Proceedings of the Ninth Meeting on Magneto-hydrodynamic Electrical Power Generation*, Tokyo.

Phillips, T. (1975). *Physical Traces Associated with UFO Sightings*. Evanston, IL: Center for UFO Studies.

Planck, M. (1950). *Scientific Autobiography*. London: London, Williams and Norgate, p. 33.

Poher, C. (1973). *Études Statistiques Portant Sur 1,000 Témoignages d'Observation d'U.F.O.* Toulouse, France: CNES.

Powell, J. (1981). *Aircraft Radio Systems*. London: Pitman.

Project Blue Book (1955). Special Report No. 14. Air Technical Intelligence Center. Dayton, OH: Wright-Patterson Air Force Base.

Project Grudge (1949). Air Material Command report. Dayton, OH: Wright-Patterson Air Force Base.

Project Sign (1949). *Unidentified Aerial Objects, Technical Report No. F-TR-2274-IA*. Air Material Command report. Dayton, OH: Wright-Patterson Air force Base.

Randles, J., and Warrington, P. (1979). *UFOs: A British Viewpoint*. London: Robert Hale.

Rodeghier, M. (1981). *UFO Reports Involving Vehicle Interference*. Evanston, IL: Center for UFO Studies.

Ruppelt, E. J. (1956). *The Report on Unidentified Flying Objects*. Garden City, NY: Doubleday & Co.

Sagan, C. (ed.) (1973). *Communication with Extraterrestrial Intelligence*. Cambridge, MA: MIT Press.

Saunders, D. R., and Harkins, R. R. (1968). *UFOs? Yes!* New York: New American Library.

Schuessler, J. F. (1981). "Cash-Landrum Radiation Case." *MUFON UFO Journal*, no. 165, November, p. 3.

Schuessler, J. F. (1988). "Medical Injuries Resulting from a UFO Encounter." *Proceedings of the Second CUFOS Conference*, Chicago, Illinois, September 25–27, 1981, M. Hynek, (ed.). Chicago, Illinois: CUFOS, p. 59.

Schuessler, J. F. (1996). *UFO-Related Physiological Effects*. La Porte, Texas: Geo Graphics Printing Co.

Schuessler, J. F. (1998). *The Cash-Landrum Incident*. LaPorte, Texas: Geo Graphics Printing Co.

Sentman, D. D., and Westcott, E. M. (1995). "Red Sprites and Blue Jets: Thunderstorm Excited Optical Emissions in the Stratosphere, Mesophere, and Ionosphere." *Physics of Plasmas*, 2, p. 254.

Smith, W. (1996). "A Reference Guide for the Condon Report." *Journal of UFO Studies*, New Series, 6, pp. 185–194.

SOBEPS (1991). Vague d'OVNI sur la Belgique SOBEPS asbi, 74, Avenue Paul Janson, Bruxelles.

Southall, H. L., and Oberly, C. E. (1979). "System Considerations for Airborne, High Power Superconducting Generators" *Institute of Electrical and Electronics Engineering Magazine*, 15, 1, p. 711.

Story, R. (1980). *The Encyclopedia of UFOs*. Garden City, New York: Doubleday.

Sturrock, P. A. (1974a). *Evaluation of the Condon Report on the Colorado UFO Project*. Stanford University Institute for Plasma Research Report SUIPR 599.

Sturrock, P. A. (1974b). "UFO Reports from AIAA Members." *Astronautics and Aeronautics*, 12, 5, pp. 60–64.

Sturrock, P. A. (1977a). *Report on a Survey of the Membership of the American Astronomical Society Concerning the UFO Problem*, SUIPR Report No. 681, Stanford (January 1977).

Sturrock, P. A. (1977b). *Report on a Survey of the Membership of the American Astronomical Society Concerning the UFO Problem* (Revised), SUIPR Report No. 681R, Stanford (November 1977).

Sturrock, Peter A. (1984). "Brazil Magnesium Study," paper presented at the Third Annual Meeting of the Society for Scientific Exploration, Princeton, New Jersey.

Sturrock, P. A. (1987). "An Analysis of the Condon Report on the Colorado UFO Project." *Journal of Scientific Exploration*, 1, pp. 75–100.

Sturrock, P. A. (1994a). "Report on a Survey of the Membership of the American Astronomical Society Concerning the UFO Problem: Part I." *Journal of Scientific Exploration*, 8, p. 1.

Sturrock, P. A. (1994b). "Report on a Survey of the Membership of the American Astronomical Society Concerning the UFO Problem: Part 2." *Journal of Scientific Exploration*, 8, p. 153.

Sturrock, P. A. (1994c). "Report on a Survey of the Membership of the American Astronomical Society Concerning the UFO Problem: Part 3." *Journal of Scientific Exploration*, 8, p. 309.

Sturrock, P. A. (1994d). "Applied Scientific Inference." *Journal of Scientific Exploration*, 8, 4, pp. 491–508.

Swift, D. W. (1990). *SETI Pioneers*. Tuscon, AZ: University of Arizona Press.

Swords, M. D. (1996). "The University of Colorado UFO Project: The 'Scientific Study of UFOs.'" *Journal of UFO Studies*, 6, 149–184.

Thayer, G. D. (1971). "UFO Encounter II, Sample Case Selected by the UFO Subcommittee of the AIAA, Lakenheath, England: Radar-Visual Case, August 13-14, 1956." *Astronautics and Aeronautics*, 9, No. 9, pp. 60–70.

Vallee, J. F. (1990a). *Confrontations*. New York: Ballantine. Appendix, pp. 231–244.

Vallee, J. F. (1990b). "Return to Trans-en-Provence." *Journal of Scientific Exploration*, vol. 4, no. 1, pp. 19–25.

Velasco, J.-J. (1990). "Report on the analysis of anomalous physical traces: The 1981 Trans-en-Provence UFO Case." *Journal of Scientific Exploration*, 4, 1, pp. 27–48.

Von Ludwiger, I. (1983). MUFON-CES-Bericht Nr. 9. Mutual UFO Network-Central European Section.

Von Ludwiger, I. (1998). *Investigating a Mystery* (unpublished book manuscript). Personal communication, courtesy of the National Institute of Discovery Science.

Watt, D. A. (1958). *The Development and Operation of a 10 Kw Homopolar Generator with Mercury Brushes*, IEE paper 2606U, p. 233.

Weinstein, D. (1997). *UFO/Aircraft Encounters: Military, Airliner, Private Pilots UFO Sightings 1942 to 1996* (privately published).

Zeidman, J. (1979). *A UFO-Helicopter Encounter Over Ohio*. Center for UFO Studies.

Zeidman, J. (1988). "Green Light over Mansfield," *International UFO Reporter* Nov./Dec. 1988 issue, p. 13.

Ziman, J. (1978). *Reliable Knowledge: An Exploration of the Grounds of Belief in Science*. Cambridge, UK: Cambridge University Press.

A BRIEF GUIDE TO
UFO LITERATURE

U.S. OFFICIAL DOCUMENTS
Important, but not easy to find

Smith, M., and Havas, G. D. 1983, Report No. 83–205 SPR: The UFO Enigma (Washington DC: Congressional Research Service).

U.S. Air Force Air Material Command 1949, Project SIGN (Dayton, OH: Wright-Patterson AFB).

U.S. Air Force Air Material Command 1949, Project GRUDGE (Dayton, OH: Wright Patterson AFB).

U.S. Air Force Air Material Command 1951, Project Twinkle Final Report (Dayton, OH: Wright-Patterson AFB).

U.S. Air Force Air Material Command 1951–1953, Project Blue Book Reports No. 1–12 (Dayton, OH: Wright-Patterson AFB).

U.S. Air Force Air Material Command 1955, Special Report No. 14: Analysis of Reports of Unidentified Flying Objects (Dayton, OH: Wright-Patterson AFB).

U.S. Air Force Air Material Command 1966, Special Report of the O'Brien Committee (Washington, DC: U.S. Air Force).

U.S. Central Intelligence Agency 1953, Report of Meetings of Scientific Advisory Panel on Unidentified Flying Objects convened by Office of Scientific Intelligence (Washington, DC: Central Intelligence Agency).

U.S. Congress 1968, 90th Congress, 2nd Session, House Committee on Science and Astronautics, Symposium on Unidentified Flying Objects (Washington DC: Government Printing Office).

ENCYCLOPEDIAS

Clark, J. 1998, *The UFO Encyclopedia*, 2nd Edition, 2 volumes (Detroit, MI: Omnigraphics).

Sachs, M. 1980, *The UFO Encyclopedia* (New York: Putnam's Sons).

Story, R. D. 1980, *The Encyclopedia of UFOs* (New York, Doubleday and Co.).

EDITED VOLUMES

Condon, E. U., and Gillmor, D. S. 1969, *Scientific Study of Unidentified Flying Objects* (New York: Bantam Books).

Evans, H., and Spencer, J. (eds.) 1987, *UFOs 1947–1987: The 40-Year Search for an Explanation* (London, UK: Fortean Tomes).

Haines, Richard F. (ed.) 1979, *UFO Phenomena and the Behavioral Scientist* (Metuchen, NJ: Scarecrow Press Inc.)

Sagan, C., and Page, T. (eds.) 1972, *UFO's—A Scientific Debate* (Ithaca, NY: Cornell University Press).

CASE STUDIES

Haines, R. F. 1987, *Melbourne Episode: Case Study of a Missing Pilot* (Los Altos, CA: L.D.A. Press).

Salisbury, F. 1974, *The Utah UFO Display: A Biologist's Report* (Old Greenwich, CT: Devin-Adair).

Schuessler, J. F. 1998, *The Cash-Landrum UFO Incident* (LaPorte, TX: Geo Graphics).

MONOGRAPHS

Dick, S. J. 1994, *The Biological Universe: The Twentieth-Century Extraterrestrial Life Debate and the Limits of Science* (New York: Cambridge University Press).

Fowler, R. E. 1974, *UFOs: Interplanetary Visitors* (Jericho, NY: Exposition Press).

Haines, R. F. 1980, *Observing UFOs: An Investigative Handbook.* (Chicago: Nelson-Hall).

Hendry, A. 1979, *The UFO Handbook: A Guide to Investigating, Evaluating and Reporting UFO Sightings* (New York: Doubleday and Co.).

Hill, P. R. 1995, *Unconventional Flying Objects: A Scientific Analysis* (Charlottesville, VA: Hampton Roads Publishing Co. Inc.).

Hynek, J. Allen 1972, *The UFO Experience* (Chicago, IL: Henry Regnery).

Hynek, J. Allen 1977, *The Hynek UFO Report* (New York: Dell Publishing).

Jacobs, D. M. 1975, *The UFO Controversy in America* (Bloomington, IN: Indiana University Press).

Klass, P. J. 1975, *UFOs—Explained.* (New York: Random House).

Klass, P. J. 1983, *UFOs—The Public Deceived.* (Buffalo, NY: Prometheus Books).

Klass, P. J. 1997, *Bringing UFOs Down to Earth.* (Buffalo, NY: Prometheus Books).

Lorenzen, Coral E. 1962, *The Great Flying Saucer Hoax* (New York: The Williams-Frederick Press).

Menzel, D. H. 1953, *Flying Saucers* (Cambridge, MA: Harvard University Press).

Menzel, D. H., and Boyd, L. G. 1963, *The World of Flying Saucers: A Scientific Examination of a Major Myth of the Space Age* (Garden City, NY: Doubleday and Co.).

Menzel, D. H., and Taves, E. H. 1977, *The UFO Enigma: The Definitive Explanation of the UFO Phenomenon* (Garden City, NY: Doubleday and Co.).

Oberg, James E. 1981, *UFOs and Outer Space Mysteries: A Sympathetic Skeptic's Report* (Norfolk, VA: Donning Company).

Randles, Jenny 1987, *The UFO Conspiracy* (Poole, Dorset, UK: Blandford Press).

Ruppelt, E. J. 1956, *The Report on Unidentified Flying Objects* (Garden City, NY; Doubleday and Co.).

Rutledge, Harley D. 1981, *Project Identification: The First Scientific Study of UFO Phenomena* (Englewood Cliffs, NJ: Prentice Hall).

Saunders, D. R., and Harkins, R. R. 1968, *UFOs? Yes! Where the Condon Committee Went Wrong* (New York: New American Library).

Schuessler, J. F. 1996, *UFO-Related Human Physiological Effects* (LaPorte, TX: GeoGraphics Publishing Co.).

Sheaffer, R. 1981, *The UFO Verdict: Examining the Evidence* (Buffalo, NY: Prometheus Press).

Vallee, J. 1967, *The Anatomy of a Phenomenon* (Chicago, IL: Henry Regnery).

Vallee, J. 1969, *Passport to Magonia* (Chicago, IL: Henry Regnery).

Vallee, J., and Vallee, J. 1966, *Challenge to Science: The UFO Enigma* (Chicago, IL: Henry Regnery).

JOURNALS

Journal of Scientific Exploration (Editorial Office: P.O. Box 5848, Stanford, CA 94309–5848).

Journal of UFO Studies (Editorial Office: J. Allen Hynek Center for UFO Studies, 2437 W. Peterson Ave., Chicago, IL 60659).

MUFON Journal (Editorial Office: 103 Oldtowne Road, Seguin, TX 75188).

CATALOG

U Database. 1999. For information, see Larry Hatch's web site: *www.jps.net/larryhat*

ACKNOWLEDGMENTS

Some of the material in this book is based on articles and reports previously published elsewhere. I wish to thank the Center for UFO Studies and the Society for Scientific Exploration for their generous cooperation in this matter. I also wish to thank the following authors who have generously given me their permission to draw upon their articles and reports: Von R. Eshleman, Richard F. Haines, Thomas Holzer, J. R. (Randy) Jokipii, François Louange, J. J. (Jay) Melosh, James J. Papike, Guenther Reitz, Charles R. Tolbert, Jacques Vallee, Jean-Jacques Velasco, Bernard Veyret, and Jennie Zeidman.

This material is contained in the following chapters:

Chapter 3: Sturrock, P. A. 1987, "An Analysis of the Condon Report on the Colorado UFO Project," *Journal of Scientific Exploration* 1, pp. 75–100.

Chapters 6–16: Sturrock, P. A. 1998, "Physical Evidence Related to UFO Reports," Sections 2–13, *Journal of Scientific Exploration* 12, pp. 185–210.

Chapter 18: Eshleman, V., Holzer, T., Jokipii, J. R., Louange, F., Melosh, H. J., Papike, J. J., Reitz, G., Tolbert, C. R., and Veyret, B. 1998, "Physical Evidence Related to UFO Reports, Section 1, Summary Report of the Scientific Review Panel," *Journal of Scientific Exploration* 12, pp. 183–185.

Chapter 19: Sturrock, P. A. 1998, "Physical Evidence Related to UFO Reports, Section 14, Recommendations Concerning Implementation," *Journal of Scientific Exploration* 12, pp. 210–214.

Chapter 20: Louange F., and Velasco, J.-J., 1998, "Physical Evidence Related to UFO Reports, Appendix 1, Official UFO Investigations in France: The GEPAN/SEPRA Project," *Journal of Scientific Exploration* 12, pp. 214–217.

Chapter 21: Louange F., 1998, "Physical Evidence Related to UFO Reports, Appendix 2, Procedures for Analysis of Photographic Evidence," *Journal of Scientific Exploration* 12, pp. 217–219.

Chapter 22: Eshleman, V. R. 1998, "Physical Evidence Related to UFO Reports, Appendix 4, Electromagnetic-Wave Ducting, and Appendix 5, Sprites," *Journal of Scientific Exploration* 12, pp. 220–222.

Chapter 23: Eshleman, V. R. 1998, "Physical Evidence Related to UFO Reports, Appendix 6, SETI and UFO Investigations Compared" *Journal of Scientific Exploration* 12, pp. 222–225. Louange, F. 1998, "Physical Evidence Related to UFO Reports, Appendix 7, Further Thoughts on SETI and UFO Investigations," *Journal of Scientific Exploration* 12, pp. 225–226.

Chapter 25: Haines, R. F. 1987, "An Analysis of a UFO Photograph," *Journal of Scientific Exploration* 1, pp. 129–147. Haines, R. F., and Vallee, J. 1989, "Photo Analysis of an Aerial Disk over Costa Rica," *Journal of Scientific Exploration* 3, pp. 113–131. Haines, R. F., and Vallee, J. 1990, "Photo Analysis of an Aerial Disk over Costa Rica: New Evidence," *Journal of Scientific Exploration* 4, pp. 71–74.

Chapter 26: Vallee, J. 1998, "Estimates of Optical Power Output in Six Cases of Unexplained Aerial Objects with Defined Luminosity Characteristics," *Journal of Scientific Exploration* 12, pp. 345–358.

Chapter 27: Vallee, J. 1998, "Physical Analysis of Ten Cases of Unexplained Aerial Objects with Material Samples," *Journal of Scientific Exploration* 12, pp. 359–375.

Chapter 28: Velasco, J.-J. 1990, "Report on the Analysis of Anomalous Physical Traces: The 1981 Trans-en-Provence Case," *Journal of Scientific Exploration*, 4, pp. 27–48. Vallee, J. 1990, "Return to Trans-en-Provence," *Journal of Scientific Exploration* 4, pp. 19–25.

Chapter 29: Zeidman, J. 1979, *A Helicopter-UFO Encounter over Ohio*, Center for UFO Studies Report.

LIST OF ACRONYMS

AAS	American Astronomical Society
ADF	automatic direction finder
AFB	air force base
AFOSR	Air Force Office of Scientific Research
AIAA	American Institute of Aeronautics and Astronautics
ALAT	Aviation Léger de l'Armée de Terre (Army Light Aviation)
AN	anomalies
AP	anomalous propagation
ATC	air traffic control
CCAP	Civil Commission on Aerial Phenomena
CCD	charge-coupled device
CE	close encounter
CIA	Central Intelligence Agency
CNES	Centre National d'Études Spatiales (National Center for Space Research)
CUFOS	Center for UFO Studies
CW	clockwise
DG	directional gyrocompass
EM	electromagnetic
ESA	European Space Agency
EST	eastern standard time
ETA	extraterrestrial actuality
ETH	extraterrestrial hypothesis
ETI	extraterrestrial intelligent
ETIL	extraterrestrial intelligent life
ETL	extraterrestrial life
FAA	Federal Aviation Administration

FB	flyby
fpm	feet per minute
ft-L	foot-lumen
GCA	ground-controlled approach
GEPAN	Groupe d'Études des Phénomènes Aérospatiaux Nonidentifiés (Aerial Phenomena Research Group)
ICRP	International Commission for Radiological Protection
IFA	International Frisbee Association
IFR	instrument flight rules
INRA	Institut National de Recherche Agronomique (National Institute of Agronomic Research)
LDP	Laboratoire d'Analyses Physiques (Physical Analysis Laboratory)
MA	maneuver
msl	mean sea level
MTF	modulation transfer function
MUFON	Mutual UFO Network
MUFON-CES	MUFON Central European Society
NAS	National Academy of Science
NASA	National Aeronautics and Space Administration
NDB	nondirectional beacon
NOAA	National Oceanographic and Atmospheric Administration
NPIC	National Photographic Interpretation Center
OVNI	objet volant non-identifié (unidentified flying object)
PIO	public information officer
RAF	Royal Air Force
RMI	radio magnetic indicator
RPM	revolutions per minute
SEM	scanning electron microscope
SEPRA	Service d'Expertise des Phénomènes de Rentrées Atmosphériques (Atmospheric Re-entry Phenomena Expertise Department)
SETI	search for exterrestrial intelligence
SIMS	secondary ion mass spectrometer
SLR	single-lens reflex
SNEPA	Syndicat National de l'Enseignment Agricole Public (National Sydicate for Agricultural Instruction)
SOBEPS	Sociéte Belge d'Étude des Phénomènes Spatiaux
UFO	unidentified flying object
UHF	ultra high frequency
URS	unidentified radio signals
USAF	United States Air Force
VHF	very high frequency
VOR	very-high-frequency omnidirectional radio range

INDEX

• • •

ABOUT THE AUTHOR

Peter A. Sturrock studied mathematics at Cambridge University, England, with a three-year interruption (1943–1946) to work on radar. He was awarded the University Rayleigh Prize for mathematics. Research work on electron physics carried out at the Cavendish Laboratory in Cambridge, the National Bureau of Standards in Washington, and the École Normale Supérieure in Paris earned him a Ph.D. in 1951. His Ph.D. dissertation was later expanded and published as a monograph entitled *Static and Dynamic Electron Optics* in 1955.

Sturrock subsequently pursued research in nuclear physics as Harwell Research Fellow at the Atomic Energy Research Establishment, England; research on plasma physics as Fellow of St. Johns' College, Cambridge; research on microwave tubes as Research Associate in the Microwave Laboratory at Stanford University; and research on accelerator physics as Ford Foundation Fellow at the European Center for Nuclear Research (CERN), Geneva. During this period, Sturrock made a number of inventions, one of them being a microwave tube that operates on a principle subsequently rediscovered and named the "free-electron laser."

Sturrock was appointed Professor of Engineering Science and Applied Physics in the School of Engineering and the Physics Department at Stanford University in January 1961, but subsequently transferred to become Professor of Space Science and Astrophysics in the Applied Physics Department and, by courtesy, in the Physics Department. His teaching duties ended in 1998, and he now spends full time on research. Sturrock was Chair of the Founding Committee of the Institute for Plasma Research and served as Director from 1964–74 and from 1980–83. He subsequently served as Chair of the Founding Committee of the Center for Space Science and Astrophysics and served as Deputy Director from 1983–92 and as Director from 1992 to 1998. He also served as chair of the committees that established the Stanford-NASA-Ames Institute for Space Research, and the Stanford-Lockheed Institute for Astrophysical and Space Research. Since 1961, he has worked primarily on plasma physics, solar physics, and astrophysics. He has published over two hundred scientific articles and two monographs, and has edited five volumes that review plasma physics, solar physics, and astrophysics. His recent monograph, *Plasma Physics, an Introduction to the Theory of Astrophysical, Geophysical and Laboratory Plasmas*, is based on a graduate level course that he has taught at Stanford for over twenty years.

From 1965–66, Sturrock served as Chairman of the Division of Plasma Physics of the American Physical Society, and from 1974–75 as Chairman of the Solar Physics Division of the American Astronomical Society. He was Director of the Summer School on Plasma Astrophysics at Varenna, Italy, in 1966; Chairman of the Organizing Committee of the Conference on Plasma Instabilities in Astrophysics held at Asilomar in 1968; and Director of the Skylab Workshop on Solar Flares held at Boulder in 1977. He has also served on many national panels and committees, notably (1984–85) as Chairman of the Advocacy Panel that reviewed Solar Physics for the National Academy of Sciences.

Sturrock is a member of the American Astronomical Society, the American Institute of Aeronautics and Astronautics, the International Academy of Astronautics, and the International Astronomical Union, and is a Fellow of the American Association for the Advancement of Science, the American Physical Society, and the Royal Astronomical Society. He was chair of the Founding Committee of the Society for Scientific Exploration, and has served as President since its formation in 1982. In 1967, Sturrock received the Gravity Prize (for gravitational research) from the Gravity Research Foundation; in 1977, the Lindsay Award from NASA Goddard Space Flight Center; in 1986 the Hale Prize for solar physics from the American Astronomical Society; in 1990, the Arctowski Medal for solar-terrestrial research from the National Academy of Sciences; and in 1992, the Space Sciences Award from the American Institute of Aeronautics and Astronautics.

Sturrock has served as consultant to the British Atomic Energy Research Establishment, Boeing Aircraft Company, Brookhaven National Laboratory, CERN, General Atomic, NASA Ames Research Center, NASA Goddard Space Science Center, and Varian Associates.